America
TRANSFORMED

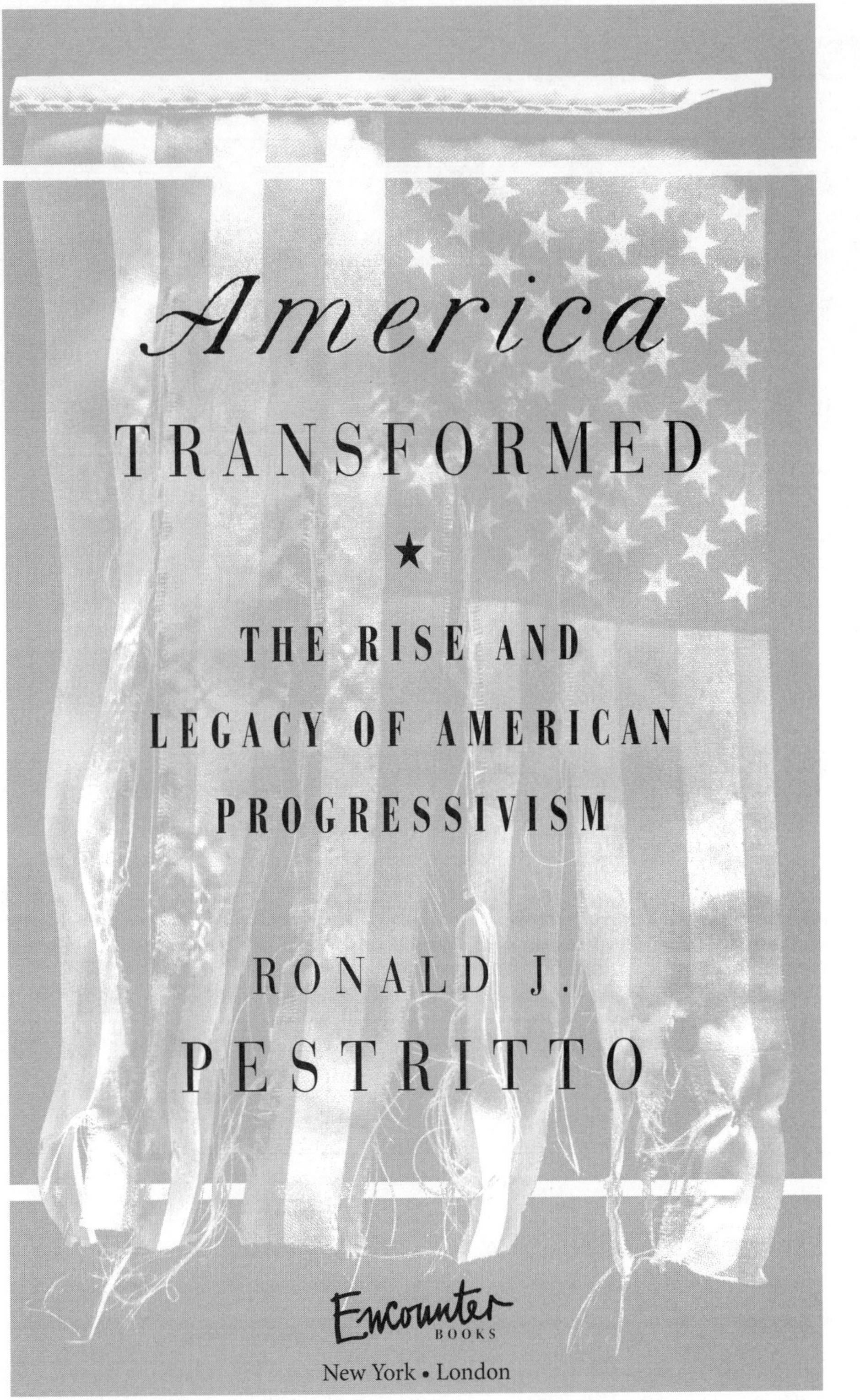

America Transformed

★

The Rise and Legacy of American Progressivism

Ronald J. Pestritto

Encounter Books
New York • London

First American edition published in 2021 by Encounter Books, an activity of Encounter for Culture and Education, Inc., a nonprofit, tax-exempt corporation.
Encounter Books website address: www.encounterbooks.com

Manufactured in the United States and printed on acid-free paper. The paper used in this publication meets the minimum requirements of ANSI/NISO Z39.48-1992 (R 1997) (*Permanence of Paper*).

FIRST AMERICAN EDITION

LIBRARY OF CONGRESS CATALOGING-IN-PUBLICATION DATA

Names: Pestritto, Ronald J., 1968– author.
Title: America transformed : the rise and legacy of American progressivism / Ronald J. Pestritto.
Description: First American edition. | New York, New York Encounter Books, 2021. | Includes bibliographical references and index.
Identifiers: LCCN 2020036871 (print) | LCCN 2020036872 (ebook) ISBN 9781641771689 (hardcover) | ISBN 9781641771696 (ebook)
Subjects: LCSH: Progressivism (United States politics)—History. United States—Politics and government—1865-1933.
Classification: LCC E661 .P47 2021 (print) | LCC E661 (ebook) DDC 324.2732/7—dc23
LC record available at https://lccn.loc.gov/2020036871
LC ebook record available at https://lccn.loc.gov/2020036872

Interior page design and typesetting by Bruce Leckie

To Charles R. Kesler

CONTENTS

Acknowledgments

Charles R. Kesler, to whom this book is dedicated, is owed a substantial debt of gratitude for showing me the importance of the progressives, for all that he taught me, and for serving as a model teacher and friend. I hesitate to say this, as it may well bring him more blame than praise from some quarters, but he's been living with that prospect for a long time now. This gratitude must be extended to the broader group of scholars and leaders of the Claremont Institute, from whom I have learned much and where I am privileged to serve as a Senior Fellow. I thank especially the current leadership of the Institute—president Ryan Williams and chairman Tom Klingenstein—for their indispensable support and friendship. I have no idea when this book would have come out were it not for Ryan's persistence.

My home institution, Hillsdale College, is gratefully acknowledged as an ideal environment in which to study the principles of free government. In a time when higher education has become overtly hostile to those principles, the College remains steadfast in its commitment to genuine academic freedom and to the pursuit of truth through a study of the liberal arts and the American experiment of self-government under law. I thank my colleagues and my students, and I extend a special thanks to the College's indefatigable president, Larry Arnn, for all of the opportunities he has given me.

Other organizations and individuals have also provided support for the work represented in this book. I am particularly grateful to the Social Philosophy and Policy Foundation—under the leadership of Fred Miller and Jeff Paul—for the support and encouragement given to a number of my projects on the progressives. The Earhart Foundation is also gratefully acknowledged.

I thank Mariel Stauff, Tom Tacoma, and Stephen Goniprow for their excellent work on the manuscript. Roger Kimball and the staff at Encounter Books have been a pleasure to work with.

As indicated in the Introduction, parts of this volume consist of revisions to work I originally published elsewhere. The two most common outlets for my original pieces were *Social Philosophy and Policy* and Rowman & Littlefield Publishing Group, and I thank both, as well as Cambridge University Press and the University Press of Kentucky. Some of the originals were also collaborations, and I offer my thanks to co-authors William J. Atto, Jason R. Jividen, and Taylor Kempema for allowing me to revise those original pieces and especially for how much I learned and profited from working with them.

INTRODUCTION

PROGRESSIVISM'S ENDURING RELEVANCE

This book marks the culmination of years of writing about American progressivism since the 2005 publication of my monograph on Woodrow Wilson's political thought, and the related publication of two edited volumes of Progressive Era writings in 2005 and 2008. After the original Wilson project, my work dug deeper into Wilson's thought itself, into the thought of other important progressives, and into the effect of all of this on American politics and law today. A selection of those essays and articles forms the backbone of the present volume; the essays have been substantially revised for the book, with new work woven in, and have been arranged to make a coherent case proceeding from first principles to the practical politics of our own day. The aim is to demonstrate how an understanding of Progressive Era thought is essential to grasping the stakes of our present political debates.

Like many students of American political thought, I was initially interested in studying the American Constitution and the first principles of the American founding—a period on which I wrote my first book. Since I had been trained in political philosophy, the founding period was compelling, due in part to the facts that its leading figures were well-versed in the tradition of Western political thought and that one could see ample evidence of this in their major speeches and writings.

The circumstances of the founding also provided a unique opportunity to see how some of the most important ideas from the Western tradition played out in the crucible of real events. My scholarly interest was in statesmanship, in other words, as much as it was in a more abstract understanding of the ideas that provide statesmanship with its ultimate ends. These scholarly interests coincided with my interests as a citizen: being disposed to think both that the Constitution was good and that it should continue to matter in the politics of our own day, the ideas that gave rise to it came to occupy the bulk of my attention as a student and as a young scholar.

Yet neither a scholar nor a citizen can ignore the reality that today's political world is vastly different from that of the founding, and the prevailing political ideas and culture mark a sharp departure from the regime's original principles. Much of this departure is due to the ordinary passage of time and the onset of circumstances that could not possibly have been foreseen hundreds of years ago. The founders themselves understood this inevitability perfectly well. Yet certain core principles were understood by them to be permanent, meant to endure through the unforeseeable exigencies of historical events. This is because they believed—in keeping with much of the Western tradition of thought—that core political ideas were grounded in the very nature of man, and thus that certain first principles of government were "applicable to all men and all times," to use the words that Abraham Lincoln once used to describe the founders' ideas.[1] But that way of looking at politics does not prevail today, as even the core first principles spoken of by the founders and by Lincoln have lost their influence on our culture and our political institutions. This is where the progressives come in. As a student of the founding, I became interested in why its principles no longer held sway in the world in which I was engaged as a citizen, and this interest led me to the study of American progressivism.

In this quest to learn more about the fate of America's first principles in contemporary culture and government, I was fortunate to be studying among Harry Jaffa and his students at Claremont, and within the orbit of scholars associated with the Claremont Institute. This was not only an excellent setting in which to learn about the founding itself; it

---

1 Abraham Lincoln to Henry L. Pierce and Others, April 6, 1859, in *Abraham Lincoln: Speeches and Writings, 1859–1865*, ed. Don E. Fehrenbacher (New York: Library of America, 1989), 19.

was also about the only environment of political theorists at that time where some initial work was being done on the American progressives. It was my teacher Charles R. Kesler, along with other Claremont scholars like John Marini, who first pointed me to the critical role played by the progressives in transforming the core ideas of the American regime, and thus in helping to give rise to modern liberalism. Other than this very small school of political theorists, the only scholarly work that had been done on the progressives prior to the last decade was by historians. The consensus in the major historical works was that there was nothing really radical about American progressivism; it represented, instead, the inevitable adjustments by statesmen in response to the onset of the profoundly new social and economic circumstances that emerged at the turn of the twentieth century. But the political theorists saw something different, deeper, and more radical at work: for them, American progressivism had been a direct assault on the core ideas of the American founding and was thus uniquely influential in the change of the country's direction and the rise of the modern state. My own work on the progressives took off from this basic way of seeing things—first in a book on Woodrow Wilson,[2] and later expanding into writings on progressivism more broadly, culminating in the present volume.

It would be difficult to understate the size of that original group of political theorists who had been pointing to the transformative role of American progressivism. Before the likes of Kesler,[3] Marini,[4] and (eventually) myself, Paul Eidelberg's *Discourse on Statesmanship* may have been among the first to make the case for progressivism's transformative role in the American political tradition.[5] James Ceaser emerged as a lead scholar in the "modern presidency" school, which attributed major changes in

2 Ronald J. Pestritto, *Woodrow Wilson and the Roots of Modern Liberalism* (Lanham, MD: Rowman & Littlefield, 2005).

3 Charles R. Kesler, "Woodrow Wilson and the Statesmanship of Progress," in *Natural Right and Political Right*, ed. Thomas B. Silver and Peter W. Schramm (Durham, NC: Carolina Academic Press, 1984), 103–27.

4 John Marini, "Theology, Metaphysics, and Positivism: The Origins of the Social Sciences and the Transformation of the American University," in *Challenges to the American Founding: Slavery, Historicism, and Progressivism in the Nineteenth Century*, ed. Ronald J. Pestritto and Thomas G. West (Lanham, MD: Lexington Books, 2005), 163–194; Marini and Ken Masugi, eds., *The Progressive Revolution in Politics and Political Science: Transforming the American Regime* (Lanham: Rowman & Littlefield, 2005). Much of this earlier work is incorporated in Marini's recent book, *Unmasking the Administrative State* (New York: Encounter Books, 2019).

5 Paul Eidelberg, *Discourse on Statesmanship: The Design and Transformation of the American Polity* (Urbana: University of Illinois Press, 1974).

the institution of the presidency to progressive statesmen;[6] Dennis J. Mahoney (another Jaffa student) did pioneering work on the connection between progressivism and the development of political science as a discipline;[7] and later Bradley C. S. Watson wrote on the progressive turn in constitutional jurisprudence.[8] There were others who are inevitably left out in lists such as this, but not many. This situation of relative obscurity changed with the national political cycle of 2008, which brought with it the prominent embrace by the Left of its Progressive Era roots and culminated in the election of President Barack Obama. Progressivism—theretofore an object of interest occupying a *very* small corner in the discipline of political theory—went mainstream, both in academic circles and in the public discourse.

In the national political debates of the 1980s the term "liberal" had become a dirty word, and thus in the new millennium those who once called themselves "liberals" embraced the term "progressive" instead. This embrace went deeper than a mere re-packaging: progressive politicians pointed to the original Progressive Era as the source of their principles. Hillary Clinton specifically mentioned Woodrow Wilson and Theodore Roosevelt as the inspirations for her progressivism during the 2008 primary debates, and Obama later launched a major economic initiative by making a speech at Osawatomie, Kansas[9]—where Roosevelt had

6 James W. Ceaser, *Presidential Selection: Theory and Development* (Princeton: Princeton University Press, 1979); Ceaser, Glen E. Thurow, Jeffrey K. Tulis, Joseph M. Bessette, "The Rise of the Rhetorical Presidency," *Presidential Studies Quarterly* 11, no. 2 (Spring 1981): 158–171. For additional examples of work in the "modern presidency" school, see also Tulis, *The Rhetorical Presidency* (Princeton: Princeton University Press, 1987); Robert Eden, "Opinion Leadership and the Problem of Executive Power: Woodrow Wilson's Original Position," *Review of Politics* 57, no. 3 (Summer 1995): 483–503; Eden, "The Rhetorical Presidency and the Eclipse of Executive Power: Woodrow Wilson's *Constitutional Government in the United States*," *Polity* 28, no. 3 (Spring 1996): 357–378; Charles R. Kesler, "Separation of Powers and the Administrative State," in *The Imperial Congress*, ed. Gordon S. Jones and John A. Marini (New York: Pharos Books, 1988), 20–40; Charles R. Kesler, "The Public Philosophy of the New Freedom and the New Deal," in *The New Deal and Its Legacy*, ed. Robert Eden (New York: Greenwood Press, 1989), 155–66; Kesler, "Woodrow Wilson and the Statesmanship of Progress," 103–127.

7 Dennis Mahoney, *Politics and Progress: The Emergence of American Political Science* (Lanham, MD: Lexington Books, 2004).

8 Bradley C. S. Watson, *Living Constitution, Dying Faith: Progressivism and the New Science of Jurisprudence* (Wilmington: ISI Books, 2009). Paul D. Moreno has also recently written on the progressive influence on constitutional history; see Moreno, *The American State from the Civil War to the New Deal: The Twilight of Constitutionalism and the Triumph of Progressivism* (Cambridge: Cambridge University Press, 2013); and Moreno, *The Bureaucrat Kings: The Origins and Underpinnings of America's Bureaucratic State* (Santa Barbara: Praeger, 2017).

9 Barack Obama, "Remarks at Osawatomie High School in Osawatomie, Kansas," December 6, 2011, accessed February 8, 2020, https://www.presidency.ucsb.edu/documents/remarks-osawatomie-high-school-osawatomie-kansas.

delivered his famous "New Nationalism" speech in 1910. Among other things, the embrace of the progressive mantle helped to clear up any confusion that might have existed between *modern* liberals—those who favor an expansive and active central government of the kind we have seen in America since the early part of the twentieth century—and those whom we might call *classical* liberals, who see the fundamental purpose of government as the protection of individual rights and thus view with suspicion any extension of governmental power into spheres beyond this limited purpose. More important, by increasingly identifying themselves as progressives, modern liberals had come home. The most influential think tank on the Left—founded by former Clinton aide John Podesta—came to be the Center for American Progress; and Podesta published a popular book titled *The Power of Progress: How America's Progressives Can (Once Again) Save Our Economy, Our Climate, and Our Country.*[10]

Faced with this unapologetic embrace of progressive ideas and policies, which was backed with the real political power of Obama's ascension to the presidency, conservatives suddenly became interested in understanding progressivism and in finding ways to battle it in public discourse. The new energy on the Left was met with new energy on the Right, as conservatives realized that Obama and the new progressives were quite serious in their stated goal to "change" and "transform" America. This progressive argument that new principles were needed for new times, and that history had passed by the old American ideas, found its perfect intellectual antecedent in the original Progressive Era. And the perfect antecedent of the conservative counterargument was to be found in the principles of the American Revolution, which had proclaimed permanent truths about human nature and correspondingly timeless ends of government that were not subject to redefinition from age to age. It was in this way that the Tea Party movement became the popular manifestation, on the Right, of a deeper and more thoughtful commitment among conservative intellectuals to engage progressive ideas with a renewed explication of those of the American founding. And this is why those of us who had, until then, been talking about American progressivism within small academic circles, came to be drawn into the major debates of the public square—writing in popular outlets and even going on television to shed light on the progressive

10 John Podesta, *The Power of Progress: How America's Progressives Can (Once Again) Save Our Economy, Our Climate, and Our Country* (New York: Crown, 2008).

origins of contemporary liberalism and to explain how progressivism had played a central role in the loss of our constitutional culture.[11] And while the Tea Party phenomenon itself faded after a couple of election cycles, the deeper commitment in at least some circles on the Right to bringing constitutional principles to bear on public policy remains. As progressives have come to rely more on the organs of the administrative state as the primary means of pursuing their policy goals, conservatives have increasingly fallen back on reasserting the role of the Constitution's traditional branches of government and its principle of the separation of powers. President Trump's advisor Stephen Bannon famously articulated a main goal of the administration as the "deconstruction of the administrative state,"[12] and politicians and judges on the Right have come to question the very legitimacy of the post-New Deal order in ways that were not common just a generation earlier. Put differently, the disputes that we see in national politics are, increasingly, fundamental disputes, reflecting a deep divide over first principles. This reality explains, perhaps more than any other factor, the renewed interest in the core principles of the founding order, and the core arguments made by the original progressives for a transformation of that order. It also helps to explain the rapid rise in scholarship on American progressivism, from both sides of the divide.

This divide, however, is more complicated than "Right vs. Left." While conservatives are quite united in opposition to the policies of the contemporary progressives, intellectuals on the Right are of diverse views on the role of the original progressives, and on the progressives' relationship to the American founding. To know what one thinks of the progressives, one must first know what to make of the founding, since the original progressives defined their movement as a fundamental move away from the founders' political thought. And conservative intellectuals have never agreed on what to make of the founding. The different

---

11 For an instructive account, see Robert D. Johnston, "Long Live Teddy/Death to Woodrow: The Polarized Politics of The Progressive Era in the 2012 Election," *Journal of the Gilded Age and Progressive Era* 13, no. 3 (July 2014): 411–443. For those interested in a broader historiography of work on the progressives, Johnston has a thorough one: Johnston, "Re-Democratizing the Progressive Era: The Politics of Progressive Era Political Historiography," *Journal of the Gilded Age and Progressive Era* 1, no. 1 (2002): 68–92.

12 Philip Rucker and Robert Costa, "Bannon Vows a Daily Fight for 'Deconstruction of the Administrative State,'" *The Washington Post*, February 23, 2017, accessed February 8, 2020, https://www.washingtonpost.com/politics/top-wh-strategist-vows-a-daily-fight-for-deconstruction-of-the-administrative-state/2017/02/23/03f6b8da-f9ea-11e6-bf01-d47f8cf9b643_story.html.

strands of the conservative intellectual movement have, for decades, had sharply and fundamentally different views of the American founding, and of just who is to blame for the rise and victory of the modern liberal state. When the Tea Party movement rose up in 2009 and the energy in conservative politics (not to mention the fundraising opportunities) became focused on a return to founding principles and on resisting the progressive transformation of those principles, conservative organizations scrambled to promote projects on the founding or on progressivism. For many of them, this was new territory. Just a few years prior, many of the same organizations were not at all sure that they liked anything about the founding and would have had trouble identifying any but the most obvious among American progressives. Even today, as coalescing around the Constitution and against progressivism has become ubiquitous in the *popular* politics of the Right, conservative *intellectuals* still sharply diverge on this question.

I have argued, and will continue to argue in this book, that the turn in American politics toward the modern liberal state was grounded in the progressive rejection of the founders' political principles. The major challenge to that argument within conservative intellectual circles has come from those who agree that the turn to modern liberalism has been disastrous for America, but disagree that the progressives are principally to blame for this development. It's not that these conservatives embrace progressivism; rather, they see progressivism as the inevitable result of dangerous ideas and trends that have much earlier origins in American political development. These scholars are profoundly uncomfortable with the founding itself—with the alleged modernism of its political philosophy or with the fact that the Federalists rather than the Anti-Federalists emerged with the upper hand. From this perspective, the fault in my argument lies in failing to view the founding with a sufficiently critical eye—in blaming the progressives for developments which grew out of defects that the founders themselves baked into the system from the beginning, even if unwittingly. The most well-known recent example would have to be Patrick Deneen,[13] though this uneasiness with the founding is hardly novel in the history in the conservative movement.[14]

---

13 Patrick J. Deneen, *Why Liberalism Failed* (New Haven: Yale University Press, 2018); for an opposing view, see Dennis Hale and Marc Landy, "Blame the Fathers," review of *Why Liberalism Failed*, by Patrick J. Deneen, *Claremont Review of Books* (Summer 2018).

14 See, for example, Robert H. Bork, *Slouching Toward Gomorrah* (New York: ReganBooks, 1996); Peter Lawler, "Natural Law, Our Constitution, and Our Democracy," in *Modern*

There are many facets to this conservative critique and a serious account of it lies beyond the purpose of this book, though oddly Alexis de Tocqueville is often employed in making the criticism. Tocqueville is the principal authority on American government for this group of conservative intellectuals, because he saw the potential in democratic individualism for the rise of the soft despotism of the modern state. And so those of us who primarily blame the progressives for America's wrong turn (with an assist from the German ideas they imported) make matters worse by failing to give Tocqueville's analysis of America's defects pride of place. This failure, the critique continues, causes us to look outside of the American tradition—to the German ideas of the progressives—for the source of our wrong turn, when the real source lies with the Americans themselves, as Tocqueville allegedly taught us. As Deneen has written, *Democracy in America* "perceived the seeds of progressivism's major tenets already embedded in the basic features and attributes of liberal democracy as established at the founding."[15] Yet this contention that Tocqueville sees the defects of "liberal democracy *as established at the founding*" seems to conflate his general account of democracy with the American version of it. The point of Tocqueville's book is to praise American democracy by distinguishing it from other, purer forms, and by showing how it cuts against the general trends of democratic times. Far from seeing a future progressive utopia baked into the principles of American democracy, Tocqueville mimics *The Federalist* on what it will take to make self-government work. He, like the Federalist framers of the Constitution, understands that the gravest threat to republicanism is majority tyranny.[16] And of course it is the Constitution's protections against majority tyranny that are the greatest source of irritation to America's progressives, as this book will show. Tocqueville distinguishes American constitutionalism, in other words, from the very form of anti-constitutionalist democracy that progressives would later champion.

And the contention that the progressives were simply taking advantage of principles that were present all along in American government

---

America and the Legacy of the Founding, ed. by Ronald J. Pestritto and Thomas G. West (Lanham, MD: Lexington Books, 2005), 207–237.

15 Patrick J. Deneen, "Tocqueville on the Individualist Roots of Progressivism," *The Imaginative Conservative*, November 29, 2013, accessed February 8, 2020, https://theimaginativeconservative.org/2013/11/tocqueville-individualist-roots-progressivism.html.

16 Alexis de Tocqueville, *Democracy in America*, ed. and trans. Harvey C. Mansfield and Delba Winthrop (Chicago: University of Chicago Press, 2002), 249.

runs up against another stubborn fact: the progressives themselves. There is a reason that almost every theoretical work written by an American progressive—and many practical ones as well—begins with a sustained and direct attack on the philosophy of the American founding and on the principles of the American Constitution—and that reason is *not* that the progressives saw in the founding the secret source of their own vision for the modern state. This isn't to suggest that there weren't native influences on the rise of progressivism, or that there weren't receptive elements of the American political tradition which made the importation of German state theory more plausible[17]—history is complicated and shifts of this magnitude almost always involve a combination of factors that can be difficult to disentangle. But the social compact principles of the founding provide a clear contrast to the ideas and philosophers championed by the progressives, and the progressives themselves knew it.

This book grounds itself on that fact and will detail how and why American progressives saw the principles of the founding as ideas that had to be refuted and replaced if their vision for the modern state was to be fulfilled.

It will do so in Part I by beginning with an overview of progressivism and the Progressive Era—an essential primer, before more focused analyses follow in subsequent chapters. In showing how progressivism can be understood as a single, coherent, identifiable idea or principle, one runs the risk of criticism from those who would point to important differences among the prominent progressives on the major issues of the day. Most obviously, the two most prominent national progressives addressed in this book—Roosevelt and Wilson—not only were from different political parties but opposed one another in a hard-fought presidential election. Perhaps even more importantly, there was a split among national progressives about the viability of the two-party system itself, to mention just one of the differences on the issues that characterized Progressive Era debates. Nonetheless, the book will contend that progressivism can be understood as a coherent set of principles, with a common purpose. The differences among progressives over issues like reforming the party system were, in

---

17 There is little secondary scholarship on the potential pre-Civil War sources of progressive thought from within the American tradition itself, though in an as-yet unpublished dissertation, Nathan E. Gill credibly points to New England intellectuals and politicians as one possibility. Gill, *The Decline and Rejection of Social Contract Theory in Antebellum New England* (Doctoral Dissertation, Hillsdale College, 2018).

the end, differences over particular means, not over fundamental ideas of what government is or ought to be, and certainly not over the need with which all progressives identified to revolutionize both the theory and practice of American government.

Because of the coherent set of principles that characterizes this movement, we can think of it as an "-ism" as much as we think of it as an "era." The meaning of progressivism, and its profound relevance for American politics today, transcends any boundaries that might be placed upon it by a particular set of dates or figures. Progressivism and the ideas that constitute it are alive and well today, as is evidenced by the reclaiming of that title by today's liberals. Understanding progressivism thus requires both an historical and a theoretical perspective. One cannot comprehend progressivism without paying careful attention to the particular events and figures of the Progressive Era and thinking about how these shaped the character of the movement; nor can one comprehend the progressives without perceiving the core ideas that gave them their identity and thinking about the relevance of these ideas in their own right.

After the opening chapter provides a primer on progressivism and the Progressive Era, Part I will continue with a deeper dive into the political philosophy of progressivism, showing in two chapters what the first principles of the movement were and the way in which these principles departed from the political theory of the American Constitution. Chapter Two will lay out the contrast by showing how liberalism underwent a fundamental transformation—from classical to modern—in the works of the most important progressive thinkers. Chapter Three will look at two of these thinkers—Roosevelt and Wilson—in greater detail, concentrating on their democratic theory, which aimed to popularize American government but also delegate power to expert administrators.

Part II of the book moves from progressive first principles to the actual development of progressive politics in American history. Progressive changes to American government did not take place in a vacuum, or as a merely theoretical exercise; they played out in real time and were shaped by the important events and figures of American history. This part of the book examines the manner in which key figures and events affected the progressive transformation described in Part I. Specifically, Chapter Four shows how the major transformative event of the nineteenth century—the Civil War—and its central figure—Abraham Lincoln—influenced progressive thinking and how the progressives' ideas developed out of a view they had of Lincoln and the sectional conflict. Progressivism was also deeply intertwined with a major cultural and religious movement coming out of the nineteenth century—the Social Gospel movement—and Chapter Five shows how the major progressive figures were part of, and influenced by, that movement. Richard T. Ely and Walter Rauschenbusch played major roles here, in addition to more well-known figures like Roosevelt—though there was tension between religious and secular progressives that will also be addressed. Finally, in addition to the Civil War and the Social Gospel, America's emergence as a major player in international affairs was a critical historical setting for the progressives; indeed, international involvement is arguably the context in which progressive figures like Wilson are best-known. Chapter Six will detail the critical international events in which progressives were involved, and will also show how the conventional understanding of progressive internationalism stands at odds, on key points, with the progressive principles outlined in Part I.

And while these historical events are important to understanding American progressivism, the recent explosion of interest in progressivism comes not from an antiquarian curiosity in a bygone era but from the relevance that Progressive Era changes have for the practice of government today. Part III will look to the connection between the original theory and development of progressivism and the shape of American government today. The rise and dominance of the administrative state will draw the most attention, given its obvious relevance in today's politics and the connection to the progressives' first principles. Chapter Seven looks to the origins of the administrative state in the institutional arguments of Wilson, Frank Goodnow, and James Landis, while Chapter Eight carries the analysis into present national policy disputes, identifying the key holdings in constitutional and administrative law that have set the stage for contemporary administrative discretion. Finally, Chapter Nine concludes the book by looking to the area of government which was most immediately impacted by the Progressives, in which the most obvious structural changes took place: state and local politics. This is a major legacy of progressivism today, and it seems the most suitable way to conclude a book on the movement's transformative effect. At the state and local level—which is where the vast majority of Americans have any regular interaction with government—the effects of progressivism are so thorough and so long-established that they are barely noticed; for this reason they are also a good place to underscore the transformative role and enduring relevance of American progressivism.

PART I

★

PROGRESSIVE FIRST PRINCIPLES

CHAPTER ONE

★

A PRIMER ON PROGRESSIVISM AND THE PROGRESSIVE ERA

What is progressivism?[1] The chapters in this book will lay out its characteristics in detail, but to begin we can think of it as an argument to move beyond the political principles of the American founding. It is an argument to enlarge vastly the scope of national government for the purpose of responding to a set of economic and social conditions which, progressives contend, could not have been envisioned at the founding and for which the founders' limited, constitutional government is inadequate. Whereas the founders posited what they held to be a permanent understanding of just government, based upon a permanent account of human nature, progressives have countered that the ends and scope of government are to be defined anew in each historical epoch. They have coupled this belief in historical contingency with a deep faith in historical progress, suggesting that, due to historical evolution, government was becoming less of a danger to the governed and more capable of solving the great array of problems besetting the human race. Historically, these ideas formed a common thread among the most important American

1 This chapter is Ronald J. Pestritto's revision of an essay originally co-authored with William J. Atto. The original version was genuinely collaborative, making it difficult to parcel out responsibility for the different parts, though the sections on progressive interpretations of history and on social justice and education profited most of all from Atto's work.

thinkers from the 1880s into the 1920s and beyond, manifesting themselves in the writings and speeches of Theodore Roosevelt, Woodrow Wilson, Herbert Croly, John Dewey, Robert La Follette, and several others. The arguments of these central figures will be explored in the following chapters; the task here is to speak more generally to the fundamental characteristics in the thought of these figures that gave them common cause as progressives.

THE PRINCIPLES OF PROGRESSIVISM

The Progressive Era was the first major period in American political development to feature, as a primary characteristic, the open and direct criticism of the Constitution. While criticism of the Constitution can be found during any period of American history from 1787 onward, the Progressive Era was unique in that such criticism formed the backbone of the entire movement. Progressive Era criticism of the Constitution came not from a few fringe figures, but from the most prominent thinkers and politicians of that time. Readers are reminded, in almost any progressive text they will pick up, that the Constitution is old, and that it was written to deal with circumstances that had long ago been replaced by a whole new set of pressing social and economic ills. The progressives understood the intention and structure of the Constitution very well; they knew that it established a framework for limited government, and that these limits were to be upheld by a variety of institutional restraints and checks. They also knew that the limits placed on the national government by the Constitution represented major obstacles to implementing the progressive policy agenda. Progressives had in mind a variety of legislative programs aimed at regulating significant portions of the American economy and society, and at redistributing private property in the name of social justice. The Constitution, if interpreted and applied faithfully, stood in the way of this agenda.

The Constitution, however, was only a means to an end. It was crafted and adopted for the sake of achieving the natural rights principles of the Declaration of Independence. The progressives understood this very clearly, which is why many of the more theoretical works written by progressives feature sharp attacks on social compact theory and on the notion that the fundamental purpose of government is to secure the individual natural rights of citizens. While most of the founders and nearly all ordinary Americans did not subscribe to the radical epistemology of the social compact theorists, they did believe, in Lockean fashion, that men as individuals possessed rights by nature—rights that any just government was bound to uphold and which stood as inherent limits to the authority of government over individual liberty and property. The regulatory and redistributive aims of the progressive policy agenda, therefore, were on a collision course with the political theory of the founding. This basic fact makes understandable Woodrow Wilson's[2] admonition—in an address ostensibly honoring Thomas Jefferson—that "if you want to understand the real Declaration of Independence, do not repeat the preface."[3] Do not, in other words, repeat that part of the Declaration which enshrines natural rights as the focal point of American government.

Taking Wilson's advice here would turn our attention away from the timelessness of the Declaration's conception of government and would focus us instead on the litany of grievances made against George III; in other words, it would show the Declaration as a merely practical document, to be understood as a specific, time-bound response to a set of specific historical circumstances. Once the circumstances change, so too must our conception of government. It is with this in mind that Wilson urged that "we are not bound to adhere to the doctrines held by the signers of the Declaration of Independence," and that every Fourth of July, instead of a celebration of the timeless principles of the Declaration, should instead "be a time for examining our standards, our purposes, for determining afresh what principles, what forms of power we think most likely to effect our safety and happiness."[4] Like Wilson, the progressive academic Frank Goodnow[5] acknowledged that the founders' system of

---

2 The twenty-eighth president of the United States, who also served as governor of New Jersey, Wilson (1856–1924) is known best for his public life and especially for his leadership during and after World War I. But Wilson was also a prolific academic long before he became a politician, having held professorships at Bryn Mawr, Wesleyan, and finally Princeton (his alma mater).

3 Woodrow Wilson, "An Address to the Jefferson Club of Los Angeles," May 12, 1911, in *The Papers of Woodrow Wilson* (hereafter cited as *PWW*), 69 vols., ed. Arthur S. Link (Princeton: Princeton University Press, 1966–1993), 23:34.

4 Woodrow Wilson, "The Author and Signers of the Declaration of Independence," September 1907, in *PWW*, 17:251.

5 Goodnow (1859–1939) was the first president of the American Political Science Association. A student of John Burgess, he taught at Columbia University prior to his term as president of Johns Hopkins University. Most of Goodnow's work came in the field of administrative law,

government "was permeated by the theories of social compact and natural right," and he complained that such theories were "worse than useless," since they "retard development"[6]—that is, that the protections for individual liberty and property inhibit the expansion of government. In contrast to the principle of natural rights that undergirded the American system, Goodnow praised political systems in Europe where, he explained, "the rights which [an individual] possesses are, it is believed, conferred upon him, not by his Creator, but rather by the society to which he belongs. What they are is to be determined by the legislative authority in view of the needs of that society. Social expediency, rather than natural right, is thus to determine the sphere of individual freedom of action."[7]

Goodnow, Wilson, and other progressives championed historical contingency against the Declaration's talk of the permanent principles of just government. The natural rights understanding of government may have been appropriate, they conceded, as a response to the prevailing tyranny of that day, but, they argued, all government has to be understood as a product of its particular historical context. The great sin committed by the founding generation was not, then, its adherence to the doctrine of natural rights, but rather its notion that that doctrine was meant to transcend the particular circumstances of that day. It was this very facet of the founders' thinking that Abraham Lincoln recognized, and praised, in 1859 when he wrote of the Declaration and its primary author: "All honor to Jefferson—to the man who, in the concrete pressure of a struggle for national independence by a single people, had the coolness, forecast, and capacity to introduce into a merely revolutionary document, an abstract truth, applicable to all men and all times."[8] Recognizing the very same characteristic of the founders' thought, John Dewey[9] complained, by

---

where he pioneered (along with Wilson) a science of administration separated from the limits of constitutional government. His most comprehensive work in this regard was *Politics and Administration* (1900).

6 Frank J. Goodnow, *Social Reform and the Constitution* (New York: Macmillan, 1911), 1, 3.

7 Frank J. Goodnow, *The American Conception of Liberty and Government* (Brown University Colver Lectures, 1916), 11.

8 Abraham Lincoln to Henry L. Pierce and Others, April 6, 1859, in *Abraham Lincoln: Speeches and Writings, 1859–1865*, ed. Don E. Fehrenbacher (Library of America, 1989), 19.

9 A professor of philosophy at Columbia University and prolific author of philosophical, educational, and reform treatises, Dewey (1859–1952) made his greatest contribution to the progressive movement through his works on educational theory and reform. Among these, his best-known works are *The School and Society* (1899) and *Democracy and Education* (1916), the latter of which gives the most comprehensive statement of his radical reconstruction of the theory and purposes of education as traditionally understood.

contrast, that the founding generation "lacked historic sense and interest" and that it had a "disregard of history." As if speaking directly to Lincoln's praise of the founding, Dewey endorsed, instead, the doctrine of historical contingency. Natural rights theory, Dewey argued, "blinded the eyes of liberals to the fact that their own special interpretations of liberty, individuality and intelligence were themselves historically conditioned, and were relevant only to their own time. They put forward their ideas as immutable truths good at all times and places; they had no idea of historic relativity."[10] The idea of liberty was not frozen in time, Dewey argued, but had instead a history of evolving meaning. The history of liberalism, about which Dewey wrote in *Liberalism and Social Action*, was progressive—it told a story of the move from more primitive to more mature conceptions of liberty. Modern liberalism, therefore, represented a vast improvement over classical (or what Dewey called "early") liberalism.

This coupling of historical contingency with the doctrine of progress—shared by all progressives to one degree or another—reveals how the progressive movement became the means by which German historicism was imported into the American political tradition. The influence of German political philosophy is evident not only from looking at the ideas espoused by progressives, but also from the historical pedigree of the most influential progressive thinkers. Almost all of them were either educated in Germany in the nineteenth century or had as teachers those who were. This fact reflects the sea change that had occurred in American higher education in the second half of the nineteenth century, a time when most Americans who wanted an advanced degree went to Europe to get one. By 1900, the faculties of American colleges and universities had become populated with European Ph.D.s, and the historical thinking which dominated Europe (especially Germany) in the nineteenth century came to permeate American higher education. Johns Hopkins University, founded in 1876, was established for the express purpose of bringing the German educational model to the United States. It produced several prominent progressives, including Wilson, Dewey, and Frederick Jackson Turner.[11]

---

10 John Dewey, *Liberalism and Social Action* (Buffalo, NY: Prometheus Books, 2000), 40–41.

11 Among the most influential of American historians, Turner (1861–1932) largely rejected the "germ theory" of his mentor, Herbert Baxter Adams, which held that American institutions were derivatives of Germanic origin. Turner formulated his own "frontier thesis" as a means of explaining American development. Central to his methodology was his willingness to make use

Among other things, American progressives took from the Germans—and especially from the German philosopher G. W. F. Hegel and his disciples—their critique of individual rights and social compact theory, and their organic or "living" notion of the national state. Wilson, in reflecting on what it meant to be a progressive, wrote of government as a "living thing," which was to be understood according to "the theory of organic life." This "living" notion of a constitution, Wilson contended, was far superior to the founders' model, which had considered government a kind of "machine" which could be constantly limited through checks and balances.[12] As a living entity, the progressives reasoned, government had to evolve and adapt in response to changing circumstances. While early American conceptions of national government had carefully circumscribed its power due to the perceived threat to individual liberties, progressives argued that history had brought about an improvement in the human condition, such that the will of the people was no longer in danger of becoming factious. Citing a whole new host of economic and social ills that called out for a governmental remedy, progressives took this doctrine of progress and translated it into a call for a sharp increase in the scope of governmental power.

There may be no greater example of this phenomenon than Theodore Roosevelt's speech on the New Nationalism in 1910, which became the foundation for his 1912 campaign to regain the presidency. The speech reflects Roosevelt's turn, after his presidency, to a more radical brand of progressivism, demonstrating the extent to which other progressives like Herbert Croly had come to influence his thinking. In the New Nationalism speech, Roosevelt called for the state to take an active role in effecting economic equality by way of superintending the use of private property. Private property rights, which had been serving as a brake on the more aggressive progressive policy proposals, were to be respected, Roosevelt argued, only insofar as the government approved of the property's social utility:

---

of multiple disciplines such as sociology, statistics, and geography in his work. Though he wrote a number of important works including *The Rise of the New West* (1906) and the posthumously published *The Significance of Sections in American History* (1932), which was awarded a Pulitzer prize, none equaled the influence of his 1893 essay "The Significance of the Frontier in American History."

12 Woodrow Wilson, *The New Freedom* (New York: Doubleday, Page & Company, 1913), 46–47.

> We grudge no man a fortune in civil life if it is honorably obtained and well used. It is not even enough that it should have been gained without doing damage to the community. We should permit it to be gained only so long as the gaining represents benefit to the community. This, I know, implies a policy of a far more active governmental interference with social and economic conditions in this country than we have yet had, but I think we have got to face the fact that such an increase in governmental control is now necessary.[13]

New circumstances, Roosevelt argued, necessitated a new conception of government, and natural rights were no longer to serve as a principled boundary that the state was prohibited from crossing. Wilson had outlined a similar view of the extent of state power in a concise but revealing essay on the relationship between socialism and democracy. Wilson's essay starts out by defining socialism, suggesting that it stands for unfettered state power, which trumps any notion of individual rights. It "proposes that all idea of a limitation of public authority by individual rights be put out of view" and "that no line can be drawn between private and public affairs which the State may not cross at will." After laying out this definition of socialism, Wilson explained that he found nothing wrong with it in principle, since it was merely the logical extension of genuine democratic theory. It gives all power to the people, in their collective capacity, to carry out their will through the exercise of governmental power, unlimited by any undemocratic idea like individual rights. He elaborated:

> In fundamental theory socialism and democracy are almost if not quite one and the same. They both rest at bottom upon the absolute right of the community to determine its own destiny *and that of its members.* Limits of wisdom and convenience to the public control there may be: limits of principle there are, upon strict analysis, none.[14]

In this view, rights-based theories of self-government, such as the republicanism to which the American founders subscribed and of which Wilson

13 Theodore Roosevelt, "The New Nationalism," in *The New Nationalism* (New York: The Outlook Company, 1910), 17–18.

14 Woodrow Wilson, "Socialism and Democracy," August 22, 1887, in *PWW*, 5:561. Emphasis added.

was sharply critical, are far less democratic than socialism. As Wilson and his fellow progressives believed, rights-based theories of government limit the state's sphere of action, thus limiting the ability of the people to implement their collective will and consequently representing something less than a real democracy.

PROGRESSIVE INTERPRETATIONS OF HISTORY

Given their reliance on the doctrine of progress, a significant number of leading national progressives placed critical emphasis upon historical interpretation. Both Roosevelt and Wilson had a keen sense of history and were, in fact, historians in their own right, each producing a number of scholarly historical works. And both were dramatically influenced by the changes that accompanied the professionalization of historical study in the academy in the late nineteenth century. By the time Roosevelt became president in 1901, a quarter-century of change had stripped the field of its attachment to purely literary narrative and Romantic expression; the prose of Francis Parkman and the celebratory works of George Bancroft (though Bancroft often praised the values progressives cherished, such as popular democracy and individual autonomy) yielded to the "new learning." To assert their legitimate place in the university, historians maintained, they must adopt new methodologies and incorporate the multitudes of information and the insights provided by the new fields of sociology, psychology, and statistics.

Among the earliest of the new approaches to historical methodology was the "Teutonic-germ theory" of Herbert Baxter Adams at Johns Hopkins University. Adams's assertion that democratic institutions in America owed their existence to Germanic developments centuries earlier held sway briefly among historians in the 1880s. Among Adams's closest students were Wilson and Turner, and Turner's early writings clearly suggest the influence of Adams and the Germanic model. As late as 1891, Turner published an article entitled "The Significance of History" that quoted Adams extensively and demonstrated his support for Adams's ideas. Turner wrote:

> The story of the peopling of America has not yet been written. We do not understand ourselves.... One of the most fruitful fields of study in our country has been the process of growth of our own institutions,

> local and national. The town and the country, the germs of our political institutions, have been traced back to old Teutonic roots.[15]

Nonetheless, Turner ultimately rejected the germ theory as an inadequate explanatory model and replaced it in 1893 with one far more influential. He posited the "frontier thesis" as the means to understand American development, and the thesis, with its emphasis on democratic individualism, sparked a reinterpretation of American history that served progressives well. The American was a new man, Turner maintained, refashioned by the transforming influence of frontier life. America's development was "not simply the development of Germanic germs" but was unique and resulted in "a new product that is American." The innovative, self-reliant farmer of Turner's frontier epitomized the democratizing effect of the westward movement, and thus Turner's work was congenial to supporters of an aggressive popular movement that stressed democratic means to realize political and social reform.

Equally, and perhaps more, important for progressives' attempt to break with the past in favor of a more egalitarian polity was the emergence of a body of scholarly work that questioned the longstanding view of the Revolutionary generation as one motivated mostly by a sense of selfless duty to country and commitment to natural-law principles as enshrined in the Declaration of Independence. It was Charles Beard's[16] *An Economic Interpretation of the Constitution of the United States*, published in 1913, that undoubtedly did the most to aid the progressive reform agenda on this front, but there were a number of significant works by progressive scholars that preceded Beard and, to a degree, set the stage for his dramatic interpretation of the constitutional convention. The political scientist J. Allen Smith, for example, published *The Spirit of American Government* six years before Beard's *Economic Interpretation*.

---

15 Frederick Jackson Turner, "The Significance of History," in Harvey Wish, ed. *American Historians: A Selection* (Oxford: Oxford University Press, 1962 [orig. pub. 1891]), 299.

16 Through his controversial writings on the Constitution, the Civil War, and American foreign policy during Franklin Roosevelt's presidency, Beard (1874–1948) established his reputation as a maverick in the disciplines of political science and history. He completed his doctorate in political science at Columbia University in 1904 and held professorships there and at several other universities during his career. He was a prolific author whose most important works included *An Economic Interpretation of the Constitution of the United States* (1913), *Rise of American Civilization* (1927), co-authored with his wife, Mary, and *President Roosevelt and the Coming of War, 1941* (1948).

Smith maintained that the delegates to the constitutional convention were best understood, not as a group of disinterested patriots pursuing the common good, but as a distinct group with definable economic interests.[17] James Harvey Robinson, an intellectual historian and leading light of the "New Historians" at Columbia University, which included a significant number of progressive luminaries such as Beard, called upon scholars to provide a usable history, one that embraced the new learning and illuminated potential solutions to the ills of industrial society.[18] Even Turner, oftentimes considered the least radical of the leading progressive historians, criticized "Gladstone's remark that 'The American Constitution is the most wonderful work ever struck off at a given time by the brain and purpose of man.'" That statement, Turner contended, "has been shown to be misleading, for the Constitution was, with all the constructive powers of the fathers, still a growth; and our history is only to be understood as a growth from European history under the new conditions of the new world."[19]

It was Beard, however, who provided the most radical break with the standard interpretation of the proceedings at the Philadelphia convention. The *Economic Interpretation* was received like a thunderclap, with denunciations (and some praise) from many of Beard's colleagues. The delegates at Philadelphia, Beard contended, were motivated by personal economic concerns and determined to produce a document that strengthened their control of government and thus assured their continued financial success. While Beard's assertion was similar to Smith's, his methodology, which seemed to substantiate the charge of avarice in a way that Smith's had not, combined with the charge that the framers should be condemned for reprehensible self-seeking, was a direct assault on the previously sacrosanct Constitution and its authors. Jefferson may have believed that the delegates assembled in Philadelphia were "demi-gods," but Beard thought otherwise. In Beard's analysis, even Madison—perhaps especially Madison—was charged with subscribing to "the theory of economic determinism in politics."[20]

---

17 J. Allen Smith, *The Spirit of American Government*, ed. Cushing Strout (Cambridge: The Belknap Press of Harvard University Press, 1965), 27–39.

18 James Harvey Robinson, *The New History: Essays Illustrating the Modern Historical Outlook* (Mishawaka, IN: Palala Press, 2015), 16–25.

19 Turner, "The Significance of History," 299.

20 Charles Beard, *An Economic Interpretation of the Constitution of the United States* (New York: Macmillan, 1935), 15.

The implications of Beard's thesis were clear and significant for advocates of progressive reform: there had been no popular control of government from the founding generation to the present; a great people had been duped by the conniving of a relatively small interest group. It was, therefore, incumbent upon proponents of democracy to wrest control of government from the few and place it where, despite the rhetoric of earlier generations, it had never been, in the hands of the populace. "[O]ur fundamental law," Beard wrote, "was not the product of an abstraction known as 'the whole people,' but of a group of economic interests."[21] Though Beard, and progressive historians generally, are usually credited with positing the notion of discontinuity in America's past, there is a significant exception here. Beard sounded a clear note of continuity by maintaining that economic elites had always maintained their status by virtue of their control of the political apparatus.

Progressive interpretations of history thus supported the purposes of reformers by suggesting that America's story was one of progress, while also stressing its reliance, oftentimes, on a false understanding of the past that served to obstruct the reform agenda. Old myths and shibboleths were to be replaced with a realistic appraisal of American life, which included both an emphasis on the unique aspects of the American character and a willingness to break with an uncritical celebration of the national past.

PROGRESSIVISM AND RELIGION

History was, for the progressives, more than a series of chance events. The passing of each historical epoch marked, instead, deliberate progress on the path to genuine democracy. With this conception of history as rational and powerful, we can also see a strong religious current that runs through much of progressive thought. Like Hegel, many progressives saw the hand of God at work in the process of historical progress. History was the means by which God gradually made himself present on earth, and the end result of this divinely inspired process was to be the modern democratic state. Consequently the state, for many progressives, was a god to which all citizens owed their undivided devotion: "the Divine Idea

21 Beard, *Economic Interpretation*, 17.

as it exists on Earth," as Hegel had put it in his *Philosophy of History*.[22] Cooperation with history—willingness, in other words, to adjust one's politics and morality to the evolving pressures of the current age—thus becomes a kind of divine imperative and a test of one's faithfulness to God. Those refusing to go along with the demands of historical progress were, therefore, defying the will of God himself.[23]

Such a conception of history helps to explain the remarkably explicit religious language employed by many progressive politicians. During his speech at the Progressive Party convention in 1912, Roosevelt thundered: "Our cause is based on the eternal principles of righteousness; and even though we who now lead may for a time fail, in the end the cause itself shall triumph.... We stand at Armageddon, and we battle for the Lord."[24] The convention culminated with party stalwarts waving bibles and demonstrating to fervent chants of "Onward Christian Soldiers." Even with respect to issues as mundane as the gold standard, religious language was invoked, as when William Jennings Bryan famously clamored at the 1896 Democratic convention: "You shall not press down upon the brow of labor this crown of thorns; you shall not crucify mankind upon a cross of gold."[25] This kind of language, and the fusion it represents between Hegelianism and evangelical Protestantism, calls to mind what was, in many respects, the religious arm of progressivism: Social Gospel.

The connection between progressivism and Social Gospel will be explored more fully in Chapter Five, but in short, Social Gospel, beginning in the 1880s and lasting through the First World War, represented the response of liberal evangelical Protestantism to the great cultural and intellectual challenges of the late nineteenth century, most notably evolution and the new science. The response of the orthodox wing of the Protestant church was fundamentalism; going in the other direction, Social Gospel embraced evolutionary theory (although not its

22 G.W.F. Hegel, *The Philosophy of History*, trans. J. Sibree (Mineola, NY: Dover Publications, Inc., 1956), 39: the divinity of the state, Hegel explained, meant that "all worth which the human being possesses—all spiritual reality, he possesses only through the State."

23 For some good examples of this mode of thinking, see two of Wilson's early religious essays: "Christ's Army," August 17, 1876, in *PWW*, 1:180–181; "Christian Progress," December 20, 1876, in *PWW*, 1:235.

24 Theodore Roosevelt, "A Confession of Faith: Address Before the National Convention of the Progressive Party in Chicago, August 6, 1912," in *Progressive Principles*, ed. Elmer H. Youngman (New York: Progressive National Service, 1913), 173.

25 William Jennings Bryan, "In the Chicago Convention," in *Speeches of William Jennings Bryan, Vol. I*, ed. William Jennings Bryan (New York: Funk & Wagnalls, 1909), 249.

"survival of the fittest" determinism) and saw orthodox religion as insufficient for the times. Social Gospel posited evolution as a divine plan for rational social advancement and suggested that it had become possible, through an empowered central state, to realize the Christian hope that "thy will be done *on earth* as it is in heaven." Social Gospel adherents considered it their mission to fulfill *in this life* the New Testament's call to bring about the perfect kingdom of God. Like the progressive politicians, Social Gospel theologians asserted that government, because of progress, was now in a position to bring about such an earthly utopia, in the form of the modern democratic state. Walter Rauschenbusch,[26] arguably *the* theologian of Social Gospel, criticized orthodox religion in a manner parallel to the progressive criticism of traditional constitutionalism. Orthodox religion, contended Rauschenbusch, had become too individualized; in focusing on salvation in the next life, conservative Christianity encouraged selfishness and a turning away from the world of man. Instead, Rauschenbusch urged, Christians ought to focus on salvation in this life, in the form of social goods achieved through the state. The orthodox church had encouraged what Rauschenbusch called a "religious individualism," where "there was a subtle twist of self-seeking which vitiated its Christlikeness."[27] But man would now be judged, Rauschenbusch explained, not by his individual sins, but by the degree to which he merged his will and his life with the divine purposes of the kingdom of God on earth. As a practical matter, this meant overcoming man's attachment to private property, removing private property rights as an obstacle to social action, and "socializing property."[28]

To be sure, progressivism had its ardent secularists, especially among those associated with *The New Republic* and the more scientific wing of the movement. But like their more religiously inclined progressive brethren, this group saw orthodox Christianity as a great obstacle to progress. They especially resented the religious influence over education, because they saw in traditional religious education an encouragement of the young to focus on the private sphere, which focus detracted from the undivided devotion to the state on which progressive

---

26 Baptist minister Walter Rauschenbusch (1861–1918) was heavily influenced by his experience as a pastor in New York City's "Hell's Kitchen." He advocated Christian socialism as the means for achieving the kingdom of God here on earth.

27 Walter Rauschenbusch, *Christianizing the Social Order* (New York: Macmillan, 1913), 111.

28 Rauschenbusch, *Christianizing the Social Order*, 419–420.

democracy was to depend. Thus *The New Republic* editorialized in 1916 that there had to be a "change in the meaning of tolerance." The editors explained that, unlike eighteenth-century liberalism, "twentieth-century democracy believes that the community has certain positive ends to achieve, and if they are to be achieved the community must control the education of the young." They editorialized that "freedom and tolerance mean the development of independent powers of judgment in the young, not the freedom of older people to impose their dogmas on the young." Modern democracy, they concluded, "insists that the plasticity of the child shall not be artificially and prematurely hardened into a philosophy of life."[29] In the end, while the Social Gospel arm of progressivism seemed to speak a language quite distinct from that of the secularist arm, the same message was preached: a worship of the state as a god, and the need to overcome any attachment to the private that might stand as an obstacle to the social enterprise.

SOCIAL JUSTICE AND EDUCATION

The determination of Social Gospel advocates to remake society was part of a larger effort that originated primarily in the last twenty years of the nineteenth century. By 1900 a number of reform efforts began to coalesce around those associated with progressivism. They were a variegated group—influenced from a variety of sources including muckrakers, prohibitionists, socialists, populists, and others—though most shared the common commitment to progress through democratic education and direct social action. Advocates of social justice seemed to possess an unlimited optimism with regard to the power of public education. If they could educate the citizenry, they believed, then their reform proposals would succeed. In the language of Social Gospel, crusaders for social justice would translate the teachings of Christ into action. Jane Addams[30]

29 "Father Blakely States the Issue," unsigned editorial in *The New Republic* (July 29, 1916): 320.

30 A progressive leader of the social justice movement in America, Addams (1860–1935) is remembered chiefly for her establishment of Hull-House in Chicago, a settlement house modeled partly on Toynbee Hall in London and devoted to poor relief and aid to urban immigrants. While much of her time was spent at Hull-House, Addams took an active role in securing progressive legislation, including the Child Labor Law of 1903. She actively campaigned for Theodore Roosevelt's Progressive ticket in 1912 and shared the Nobel Peace Prize in 1931. Though she published a number of works on political thought and social reform, including *Democracy and Social Ethics* (1902) and *The Spirit of Youth and the City Streets* (1909), her best-known work remains *Twenty Years at Hull-House* (1910).

was the quintessential advocate of the social justice agenda. Her efforts in 1889 to establish Hull-House in Chicago set an example that soon spread throughout major urban centers in industrial America, resulting in the establishment of additional settlement homes such as New York's University Settlement and Boston's South End House.

Addams's "The Subjective Necessity of Social Settlements," among the most influential documents of the social justice movement, demonstrates not only the near-obsession some progressives had with the democratic panacea, it also clearly reflects their determination to ally the reform agenda with "that true democracy of the early [Christian] Church." The social settlement movement, Addams maintained, must work "to make the entire social organism democratic, to extend democracy beyond its political expression." Such sentiments were molded in part by her witness to the corruption of urban "bossism" and by a "partial" democracy that bestowed the vote and little else on immigrants and the working poor. She appealed especially to the "fast-growing number of cultivated young people who have no recognized outlet for their active faculties" to engage in the work of social reform. Many of those same young people, she maintained, rejected "the assumption that Christianity is a set of ideas which belong to the religious consciousness" in favor of a faith that manifested itself "in the social organism."[31]

The fundamental goal of these mostly middle-class reformers was to make alterations in American society in order to save it from the inevitable consequences of economic inequalities that were intensified by the combination of industrial life and the New Immigration. And despite the apparent altruism of many progressive reformers, the coercive aspects of progressivism (some called it "benevolent social control") are unmistakable in its ultimately successful demands for prohibition, as well as its attempt, partly successful, to restrict severely the New Immigration. Perhaps the most extreme example of coercion among some social justice crusaders is found in legislation such as Indiana's 1907 law requiring the forced sterilization of certain classes of inmates—primarily those deemed mentally deficient.

Addams believed that educators must work to universalize the experience of all, by which she meant that everyone should be enabled via progressive education and reform to participate fully and equally in

31 Jane Addams, *Twenty Years at Hull-House* (New York: Macmillan, 1910), 94, 98.

society. This belief was reflected in the theories of leading progressive educationalists, including most especially John Dewey. Dewey's philosophy of education made explicit what was essentially an article of faith among progressives generally: state control and regulation of numerous aspects of public life would be required to bring about the improvements progressives sought.

Dewey's view of the purpose of education was purely social—education served to integrate the pupil into the larger community that was itself characterized by the universality of its experience. This approach demanded the explicit rejection of any attempt to teach transcendent principles in the classroom and thus it was ultimately hostile to religious education which, Dewey believed, was hopelessly mired in the past. Religious education was backward-looking when the great age of democracy demanded a revolutionary change in pedagogical theory. Thus, as Dewey proclaims in his "Pedagogic Creed," "I believe that . . . the teacher is not in the school to impose certain ideas or to form certain habits in the child, but is there as a member of the community to select the influences which shall affect the child and to assist him in properly responding to these influences."[32] At least one irony in Dewey's conception of education is that despite its disdain for the "anachronistic" approach of religious education, his theory posits its own essentially religious education to replace it. The democratic faith is paramount, and the dogmatic certitude with which he proclaims the student's need to participate in the "pooled intelligence" of humanity and to be inculcated with the universalized values of the social community suggests a substantial role for both educationalists and for the state, which essentially replaced the function of the Church in education. This thoroughgoing elimination of a religious basis for education and its replacement with a secular faith in democracy, then, was the only sure means to the renewal of social life that was shared by progressive reformers and educationalists alike. As Dewey stated, "I believe that education is a regulation of the process of coming to share in the social consciousness; and that the adjustment of individual activity on the basis of this social consciousness is the only sure method of social reconstruction."[33]

---

32 John Dewey, "My Pedagogic Creed," *School Journal* 54 (January 1897): Article II.

33 Dewey, "My Pedagogic Creed," Article V.

PROGRESSIVISM AND THE CONSTITUTION

In addition to its push for social reform, the progressive policy agenda included a wide array of legislative proposals to regulate private business and property,[34] and in many states progressives had met with considerable success in winning their enactment. Yet the federal Constitution, undergirded by the principle of individual property rights, continued to prove a formidable obstacle to these legislative programs, as did several of the state constitutions. State and federal courts had, in many cases, overturned progressive legislative achievements, ruling that the new programs extended the power of government into the private sphere well beyond its constitutional limits (the most famous example was the U.S. Supreme Court's decision in *Lochner v. New York*, overturning a state law regulating bakers' hours). It was this phenomenon that Roosevelt had in mind when he frequently railed against the judiciary and called for the people to be given the power to overturn specific state judicial decisions by popular referendum. Roosevelt contended that courts had misconstrued constitutional law, "as if it prohibited the whole people of [a] State from adopting methods of regulating the use of property so that human life, particularly the lives of working men, shall be safer, freer, and happier." The judiciary, argued Roosevelt, was construing the due process clause "as if property rights, to the exclusion of human rights, had a first mortgage on the Constitution."[35] At a more general level, the real problem, as progressives saw it, was a failure of the courts to see the Constitution as a "living" organism, one whose limitations on government ought not be read strictly or literally, but instead interpreted to fit the new demands of a new age. It was in this mode that Herbert Croly[36] contrasted a government based on "law" to a government based on

34 Glen Gendzel argues that the progressive desire to wield the power of government more robustly on behalf of the common good was a unifying theme among progressives, against the many claims that the movement had no common commitments. Gendzel, "What the Progressives Had in Common," *The Journal of the Gilded Age and Progressive Era* 10, no. 3 (July 2011): 331–339.

35 Theodore Roosevelt, "The Right of the People to Rule," *The Outlook* (March 23, 1912): 619, 620.

36 Croly (1869–1930) was a founding editor of *The New Republic*, which became the chief organ for progressive opinion in the United States. His influence was wide, most notably with Theodore Roosevelt, who adopted Croly's "New Nationalism" theme as Roosevelt turned to a more radical brand of progressivism following his presidency. In addition to his scores of essays for *The New Republic*, Croly authored two substantial books: *The Promise of American Life* (1909) and *Progressive Democracy* (1914), the latter of which is considered to contain the more mature and comprehensive of its author's reflections on liberty and democracy.

"faith." Genuine democracy, Croly argued, was grounded on faith in the people's ability to rule themselves. The founders' Constitution, by contrast, elevated law—that is, legal protection for individual rights, even against the will of the majority—over faith, and thus brought into doubt the very legitimacy of democracy. Croly asked, "does not the exaggerated value which has been attached to constitutional limitations, and the apprehensive and reactionary state of mind which has in consequence possessed many patriotic Americans, tend to undermine the foundations in human nature and human will upon which the whole superstructure of a progressive democratic society must admittedly be built?"[37]

For Wilson, the structure of the Constitution itself made it nearly impossible for progressively inclined interpreters to adapt it to their agenda. The Constitution rested, at bottom, on a system of divided powers, both between federal and state levels of government and within the national government itself. While the progressive force of history had brought about an essential unity of popular will (at least in the minds of Wilson and other progressives), the Constitution divided power in such a way as to make expression of that unified will a near impossibility. It was for this reason that Wilson detested the separation of powers, and that almost everything he wrote on the American system of government contained a sharp critique of it. The ideal model for Wilson was the parliamentary one, where the legislative and executive are essentially united, both rising or falling on the evolving popular will (indeed, many of Wilson's early writings advocated converting various facets of the American system to the parliamentary model). The separation of powers, Wilson explained, had come out of the founders' obsessive fear of majority tyranny, and thus the system was outdated for the present age, where the people were no longer a danger to themselves. As Goodnow later complained, "it was the fear of political tyranny through which liberty might be lost which led to the adoption of the theories of checks and balances and of the separation of powers."[38] The problem was outlined by Wilson on the campaign trail in 1912:

> The makers of our Federal Constitution read Montesquieu with true scientific enthusiasm. They were scientists in their way,—the best way

37 Herbert Croly, *Progressive Democracy* (New York: Macmillan, 1914), 167.

38 Goodnow, *The American Conception of Liberty and Government*, 11.

> of their age,—those fathers of the nation. . . . They constructed a government as they would have constructed an orrery,—to display the laws of nature. Politics in their thought was a variety of mechanics. The Constitution was founded on the law of gravitation. The government was to exist and move by virtue of the efficacy of "checks and balances."
>
> The trouble with the theory is that government is not a machine, but a living thing. It falls, not under the theory of the universe, but under the theory of organic life. It is accountable to Darwin, not to Newton. It is modified by its environment, necessitated by its tasks, shaped to its functions by the sheer pressure of life. No living thing can have its organs offset against each other, as checks, and live.[39]

American government needed to be reformed so that it reflected the essential unity of the public mind that progressives believed had been brought about by history. Separation of powers, therefore, had to be discarded and replaced by a system which instead separated politics and administration. By this formulation, progressives like Wilson and Goodnow meant that the national political institutions—Congress, the presidency, etc.—ought to be democratized and unified, bringing them into much closer contact with public opinion and facilitating their expression of the general public will. At the same time, since progressives believed that the most contentious political questions had been resolved by historical development (the Civil War had been decisive in this regard), the real work of government was not in politics, but in administration—in figuring out the specific means of achieving what the people generally agreed they all wanted. Understanding the progressive vision for reforming national institutions requires a comprehension of their plan for both sides of the politics–administration dichotomy—that is, for democratizing and unifying national political institutions while separating and insulating administrative agencies.

Politics

The great problem for progressives was that American national politics

---

39 Wilson, *The New Freedom*, 46–47. In this particular part of the speech Wilson closely paraphrased from his book, *Constitutional Government in the United States* (New York: Columbia University Press, 1908), 56.

suffered from a lack of accountability. As the Federalists had intended, the Constitution established an indirect form of popular rule, characterized by "the total exclusion of the people, in their collective capacity" from any direct role in governing, as James Madison put it in *Federalist* 63. For the Federalists, such a construction was an essential means to secure "the public good, and private rights, against the danger" of majority tyranny, while "at the same time to preserve the spirit and the form of popular government."[40] Likewise the separation of powers system, in failing to elevate any one branch or office above the others, denied to any one branch or office the claim of exclusively representing the people as a whole, and thus prevented any one part of the government from claiming a true position of national leadership. And this was precisely the problem from the perspective of progressives, especially for the likes of Wilson, who argued that without a clear, accountable leader, government as a whole could not be held accountable to the people's will.

For the national political institutions to be genuinely democratic, Wilson contended, there had to be an identifiable leader, to whom the public could make known its will, and whom it could hold electorally accountable for success or failure in implementing that will throughout the whole of government. "Leadership and control must be lodged somewhere," Wilson urged.[41] While Wilson's early writings looked to put Congress in this role, he ultimately concluded that only the president could serve as the kind of leader he had in mind. That Wilson had the example of President Roosevelt in front of his eye surely helps to explain his turn to presidential leadership at this time. The president, Wilson pointed out, was the only politician who could claim to speak for the people as a whole, and thus he called upon the president to transcend the separation of powers—to consider himself not merely as chief of a single branch of government, but as the popular leader of the whole of national politics. Wilson even contrasted the "constitutional aspect" of the presidency—its constitutionally defined role as chief of one of the three co-equal branches of government—to the "political" function of the president, where he could use his connection to public opinion as a tool for moving all of the branches of government in the direction called for by the people.[42] It was in this

40 Publius, *The Federalist*, ed. Charles R. Kesler and Clinton Rossiter (New York: Signet Classics, 2003), 63:385, 10:75.

41 Wilson, *Constitutional Government*, 54.

42 Wilson, *Constitutional Government*, 66.

way that Wilson believed the original intention of the separation of powers system could be circumvented, and the enhanced presidency could be a means of energizing the kind of active national government that the progressive agenda required.

From the founders' perspective, the most dangerous aspect of Wilson's vision for the presidency would have been that the president's power was to come directly from the people as opposed to the Constitution. Wilson envisioned a president who, to the extent that he could claim to embody the people's will, would move the institutions of national government by the force of that popularity. Given their considerable concern about demagoguery (majority factions, *The Federalist* frequently reminds us, rarely arise spontaneously), the founders thought it paramount that the president's power be clearly understood as coming from Article II of the Constitution itself; the president, in other words, was to be both empowered by and limited by the Constitution. In this respect, Roosevelt's conception of the presidency, like Wilson's, represented a novelty in the American political tradition. In articulating what has come to be known as his "Stewardship" theory of the presidency, Roosevelt posited the idea that presidential power is not confined by the enumerated grants of power made in the Constitution. As he explained in his *Autobiography*, his presidency was defined by his

> insistence upon the theory that the executive power was limited only by specific restrictions and prohibitions appearing in the Constitution or imposed by the Congress under its Constitutional powers. My view was that every executive officer, and above all every executive officer in high position, was a steward of the people bound actively and affirmatively to do all he could for the people, and not to content himself with the negative merit of keeping his talents undamaged in a napkin. I declined to adopt the view that what was imperatively necessary for the Nation could not be done by the President unless he could find some specific authorization to do it. My belief was that it was not only his right but his duty to do anything that the needs of the Nation demanded unless such action was forbidden by the Constitution or by the laws.[43]

43 Theodore Roosevelt, *An Autobiography* (New York: Macmillan, 1913), 388-389. See David Greenberg on Roosevelt's embrace of publicity and media attention to center policymaking in the presidency. Greenberg, "Beyond the Bully Pulpit," *Wilson Quarterly* 35, no. 3 (2011): 22–29.

Roosevelt thus understood the powers of the national government, and especially those of the president, as *plenary*, not *enumerated*—defined, in other words, by the needs of the time, not by the provisions of Article II. The president was to become the interpreter of the nation's needs, and was to use his position as the people's steward to keep government responsive to those needs as they evolved from one epoch to the next. It was in this way that the presidency became, for progressives, the agent of progress in national politics.[44]

Administration

If national political institutions were to facilitate a general and unified expression of the public's will, the national administrative institutions were to translate that broad will into specific policy. And while progressives very much wanted to democratize national political institutions, their inclination in administration was just the opposite—to shield administrative agencies from political influence, so that administrators could be free to make policy on the basis of their expertise. For all their talk about historical progress and the unity of the public will, progressives complained about the corruption of politics and the dominance of special interests. Progressives took all of the contention and interest conflict in national politics, not as evidence that the Federalists had been right about the perpetual factiousness of human nature, but rather as an indication that politics itself needed to be overcome so that the true, unified will of the public could emerge. The making of actual policy, then, had to be

44 That the Progressive Era presidencies marked a turning point in American political development, particularly in their popularization of presidential rhetoric, is a thesis of the so-called "modern presidency" school of interpreters. Scholars associated with this school point to the founders' fear of demagoguery and their avoidance of a direct connection between the president and unfiltered public opinion; the founders' caution on this front is contrasted to progressive efforts to democratize the presidency. See Paul Eidelberg, *A Discourse on Statesmanship: The Design and Transformation of the American Polity* (Urbana: University of Illinois Press, 1974); James W. Ceaser, Glen E. Thurow, Jeffrey K. Tulis, Joseph M. Bessette, "The Rise of the Rhetorical Presidency," *Presidential Studies Quarterly* 11 (Spring 1981): 158–71. See also Tulis, *The Rhetorical Presidency* (Princeton: Princeton University Press, 1987), though Tulis does not see Theodore Roosevelt as a sharp departure from the nineteenth-century paradigm in the way that Wilson was. For a critique of the "modern presidency" thesis, see David K. Nichols, *The Myth of the Modern Presidency* (University Park: Pennsylvania State University Press, 1994). For an argument that the presidency was simply re-made as a consequence of changes in the public mood, see Peri E. Arnold, *Remaking the Presidency: Roosevelt, Taft, and Wilson, 1901–1916* (Lawrence, KS: University Press of Kansas, 2009).

rescued from the machinations of electoral politics, and placed in the hands of those who could regulate the special interests—on the basis of expertise—for the sake of the common good. The early roots of progressive administration, therefore, can be seen in the Mugwump agitation for civil service reform. But whereas the civil service movement was a reaction to the corruption of the spoils system, the progressive vision of administration took this reaction and developed it into a much broader and more thoughtful call for reform, one that became a primary means of facilitating much of the progressive policy agenda. The role that progressives had in mind for the national government greatly exceeded, after all, the capabilities of the traditional constitutional branches. The extent of regulatory activity in which progressives wanted the national government to engage simply could not be handled by an institution like Congress. And so the establishment of a substantial bureaucratic apparatus, largely free from the influence of electoral politics, not only became a means of facilitating government by educated experts, but also provided an institutional machinery that could take on the many new tasks that progressives had in mind for the national government. Chapter Eight details the connection between progressive political principles and the development, over the course of the twentieth century, of the modern bureaucracy.[45]

Politically, the call for an extensive, and largely independent, regulatory apparatus is most often associated with Roosevelt's campaign in 1912, where under the banner of the "New Nationalism" Roosevelt proposed extensive government supervision and regulation of the key business interests in the country. It is less well known that, in advocating the independent regulatory power of national administration, Roosevelt was actually giving concrete political shape to an idea that had long since been brought into America by Wilson, Roosevelt's opponent in the 1912 campaign. As I will show below, Wilson's criticism of the New Nationalism reflected the essential tactics of the campaign much more than it did any principled difference between the two candidates on the question of national administrative power. For it was Wilson who pioneered the idea

45 Paul D. Moreno has written two helpful monographs on the rise of the administrative state: *The American State from the Civil War to the New Deal* (Cambridge: Cambridge University Press, 2013); *The Bureaucrat Kings: The Origins and Underpinnings of America's Bureaucratic State* (Santa Barbara: Praeger, 2016). See also Joseph Postell's *Bureaucracy in America: The Administrative State's Challenge to Constitutional Government* (Columbia: University of Missouri Press, 2017), which addresses not only the historical development of the administrative state but also its uneasy coexistence with constitutional government in our time.

of separating administration from politics in the United States—an idea that was then developed into a more coherent body of work in administrative law by Goodnow.

Wilson introduced the concept of separating administration from politics in a series of essays in the 1880s, most notably "The Study of Administration," which some public administration scholars consider to have marked the founding of their discipline in this country. Goodnow, while never directly acknowledging Wilson as far as I am aware, expanded upon this Wilsonian concept in the 1890s and eventually published a book on it in 1900: *Politics and Administration*. Wilson did not assert that administration itself was a novel concept in America, but rather that the kind of administration progressives needed for their vision of the modern democratic state was clearly at odds with the principles of the founding and the traditional interpretation of the Constitution. This is because administration—as vigorous as some of the founders surely envisioned it—was confined in the original view within the executive branch. It was thus accountable to the partisan executive and confined to the exercise of executive power. Progressive administration, by contrast, was to be liberated from the influence of partisan or electoral politics, and was to engage not only in executive action, but legislative and judicial action as well. If administrative agencies were to be responsible for superintending the activities of private business—a mission of such a scope that it far exceeded the capacity and expertise of Congress—then, on the basis of their expertise, administrators would need to make rules and regulations, enforce them, and adjudicate violations of them.[46] This meant, Wilson knew, that progressive administration had a big hurdle to overcome if it was to gain legitimacy in the United States.

The essence of Wilson's "Study," accordingly, was an argument that it was not appropriate to apply constitutional analysis to the kind of administrative power he was proposing. We ought, instead, to consider constitutional and administrative questions as entirely separate and not try to drag independent administration before the bar of constitutional scrutiny. Wilson wrote of "the distinction between *constitutional* and

---

46 This is why the majority opinion for the U.S. Supreme Court in *Humphrey's Executor v. United States*—a central case in the legitimization of independent regulatory agencies—refers to the function of agencies as not only executive, but also "quasi-legislative" and "quasi-judicial." Indeed, the Court uses the legislative and judicial nature of agency decision-making to justify agency independence from presidential control. 295 U.S. 602 (1935).

administrative questions" and explained that "the field of administration is a field of business. It is removed from the hurry and strife of politics; it at most points stands apart even from the debatable ground of constitutional study." In particular, Wilson knew that the progressive conception of administration could not fit within the Constitution's separation of powers scheme, conceding that "one cannot easily make clear to every one just where administration resides in the various departments of any practicable government."[47] Wilson forthrightly admitted in the "Study" that his whole conception of administration was foreign—indeed, it was based on the Prussian bureaucratic state championed in Hegel's *Philosophy of Right* as the rational culmination of all of world history (Wilson even quoted from *Philosophy of Right* in the first part of the "Study"). But, he asked, "why should we not use such parts of foreign contrivances as we want, if they be in any way serviceable? . . . If I see a murderous fellow sharpening a knife cleverly, I can borrow his way of sharpening the knife without borrowing his probable intention to commit murder with it."[48] As Goodnow helped to elaborate, the achievement of progressive policy aims would not be possible without the ability of enlightened experts to rise above the "polluted" atmosphere of special-interest politics and regulate for the common good. Administration, in contrast to politics, was about the "truth."[49] Progressives believed that administrators, unlike ordinary politicians, could be objective and could focus on the good of the whole people—oddly, their ability to do so rested primarily on being freed from electoral accountability. The salary and life tenure of administrators would take care of any self-interested inclinations that might otherwise corrupt their decision-making, Goodnow concluded, and he explained that "such a force should be free from the influence of politics because of the fact that their mission is the exercise of foresight and discretion, the pursuit of truth, the gathering of information, the maintenance of a strictly impartial attitude toward the individuals with whom they have dealings, and the provision of the most efficient possible administrative organization."[50]

Reflecting on the question of progressivism and the reform of

47 Woodrow Wilson, "The Study of Administration" in Ronald J. Pestritto, ed., *Woodrow Wilson: Essential Political Writings* (Lexington Books, 2005), 240–241.

48 Wilson, "Study of Administration," 246–247.

49 Frank J. Goodnow, *Politics and Administration* (Macmillan, 1900), 82.

50 Goodnow, *Politics and Administration*, 85.

national institutions, we come to a central irony in progressive thought: the strong democratizing argument with respect to political institutions is coupled with an argument on administration that calls for shifting policymaking power away from popular institutions and giving it to educated elites. Independent administrators are to be given significant policymaking discretion precisely to the extent that they are free from political or electoral control, and thus the progressive argument here seems to be a distinctly elitist one that proceeds under a democratic veneer. This paradox—more fully explored in Chapter Three—is a characteristic of progressivism that runs consistently throughout the period: from Wilson and Goodnow in the 1880s and '90s, through Croly and Roosevelt with the New Nationalism of 1912, and again with President Wilson as he implemented much of the New Nationalism during his own administration.

PARTIES, DIRECT DEMOCRACY, AND THE POLITICS OF REFORM

In keeping with his argument that national political institutions had become unaccountable, and that the system lacked clear leaders through whom the public could make its will manifest in national politics, Wilson advocated at one time a system of responsible party government along the parliamentary model.[51] In so doing, Wilson was trying to come up with a way to achieve a goal shared by all progressives: the democratization of national politics. His proposed remedy, however—a reformed, but vigorous, party system—was not endorsed by most others in the movement,[52] who saw the party system itself as a root problem and thus advocated its abolition as opposed to its reform. It is important to note that this difference, while significant, was a difference in means or methods, not a difference of principle.

Croly, like Wilson, believed that the party system served to perpetuate the indirectness of American democracy, and thus stood as an obstacle to the achievement of genuine democracy. But where Wilson

51 See, for example, Wilson, "Government by Debate," December 1882, in *PWW*, 2:159–275; "Wanted—A Party," September 1, 1886, in *PWW*, 5:342; "Leaderless Government," August 5, 1897, in *PWW*, 10:288–304.

52 The exception here would be Goodnow, who makes his own call for a responsible party model in *Politics and Administration*, 199–254.

thought that developments such as the direct primary could put the people in charge of the party system and thus reform it and turn it to progressive ends, Croly saw mechanisms like the primary as mere temporary steps on the road to abolishing parties altogether. At the heart of Croly's call for abolishing the party system was the conviction that partisanship itself detracted from the exclusive devotion that an individual ought to give directly to the state. When one identified as a partisan of a particular party, one could not also be a partisan of the organic whole—the state itself. The party system, Croly reasoned, "demands and obtains for a party an amount of loyal service and personal sacrifice which a public-spirited democrat should lavish only on the state."[53] With the Progressive Party of 1912, accordingly, we see a party platform to end parties altogether. This anti-partisan attitude is also why mechanisms of direct democracy became the hallmarks of much of the progressive movement across the country, especially at the state and local level, as detailed in Chapter Nine.

Progressivism was, in many respects, a reform movement that originated first at the local level before it emerged in state and federal government. Reforms that came to typify the progressive agenda first appeared in urban America, as muckrakers such as Lincoln Steffens and Ida Tarbell worked to document evidence of political corruption and vice, including prostitution and gambling, in the pages of *McClure's*, *Cosmopolitan*, and *Success*. And in local government a number of reform mayors, such as Detroit's Hazen Pingree (later elected governor) and Samuel "Golden Rule" Jones of Toledo, supported working class demands for greater participation in local politics via opposition to urban political machines. Among the most radical of early reformers, Jones embraced public ownership of utilities as part of the cure for urban corruption and maintained that democracy, fully realized, would resolve the inequities of political and economic life.

At the city level, the progressive drive focused on the question of home rule. Too often, it was argued, local government suffered due to restrictions placed upon it at the state level—again by political machines often tied to business interests. What was required, therefore, was a drive to clean up government to make it more efficient and responsive to people's needs. A few cities in the 1890s formed citizens' associations

53 Croly, *Progressive Democracy*, 341.

to challenge the status quo in municipal government. Pingree called for equitable taxation and local regulation of public utilities. He also advocated a substantial program of social services, as did Jones, who argued that without substantial reforms such as public ownership of utilities, competitive civil service for city government positions, and civic improvements including taxpayer-funded parks and playgrounds, urban America would erupt in class warfare and democracy would be undermined. Among the most significant of the progressives' successes in local political reform was the birth of commission government in Galveston, Texas, in 1900. In the aftermath of a hurricane, the state legislature appointed a commission of individuals who were responsible for specific aspects of public life. The idea spread rapidly between 1900 and 1920. Similarly, Staunton, Virginia (Wilson's birthplace, coincidentally), adopted the city-manager form of government at this time.

The most significant programs, however, were found in the states. At the turn of the century, most parties used the caucus method for choosing their candidates for the state legislature. Political bosses dominated state capitals as they dominated much of urban political life. The quintessential state-level reformer, Robert M. La Follette[54] of Wisconsin, was determined to change this state of affairs. A member of the Republican Party, he was ostracized by the party regulars as his reform tendencies became obvious. Undaunted, he ran for governor in 1900 and won, and was reelected two more times before moving on to the U.S. Senate. His "Wisconsin experiment" in government was praised by Roosevelt (who called it a "laboratory of democracy") for its innovative use of direct-democracy devices—including the initiative, referendum, and recall—to give the people a voice in government. La Follette was convinced that his efforts in Wisconsin had, in fact, established a model that progressives could emulate throughout the country. He wrote:

> The public service of the state has been democratized by a civil service law opening it to men and women on an equal footing independent

54 Author of the "Wisconsin Idea" of efficiency in government, La Follette (1855–1925) challenged the state Republican organization in Wisconsin, eventually winning the gubernatorial contest in 1900. After five years as governor, La Follette was elected to the U.S. Senate where he quickly became known for his advocacy of progressive reform. He established a magazine, *La Follette's Weekly Magazine* (1909), which popularized such progressive devices as "The Roll Call" in order to publicize voting records of senators and representatives.

> of everything excepting qualification and fitness for office. I think the passing of this law was the only case of the kind where the employees then holding office were not blanketed into the service, but were required to take the regular competitive examinations in order to retain their jobs. The law has worked to the great advantage of the service and to the general improvement of political standards. There is no longer any political pull in Wisconsin.[55]

Of course, in the same work, La Follette detailed the methods used to ensure his machine's control of the political process in Wisconsin, an irony that could scarcely have been lost on his opponents. Nonetheless, La Follette demonstrated that the progressive agenda of direct democracy and local control, accompanied by a massive regulation of industry, could be achieved at the state level. It was his goal to bring the Wisconsin example to the rest of the nation as president, though his best chance to capture the Republican nomination failed when he suffered a nervous breakdown in the 1912 primary campaign. That chapter of the progressives' story, begun by Theodore Roosevelt, was left to Woodrow Wilson to complete.

ROOSEVELT, WILSON, AND 1912

Due partly to the differences between Roosevelt and Wilson on the question of political parties, the 1912 election is often billed as a contest between the progressive Roosevelt and the conservative Wilson. Such a characterization, while inaccurate,[56] is encouraged by several other

55 Robert M. La Follette, *La Follette's Autobiography: A Personal Narrative of Political Experiences* (Madison, WI: The Robert M. La Follette Co., 1911), 365–366.

56 Eldon J. Eisenach's *The Lost Promise of Progressivism* (Lawrence, KS: University Press of Kansas, 1994) is perhaps the most obvious example of this inaccurate understanding of Roosevelt and Wilson. Many factors contribute to this misunderstanding, as explained here, in addition to the fact that Eisenach's account rests almost entirely on a narrow sliver of Wilson's work and disregards the vast majority of what he had to say on the principles of government; the result is a facile and distorted portrayal of Wilson's politics. See 3, 31–36, 124–25. Far superior is the account of Sidney M. Milkis in *Theodore Roosevelt, the Progressive Party, and the Transformation of American Democracy* (Lawrence, KS: University Press of Kansas, 2009), which distinguishes Roosevelt and Wilson more than I would argue is warranted, but which nonetheless understands that Wilson was clearly a progressive. See 185–251. For other scholarly accounts which understand Wilson's clear commitment to progressivism, see: Kendrick A. Clements, *The Presidency of Woodrow Wilson* (Lawrence: University Press of Kansas, 1992), 2–3; and Niels Aage Thorsen, *The Political Thought of Woodrow Wilson 1875–1910* (Princeton: Princeton University Press, 1988), 219. On the consequences of the 1912 election in general, see Lewis L. Gould, *Four*

factors. Chief among these is that Roosevelt campaigned in 1912 on the New Nationalism—a call for a marked increase in the scope of national power and central-government supervision of private business interests—while Wilson campaigned on the New Freedom, a program critical of the paternalistic implications of Roosevelt's platform. The result has been a misleading dichotomy in the literature on the progressives, pitting the "Hamiltonian," big-government Roosevelt against the "Jeffersonian," small-government, states' rights Wilson. Leaving aside the very important point that Hamilton and Jefferson, their differences notwithstanding, were far more akin to each other than either of them was to any progressive, the Hamiltonian–Jeffersonian dichotomy falsely portrays Wilson as a kind of anti-progressive. In fact, nothing could be further from the truth. Part of the problem comes from the fact that the Princeton collection of Wilson's papers was published and made fully available only recently, and thus much of the twentieth-century scholarship on Wilson was based upon a very incomplete look at his body of work, missing almost entirely a consideration of those early works of Wilson's academic career where he was writing and thinking most seriously about the principles of politics. Put most simply, anyone who wrote "The Study of Administration" or *The State*, as Wilson did in 1887 and 1889, respectively, could not by any stretch of the imagination be characterized as a small-government, states' rights, conservative Jeffersonian. Those works, among the many, many others like them that Wilson produced, give a conception of a centralized, bureaucratic state of such scope that even the most ardent New Nationalist could find little with which to quarrel.

What explains, then, Wilson's occasional conservative, small-government rhetoric on the 1912 campaign trail? The first thing to note is that the extent and nature of such rhetoric is often exaggerated; *The New Freedom*, even on its surface, is certainly no defense of traditional American constitutionalism or unfettered, free-market economics. But beyond this, when one considers the practical political circumstances of 1912, the campaign rhetoric is not difficult to understand. Wilson's aim, naturally, was to win the election. He had been effectively silent on the question of regulating or breaking trusts prior to 1907 and 1908, which is when he began to contemplate seriously a future in politics and the corresponding need

Hats in the Ring: The 1912 Election and the Birth of Modern American Politics (Lawrence, KS: University Press of Kansas, 2008).

to carve out a unique position for himself in the national debate. More importantly, Wilson's electoral fortunes rested squarely on his position within the Democratic party. In particular, Wilson very clearly needed the William Jennings Bryan wing of the party. Consider that it took forty-six ballots for Wilson to win the party's nomination, which occurred only after Bryan intervened in Wilson's favor. Central to Bryan's populism was a fear of national executive power and a deep distrust of business interests in the Northeast. By campaigning against Roosevelt's plan to maintain the business trusts by bringing them into a regulatory relationship with the national government, Wilson solidified his position with the Bryan Democrats who were essential to his victory. And consider, finally, that once Wilson was elected, he lost little time turning his back on the small-government campaign rhetoric, embarking instead on a program of expanding national government and administration very much along the lines suggested by Roosevelt's New Nationalism.[57]

Wilson's turn to big government after 1912 was not, therefore, the "conversion" that it is often characterized to be. Rather, the anomaly was the 1912 campaign itself. Wilson was a big-government progressive long before 1912 and immediately after 1912, with the circumstances of the campaign forcing a brief detour. It is thus proper to consider both Roosevelt and Wilson as lions of the progressive movement. One of the most persuasive acknowledgements of this fact comes from Croly, who as a close advisor to Roosevelt and frequent critic of Wilson would be in a position of some authority on the question. Writing in 1914, Croly clearly considered Wilson to be a progressive. Croly characterized Wilson's progressivism as "ambiguous" and said that Wilson's "deliberate purpose seems to have been to keep progressivism vague." He later remarked that Wilson's real progressivism "poses as a higher conservatism." Why this intentional vagueness on Wilson's part about his progressivism? Croly understood very well not just Wilson's progressivism, but also the practical politics of the day: "Be it recognized also that in Mr. Wilson's situation a certain amount of ambiguity has a manifest practical value. He is a Democrat as well as a progressive.... He would have good reason,

57 As the historian George E. Mowry writes, Wilson's record as president was "worthy of any reformer and... exceedingly embarrassing to the Progressive Party." *Theodore Roosevelt and the Progressive Movement* (New York: Hill and Wang, 1960), 223. For my own account of Roosevelt and Wilson in 1912, including a fuller treatment of the secondary literature, see *Woodrow Wilson and the Roots of Modern Liberalism* (Lanham, MD: Rowman & Littlefield, 2005), 253–71.

consequently, for emphasizing any possible analogies between progressivism and the historic tradition of his own party."[58]

THE PROGRESSIVE PRESIDENCIES

Wilson's victory in 1912 and again in 1916 meant that progressives of both parties played a significant role in national, state, and local politics throughout the first two decades of the twentieth century. Both Roosevelt and Wilson worked to ensure that reform was brought to the forefront of American national life and, as a result of their efforts, the progressive agenda lost much of the aura of radicalism that had hobbled labor and reform efforts in the Gilded Age. Roosevelt's contribution to that achievement is immeasurable. In addition to a considerable intellect, he brought a sense of optimism to national political life. His wartime heroics and broad grin endeared him to the public, and Roosevelt had an ability to invest even seemingly mundane issues with high drama. From the time he declared his intent to enter politics—an unusual choice for somebody of his privileged background—he was clearly determined to reform the Republican Party from within. It was thus with good reason that Old Guard Republican Party bosses like Marcus Hanna were so fearful of this "cowboy" as president. And once in power, Roosevelt immediately established his determination to use the office of president more vigorously than any of his predecessors. His view of the executive as a "bully pulpit" coupled with an elastic view of the Constitution meant that Roosevelt's agenda—in both domestic and foreign-policy matters—was not typically restricted by scruples over matters of constitutionality. The era of mass industry and mass immigration meant that new approaches were needed. As Roosevelt noted in his first annual message to Congress in 1901:

> The tremendous and highly complex industrial development which went on with ever accelerated rapidity during the latter half of the nineteenth century brings us face to face, at the beginning of the twentieth, with very serious social problems. The old laws, and the old customs which had almost the binding force of law, were once quite sufficient to regulate the accumulation and distribution of wealth. Since the

58 Croly, *Progressive Democracy*, 15–18.

> industrial changes which have so enormously increased the productive power of mankind, they are no longer sufficient.[59]

In domestic policy, Roosevelt immediately demonstrated his willingness to intervene in industry by invoking the Sherman Antitrust Act against the Northern Securities Company, which was ultimately dissolved as an illegal monopoly. The same year (1902), he intervened to end an anthracite coal strike by the United Mine Workers that threatened a nationwide coal shortage. Roosevelt summoned representatives from the owners and the miners while he mediated an agreement. Not only was it the first time a president had acted to facilitate such talks, it was also memorable for Roosevelt's threats to bring in federal troops and nationalize the mining operations. Though the miners won only some of their demands, including higher wages and a shorter workday, Roosevelt's actions led to his reputation among many industrial workers as the protector of the common man. What followed was a substantial program to regulate numerous businesses and industries in America, including railroads and the meat-packing industry.

Similarly, Wilson viewed the president as the national leader and originator of the national political agenda. This view was reflected in his approach to Congress, where he revived the practice of delivering annual messages in person and carefully cultivated relationships with some individual members—a sign of his long-held affinity for the parliamentary model. If this approach to Congress differed in some respects from Roosevelt's, Wilson's determination to realize critical elements of the progressive reform agenda did not. Wilson already had a substantial record of reform as governor of New Jersey. Once inaugurated as president, he moved quickly to reduce the tariff, a measure which most progressives sought. Even more directly related to the progressive agenda, lost revenues from the tariff reduction were to be recovered by making use of the recently ratified Sixteenth Amendment, which levied an income tax on American workers. Wilson also took measures to reorganize and regulate the banking system by signing the Federal Reserve Act (1913) and sought support for stronger anti-trust legislation that ultimately resulted in the Clayton Antitrust Act (1914). Wilson also supported the creation

---

59 Theodore Roosevelt, First Annual Message, December 3, 1901, in *Messages and Papers of the Presidents* (New York: Bureau of National Literature, 1917), 6645.

of the Federal Trade Commission, an independent regulatory agency authorized to investigate corporations engaged in interstate commerce and violations of antitrust laws.

Through the realization of their agendas, Roosevelt and Wilson had made reform respectable. Federal regulation of numerous aspects of public life had become commonplace. Americans may have tired of their crusading zeal, but the progressive presidents and their supporters had inaugurated a new era in American government.

PROGRESSIVISM, WAR, AND PEACE

The energy that Presidents Roosevelt and Wilson showed in pursuing progressive goals was not confined to domestic reform measures. Both men supported active foreign policies that, if justified and applied differently, demonstrated nonetheless a similarity in the idealism that underwrote them. Both believed that a well-conceived foreign policy could spread American ideals abroad even as it enhanced the American economy. This is not to say, however, that they recommended comparable courses of action in a given situation—quite the opposite was oftentimes true. Roosevelt, for example, could scarcely restrain his scathing criticism of Wilson's policy of neutrality when, Roosevelt believed, the situation in Europe demanded American intervention in World War I. And Wilson clearly rejected Roosevelt's colonialist aspirations, which resulted in the acquisition of the Philippine Islands after the Spanish-American War. Still, there was an aggressive strain in many progressives' foreign policy, including that of Roosevelt and Wilson, which mirrored the forcefulness of their determination in matters of domestic social and political reform.

Beginning in the 1890s, America embarked upon a course of foreign intervention that clearly rejected cherished principles of American foreign policy as established both in Washington's Farewell Address and the Monroe Doctrine. The decision to embrace imperialism in the interest of establishing a network of colonial outposts and overseas holdings reflected the belief among some that America must look to a "new manifest destiny" to secure its future. If America did not expand abroad, it was argued, the ability to compete with other colonial powers would be lost. Among the most ardent of the leading progressive expansionists was Indiana Senator Albert J. Beveridge. Like Roosevelt, Beveridge was convinced that America must expand in order to sustain its national greatness and, since the continental frontier was closed according to the 1890 census and Turner's recent thesis, the logical place to look was the Pacific basin. Virtually all progressives who believed such expansion should be raised to the level of a national imperative were influenced to at least some degree by the writings of Alfred Thayer Mahan, whose publication of *The Influence of Sea Power upon History, 1660-1783* in 1890 staunchly supported overseas expansion. Indeed, Mahan's call for a canal across the isthmus of Central America, the possession of overseas coaling stations in the Pacific, and a navy powerful enough to carry such an ambitious program to completion fit perfectly with Roosevelt's energetic nationalism.

Though Wilson's foreign policy was distinguished from Roosevelt's by a clear disdain for colonialist expansion, he quickly demonstrated that, as president, he was willing to intervene forcefully to spread his vision of ideal government. The revolutions in Mexico and the instability they bred reportedly elicited from Wilson the promise to "teach the South American republics to elect good men." And Wilson twice intervened militarily in Mexico, ostensibly to uphold American rights there, but also to shape the outcome of the revolutionary contest. Before the United States entered World War I, he also dispatched marines to Haiti and the Dominican Republic.

Wilson's foreign policy is detailed in Chapter Six, though it should be emphasized here that it was Wilson's decisions regarding World War I that left an indelible mark on his presidency and caused substantial divisions among leading progressives, including Roosevelt, La Follette, and Wilson's Secretary of State, William Jennings Bryan. Wilson had steadfastly maintained his determination to keep the United States out of the calamitous war in Europe. Seeking reelection in 1916, he continued, despite the infamous sinking of the *Lusitania* and the loss of 128 American lives, to speak the language of neutrality and to offer the good offices of the United States to negotiate an end to the war. As an act of military desperation, however, Germany resumed unrestricted submarine warfare on February 1, 1917, which soon meant the loss of more American lives and Wilson's request for a declaration of war. Echoing the sentiments of Bryan, La Follette argued that Wilson had, in fact, not been impartial in thought or in action as he had called upon

Americans to be at the outset of the war. Rather, Wilson demanded that Germany observe neutral rights, warning that it would be held to "strict accountability" for violations of American neutrality, but did not require the same of Britain.

America's entry into the war was ultimately more than Germany could withstand. It sought an armistice based on Wilson's Fourteen Points, and Wilson headed for Europe to negotiate a treaty which, he believed, would usher in a new age of international peace. Wilson's progressive idealism was reflected in his calls for a "peace without victory" and a "war to end all wars." Such language was, however, lost on the victors in the peace negotiations at Versailles. When presented with Wilson's original fourteen points, British and French representatives balked. The result was a peace very different from the one Wilson had envisioned; not only did his call for the national self-determination of all peoples go unrealized, but his hope for American participation in a League of Nations was defeated in the Senate.

Wilson had called in 1917 for Congress to declare war in order to "make the world safe for democracy." In so doing, he departed from the more nationalistic views of Roosevelt and also laid the foundation for one of most enduring legacies of progressivism in our own time. In promoting worldwide democracy, Wilson made clear, America was not a self-interested actor but was instead "one of the champions of the rights of mankind." He elaborated that "we have no selfish ends to serve, we desire no conquest, no dominion. We seek no indemnities for ourselves, no material compensation for the sacrifices we shall freely make."[60] His fourteen-point program of peace called for a "general association of nations" founded on the "principle of justice" for "all peoples and nationalities."[61] The connections between this rhetoric and American pronouncements to this day are manifest (among the most notable of these was the second inaugural address of President George W. Bush, which declared that the goal of American foreign policy was "the global expansion of democracy"). We can see in the case of foreign policy, therefore, why the importance of progressivism to understanding the politics of contemporary America is widely acknowledged. Its continuing relevance to other

60 Woodrow Wilson, "An Address to a Joint Session of Congress," April 2, 1917, in *PWW*, 41:525.

61 Woodrow Wilson, "An Address to a Joint Session of Congress," January 8, 1918, in *PWW*, 45:538–539.

areas of American politics should also be evident and will be detailed in the chapters to follow. To understand this relevance properly, we must understand that the progressive influence on contemporary policy and institutions is grounded in the move to new principles of government. We turn, therefore, in the next chapter, to a deeper examination of the contrast between original and progressive liberalism.

CHAPTER TWO

★

ORIGINAL LIBERALISM VS. PROGRESSIVE LIBERALISM

In his explanation of how progressive political principles were built on a turn away from the principles of the American founding, John Dewey—arguably America's premier public philosopher for the first part of the twentieth century—employed a tale of two liberalisms: the founders' version, and the version adopted by his progressive contemporaries. This narrative appears to cut against today's political parlance, where liberalism has come to be understood as the ideology of the Left, and where those who prefer America's older, more traditional, principles are cast as conservatives. But Dewey was not off base in his nomenclature for the founding, as the founders' view of politics was predicated on the idea that individuals had rights grounded in nature that government was bound to secure. Dewey's account was, accordingly, not inconsistent with the founders' self-understanding, and some of the most important scholarship on the founding, such as Louis Hartz's *The Liberal Tradition in America*, affirms that those engaging the founders' thought are engaging, at least in part, a form of liberalism.[1]

1 Louis Hartz, *The Liberal Tradition in America: An Interpretation of American Political Thought Since the Revolution* (Boston: Brace & World, 1955). See also Bernard Bailyn, *The Ideological Origins of the American Revolution*, enlarged ed. (Cambridge: Harvard University Press, 1992);

To understand the distinction between progressive political principles and those earlier principles against which they rebelled, it is therefore necessary to contrast the two forms of American liberalism—its original version and its progressive version—while appreciating that they often employ similar terminology. The story of the move from eighteenth-century liberalism in America to the liberalism of America in the twentieth century centers on the Progressive Era and the transformation undertaken there in our understanding of equality, liberty, and rights—property rights, in particular.

The liberalism of the American founding was a liberalism of natural rights. The progressives understood this, and it is why their major intellectual works begin, almost without exception, with a critique of natural rights and the theory of social compact. The topic of natural rights and the American founding is deep enough for a lengthy study of its own; since the purpose of this chapter is to explore the progressive departure from the early American idea of rights, I will wade into the theory of the founding only to the extent that it is necessary to understand the subsequent progressive departure.

FOUNDING LIBERALISM

Progressives rightly identified the 1776 American Declaration of Independence as the preeminent statement of the new nation's governing philosophy, and they were especially troubled by the transhistorical and limited account of the purpose of government contained in the Declaration. The progressives identified the language of the Declaration with the social compact philosophy of John Locke's *Second Treatise of Government*. Because the nature of Lockean liberalism is complex, we should be careful about unequivocally equating Locke's principles with the founders'; the actual significance of Locke's principles may be distinct from how those principles were understood by America's founding generation and applied in the statesmanship of the day. Nonetheless, there can be little doubt about the founders' adoption of the political teaching of social compact theory:[2] the purpose of government, according to the

Michael P. Zuckert, *The Natural Rights Republic: Studies in the Foundation of the American Political Tradition* (Notre Dame, IN: University of Notre Dame Press, 1996).

2 On this connection, see Peter C. Myers, "Locke on the Social Compact: An Overview," in Ronald J. Pestritto and Thomas G. West, eds., *The American Founding and the Social Compact* (Lanham, MD: Lexington Books, 2003), 1–35.

Declaration, is the same for all men by virtue of their common nature; it does not change from one generation to the next. This purpose is to secure "certain unalienable rights," as the Declaration states, which all individuals possess in accord with "the Laws of Nature and of Nature's God." Natural rights are not conferred by government but by man's "Creator," and are thus not contingent upon whatever a particular society deems to be expedient at a given time. Government exists for the sake of protecting rights; without such a purpose, it becomes illegitimate and the people rightly withdraw their consent.

This logic of the Declaration emerges out of its equality doctrine. Far from a command for government to use its power for the sake of bringing about an actual material equality, the Declaration's statement that "all men are created equal" was understood to mean that no one man is the natural ruler of any other man. It was meant to counter the theory of divine right of kings or hereditary aristocracy. This meaning is evident not only from the Declaration itself, but also from the other public documents of the day, especially the many state declarations of rights. From those declarations it is clear how the founding generation understood equality. The Virginia Declaration of Rights—adopted just weeks before the Declaration of Independence—says, for example, that "all men are by nature equally free and independent." The Massachusetts Constitution of 1780, drafted by John Adams, says that "all men are born free and equal."[3] Equality for the founding generation pertained to equality of natural rights.

The Declaration's conception of natural rights is simply an extension of, or a consequence of, its equality doctrine. It is precisely because no other man is born my natural ruler that I may claim a right, by nature, to my life, liberty, and pursuit of happiness. Equality is a statement of fact in the Declaration—an observation about human nature—whereas the natural rights statement derives a moral doctrine from that observation: because no one *is* naturally born my political superior, then no one *ought* to interfere in the preservation of my life, my liberty, or my pursuit of happiness in whichever manner I choose. Because our natural equality of rights necessarily implies a duty on the part of others to respect those

3 For my understanding of how state declarations of rights help to illuminate the meaning of the Declaration of Independence, I have profited from Thomas G. West: "Jaffa vs. Mansfield: Does America Have a 'Constitutional' or 'Declaration of Independence' Soul?," *Perspectives on Political Science* 31 (Fall 2002): 235–46. See also Zuckert, *Natural Rights Republic*, 17–20, 33–34.

rights (without such a reciprocal duty, the assertion of rights becomes incoherent), this teaching of nature is also a "law" of nature, as seen in the Declaration.

The state declarations of rights are also useful in demonstrating that property was widely understood to be a fundamental natural right; private property rights are mentioned in *every* state declaration of rights. As Michael Zuckert has persuasively shown, Jefferson's employment of the "pursuit of happiness" language in the Declaration was not meant by him as a rejection of the right of property.[4] Rather, the understanding of the founding generation seems to have been that any legitimate government has an obligation to make its citizens secure in the title to the property they have earned through their labor. Without such an obligation on the part of government, individuals are not sufficiently free to pursue happiness in the means that seem best to them. The point is not only to protect wealth already earned and held, but to allow individuals to pursue a living secure in the knowledge that whatever fruits come from their pursuit will also be protected. The natural right to property, with which we are all endowed equally, may therefore lead to an inequality in the amount and kinds of property we end up with. As James Madison explains in referring to the "rights of property" in *Federalist* 10, the equal protection of our unequal faculties of acquiring property will lead to unequal results. The job of a legitimate government is not to even out these results (indeed, one of the founders' greatest fears was that the power of government would be employed in such a mission at the behest of a majority faction), but to preserve the "different and unequal faculties of acquiring property." This job is called by Madison "the first object of government."[5] As we will see below, this formulation was at the heart of what progressives found most objectionable about founding-era liberalism; they sought to undercut the recurrence to the "rights of property" as a defense against majority sentiment.

It should be acknowledged that some scholars have objected to understanding the American founding through the lens of eighteenth-century liberalism, and downplay the relevance of natural rights or social compact theory in early America.[6] Such arguments seem to defy

4 Zuckert, *Natural Rights Republic*, 79-80.

5 James Madison, "Federalist 10," in *The Federalist*, ed. George W. Carey and James McClellan (Indianapolis: Liberty Fund, 2001), 43.

6 In addition to the "republican" school of interpretation, headlined by Gordon Wood's *Creation of the American Republic, 1776–1787* (Chapel Hill: University of North Carolina Press, 1969),

the overwhelming evidence of the public documents of the founding era, as many other scholars have pointed out.[7] The relevant point for us is that the progressives certainly did not downplay the role of natural rights thinking in the American founding. Indeed, if eighteenth-century, natural rights liberalism was not central to defining the original meaning of the American regime, one has to wonder why the progressives would have wasted so much energy and ink attacking that brand of liberalism. As previously mentioned, attacking the natural rights liberalism of the founding was a signature characteristic of Progressive Era works.

THE PROGRESSIVE INTERPRETATION OF THE FOUNDING

For John Dewey, identifying and understanding the natural rights liberalism of the American founding was a critical part of understanding the crisis faced by progressive liberalism in Dewey's own day. In order to explain how liberalism faced a "crisis" in the twentieth century, Dewey employed a narrative of how liberalism had changed from the old to the new. His approach is notable, as indicated above, because his terminology implies that the changes in principle between eighteenth and twentieth-century America are intra-family—they are, in other words, "developments" within liberalism itself, as opposed to a move from liberalism to something different. Yet Dewey's description of contemporary liberalism depicts it as the principled antithesis of that which dominated the American founding era.

For Dewey, America's original liberalism was Locke's liberalism, and his proof is the Declaration. "The outstanding points of Locke's version of liberalism," wrote Dewey, "are that governments are instituted to protect the rights that belong to individuals prior to political organization of social relations. These rights are those summed up a century later in the American Declaration of Independence." The pre-political origin of these rights, Dewey went on to explain, gives primacy to the individual over the state. "The whole temper of this philosophy is individualistic in the sense in which individualism is opposed to organized social action. It held to

see Barry Alan Shain, *The Myth of American Individualism* (Princeton: Princeton University Press, 1994) and John Phillip Reid, *Constitutional History of the American Revolutions: The Authority of Rights* (Madison: University of Wisconsin Press, 1986).

7 See for example Zuckert, *Natural Rights Republic*, 108–117, 246n.17; Paul A. Rahe, *Republics Ancient and Modern* (Chapel Hill: University of North Carolina Press, 1992), 555–60; and Thomas G. West, "The Political Theory of the Declaration of Independence," in *The American Founding and the Social Compact*, 98–111, 116–20.

the primacy of the individual over the state not only in time but in moral authority." Dewey also connected the dots in looking to the intellectual origins of the founders' natural rights principles. He traced them not only to Locke, but to the older natural-law tradition; it was this connection to the broader tradition of natural law which made the founders' rights doctrine so inflexible, even in the face of strong majoritarian sentiment. The natural-law tradition, Dewey explained, "bequeathed to later social thought a rigid doctrine of natural rights." The natural rights doctrine, in turn, "gave a directly practical import to the older semi-theological and semi-metaphysical conception of natural law as supreme over positive law." Dewey put the natural right to property squarely at the center of the American founding and connected it directly to Locke's understanding. In fact, in his account of the Declaration, Dewey shifted seamlessly between it and the account of property rights from Chapter Five of Locke's *Second Treatise*. He explained that "among the 'natural' rights especially emphasized by Locke is that of property, originating, according to him, in the fact that an individual has 'mixed' himself, through labor, with some natural hitherto unappropriated object." From this Lockean natural right to property comes the natural "right of revolution," which is how Dewey tied Locke not just to the philosophy of the Declaration, but also to its immediate practical purpose.[8]

Like Dewey, Woodrow Wilson had done his graduate work at Johns Hopkins and was a prolific progressive academic before entering into public life. He shared Dewey's assessment of the founding. Before one could talk about the progressive conception of government, Wilson reasoned, one had to understand the flawed conception of government from which progressivism aimed to rescue American politics. This is why, in his most comprehensive account of the principles of government—*The State*—Wilson devoted substantial portions of the very first chapter to the theory of social compact and natural rights.[9] From the point of view of Wilson, Dewey, and nearly every other progressive intellectual, talking about American government necessitated talking first about social compact and natural rights. Wilson went on in subsequent works to trace the origins of American government to Jefferson's account of natural

8 John Dewey, *Liberalism and Social Action* (Amherst, NY: Prometheus Books, 2000 [orig. pub. 1935]), 15–16.

9 Woodrow Wilson, *The State* (Boston: D.C. Heath & Co., 1889), sections 17, 18, 21, 23.

rights; this was a narrative that Wilson often repeated even in his political speeches, as we see in the selections from his *New Freedom* that were detailed in the previous chapter.

Frank J. Goodnow—a more obscure, but influential, progressive—adopted the natural rights account of the American founding to frame his broad view of what was happening in the America of his day. Goodnow was the founding president of the American Political Science Association and a prominent academic who made his most effective contributions in the area of administrative law. Since progressives wanted to grant vast discretion to bureaucratic agencies, Goodnow pioneered the study of the kind of law that would be necessary to facilitate this delegation[10] before he went on to become president of Johns Hopkins. In lectures reflecting on progressive accomplishments, Goodnow explained how America had been born a child of eighteenth-century liberalism. "The end of the eighteenth century," Goodnow said, "was marked by the formulation and general acceptance by thinking men in Europe of a political philosophy which laid great emphasis on individual private rights.... The result was the adoption in this country of a doctrine of unadulterated individualism. Everyone had rights." In tying eighteenth-century philosophy to the origin of the American regime, Goodnow's account is interesting because of his emphasis on law and the courts. He recognized that the American understanding of rights originating in nature was distinct from the more positivistic English conception of rights, and that this distinction had profound implications for the nature of the American judiciary. "The rights of men," Goodnow explained, "of which their liberty consisted, were, as natural rights, regarded in a measure—and in no small measure—as independent of the law." By this formulation, Goodnow meant that the Americans understood their written Constitution as a manifestation of their natural rights, and thus these rights inherent in the Constitution superseded the ordinary positive law. Such a distinction between fundamental rights and the positive law placed great power in the hands of the judiciary, Goodnow reasoned, which was taken to be the safeguard of those fundamental rights.[11] This vision of the founding became crucial for progressives, especially those like Theodore Roosevelt who would

10 See Frank Goodnow, *Comparative Administrative Law* (New York: G.P. Putnam's Sons, 1903): and *Politics and Administration* (New York: Macmillan, 1900).

11 Frank Goodnow, "The American Conception of Liberty," in *American Progressivism*, ed. Ronald J. Pestritto and William J. Atto (Lanham, MD: Lexington Books, 2008), 55–59.

regularly rail against the judiciary precisely because it was employing the doctrine of natural rights (property rights in particular) as a weapon against progressive accomplishments in the arena of positive law.[12]

As clear as progressives were about the origins of the American regime in eighteenth-century liberalism, some of them were confused about eighteenth-century liberalism itself. While they properly placed Locke at the center of this older liberalism, some of them placed Jean-Jacques Rousseau there as well, often using Rousseau's conception of the social compact interchangeably with Locke's. It was because they conflated Rousseau and Locke that Wilson, and especially Goodnow, considered Rousseau to be an enemy of progressivism, when in fact he was more of a philosophic ally. Without going too far astray into a sustained discussion of social compact philosophy, it is important to note the critical difference between Lockean and Rousseauian social compact theory if we are to understand progressivism and its case against the founding and property rights. For Locke, property rights are natural and are thus a trump card which the individual carries with him into civil society. Locke's social compact has as one of its bedrock principles the necessity of protecting individual rights of property even against the will of a majority.[13] For Rousseau, at least in the *Second Discourse*, property rights are not natural at all; they are artificial, the invention of an "impostor" that mark the introduction of bourgeois society and the enslavement of man.[14] And while the status of rights in Rousseau's *Social Contract* is more ambiguous, a true social compact, for Rousseau, is liberated from its obligation to the artificial rights of property and driven, instead, by a general will. Thus, in making their case against the preeminence of property rights, America's progressives could have employed the Rousseau of the *Second Discourse* instead of vilifying him. Wilson and Goodnow seem to have assumed the following: because social compact theory is bad (they knew from Locke that it was responsible for the natural rights doctrine of private property), and because Rousseau wrote a book called "The Social Contract," therefore Rousseau (like Locke) must be an enemy

12 See, for example, Theodore Roosevelt, "The Right of the People to Rule," in Pestritto and Atto, eds., *American Progressivism*, 251–60.

13 John Locke, *Second Treatise of Government*, ed. Peter Laslett (Cambridge: Cambridge University Press, 1960), chs. 5 and 9, esp. sections 26–28, 34, 123–24.

14 Jean-Jacques Rousseau, *Second Discourse*, in *The First and Second Discourses*, ed. Roger D. Masters, trans. Roger D. and Judith R. Masters (New York: St. Martin's Press, 1964), esp. 141–42. See also Rousseau, *On the Social Contract*, ed. Roger D. Masters, trans. Judith R. Masters (New York: St. Martin's Press, 1978), esp. 46, 62.

of progress. In his account of social compact theory in *The State*, Wilson lumped Rousseau in with Richard Hooker, Thomas Hobbes, and Locke, using each interchangeably with the others[15]—in spite of the fact that Rousseau actually launched his own account of nature with a rejection of the accounts of these others.[16] Goodnow was similarly confused, laying the origins of the eighteenth century's radical individualism at Rousseau's feet and casting Rousseau as an enemy of those who would favor the good of society as a whole over the prerogatives of the individual.[17]

In spite of the occasional confusion with respect to distinctions within eighteenth-century political philosophy (and it is important to note that Dewey is guilty of no such confusion), the essential progressive understanding of eighteenth-century liberalism clearly identified it with Locke, and clearly connected Lockean natural rights with the American founding. This understanding was paradigmatic both for the original progressives and those who would later take up the progressive agenda. Franklin D. Roosevelt provides a pertinent illustration. Roosevelt consciously grounded his 1932 presidential campaign and New Deal in the ideas of the progressive generation that had preceded him, and especially in Wilson's brand of progressivism.[18] And like the progressives, Roosevelt knew that in speaking of the origins of American government, he had to begin with the natural rights doctrine of the Declaration. In his "Campaign Address on Progressive Government" (also known as the "Commonwealth Club Address"), even as Roosevelt argued for a new conception of the rights of property that would justify his New Deal, he began by identifying the old conception of these rights as the heart of the American founding. "The Declaration of Independence," Roosevelt proclaimed, "discusses the problem of Government in terms of a contract."[19] In his 1944 Annual Message to Congress, where Roosevelt famously

---

15 Wilson, *The State*, sec. 18.

16 Rousseau, *Second Discourse*, 102–03.

17 Goodnow, "American Conception of Liberty," 55, 57.

18 Franklin D. Roosevelt, "Campaign Address on Progressive Government," September 23, 1932, in Samuel I. Rosenman, ed., *Public Papers and Addresses of Franklin D. Roosevelt*, vol. 1 (New York: Random House, 1938), 749–50. For a different view—that the New Deal was a departure from progressivism—see: James A. Henretta, "Charles Evans Hughes and the Strange Death of Liberal America," *Law and History Review* 24, no. 1 (Spring 2006): 115–171; Morton Keller, *America's Three Regimes* (New York: Oxford University Press, 2007); Keller, "The New Deal and Progressivism: A Fresh Look," in *The New Deal and the Triumph of Liberalism*, ed. Sidney Milkis and Jerome M. Mileur (Amherst, MA: University of Massachusetts Press, 2002), 313–322; Elvin T. Lim, "The Anti-Federalist Strand in Progressive Politics and Political Thought," *Political Research Quarterly* 66, no. 1 (March 2013): 32–55.

19 Franklin D. Roosevelt, "Campaign Address on Progressive Government, 753.

argued for a second, economic "bill of rights" to go along with the original, he first traced the old understanding of rights to those "inalienable political rights" which had come from the Declaration.[20] And so we can see that the launching of the new liberalism in America, by the progressives and their disciples, required a clear understanding of the essence of the old liberalism. Having identified the natural rights doctrine at the heart of the old liberalism, progressives understood that that doctrine had to be undercut or at least redefined in order for the new liberalism to take hold.

THE PROGRESSIVE REJECTION OF PROPERTY RIGHTS—IN PRINCIPLE

The primary weapon the progressives employed against the principle of natural rights—and against property rights in particular—was historical contingency. Locke had argued in the *Second Treatise* that the standard for legitimate government is not to be found in history, but in nature—in particular, in the law of nature.[21] The logic of this argument is premised on the assumption that history is merely a record of human action, varying from epoch to epoch, sometimes witnessing events that are more just and sometimes witnessing those that are less so. It seems reasonable to conclude from Locke that one cannot derive a principle of what government *ought* to be from a mere record of what has been or what is; to do so would be to embrace the idea that might makes right, and to deny oneself an external standard of reference for judging the legitimacy of a particular political regime.[22] This is why Locke's articulation of natural rights was so congenial to the American colonists; nature was the ground of appeal for them that transcended the conventional laws and practices of the British regime in North America. The progressives grasped this central Lockean element of the founding and saw it for what it was: a permanent barrier

20 Franklin D. Roosevelt, "Annual Message to Congress," January 11, 1944, in Basil Rauch, ed., *The Roosevelt Reader* (New York: Holt, Rinehart and Winston, 1957), 347.

21 Locke, *Second Treatise*, section 6.

22 Locke addresses the historical critique of his state-of-nature thesis in sections 101–118 of the *Second Treatise*, although the argument I refer to here is based on the logic of the work as a whole. The notion that justice can be found in the particulars of history reminds one of Nietzsche's devastating critique of such a notion as an "idolatry of the factual" in *On the Advantage and Disadvantage of History for Life*, trans. Peter Preuss (Indianapolis: Hackett, 1980), 47—which is not to suggest that Nietzsche had much admiration for Lockean natural-rights theory either.

to changing the aim and scope of government in accord with what they believed were new historical demands.

For progressives like Dewey and Wilson, the principal difficulty with the older conception of property rights was the assertion that their foundation was natural—not contingent on history or on social convention. This meant that such rights are not subject to revision as government evolves historically, but inhere, instead, in the nature of man and are a primary motivation for human consent to the authority of government in the first place. The progressive critique, therefore, was not so much about the importance of property rights during the founding era, but rather the assertion by the founders that such rights ought to endure regardless of history's forward movement. This is why Wilson urged, for example, that the Declaration of Independence be read practically, and not as a source of enduring principle. It was "not a theory of government,"[23] Wilson explained, providing us with a clarifying contrast to Abraham Lincoln's understanding of the Declaration as positing "an abstract truth, applicable to all men and all times." Dewey also took aim at this particular view of the founding, contending in *Liberalism and Social Action* that a focus on individual property rights was a reasonable fit for the historical circumstances of late eighteenth-century America, but that same focus had become unreasonable under the radically different circumstances of modern liberalism. We can see how Dewey, instead of attacking the idea of property rights directly, placed them within the context of liberalism's development over time. In this way liberalism, according to Dewey, can come to have a meaning in one era that is exactly the opposite of its earlier meaning; property rights took pride of place only in the historically obsolete version of liberalism.[24] To put it in Wilson's terms, the Declaration was also a product of that older liberalism, and thus the rights enshrined there were best understood as a particular, practical remedy to a set of particular (and now long past) historical circumstances.[25]

In order to see property rights through the lens of history—to see that their significance is contingent upon social circumstance—one must detach them from their mooring in nature. This was the goal of

23 Wilson, "What is Progress?," in *American Progressivism*, 51.

24 Dewey, *Liberalism and Social Action*, 37–41.

25 Wilson, "The Author and Signers of the Declaration of Independence," in *PWW*, 17:251.

Wilson's account of the origin of political power in *The State*, which he offered as a "destructive dissolvent" to the social compact theory of Locke.[26] The problem with Locke was that his account of nature, upon which his entire standard of legitimate government rests, was purely speculative; the true foundation of government, Wilson countered, could only be uncovered by looking to the actual history of its development, not to conjecture or theory. Even while conceding that historical knowledge about the actual origins of government was imperfect, Wilson reasoned that even limited historical knowledge is far preferable to engaging in "a priori speculations" about the origins of government. In America, progressives believed that a natural account of individual property rights was being employed to defy the wishes of popular majorities, and the only foundation for these rights was the philosophic musing of social compact theory—a theory which, according to Wilson, "simply has no historical foundation."[27]

Wilson's model for a form of government that looked for its principles to history as opposed to nature was England. As in Goodnow's account of the distinction between the American and English conceptions of rights, Wilson worried about the American belief that permanent, abstract rights are enshrined in a written constitution that can be used to trump organic legislative development. Like Dewey, Wilson lamented the historical blindness of early liberals and thought that America's written constitution exacerbated the inflexibility of early American notions of rights. The problem was made worse by the difficulty of the constitutional amendment process, which reinforced the idea that change and adaptation—what Wilson called organic development—were to be avoided. Too many Americans really looked at their constitution as a contract—as a permanent, definite creation not subject to organic development. "We have been too much dominated," Wilson worried, "by the theory that our government was an artificial structure resting upon contract only."[28] Wilson's fear was that the ahistorical conception of rights was not only inhibiting organic growth (and the new, enlarged role that progressives had in mind for the national government), but that American government itself would ultimately burst and fall apart as a result. This fear can be traced back to his earliest days of thinking about government, as

26 Wilson, *The State*, 11.

27 Wilson, *The State*, 13–14.

28 Wilson, "The Modern Democratic State," in *PWW*, 5:65–68.

illustrated in the following 1876 entry to an early diary on the anniversary of American independence: "How much happier [America] would be now if she had England's form of government instead of the miserable delusion of a republic. A republic too founded upon the notion of abstract liberty! I venture to say that this country will never celebrate another centennial as a republic. The English form of government is the only true one."[29]

In contending for a more flexible, organic constitutionalism (in other words, the unwritten British constitution), Wilson argued that liberty and rights were concepts that could not be permanently defined. "Liberty fixed in unalterable law would be no liberty at all," he wrote. Liberty for the founding generation meant a doctrine of rights which protected the individual from tyranny in government, even when such a government might be fueled by a majority. But in his own day, Wilson reasoned, that founding-era conception of liberty was proving an impediment to liberty as it ought then to be understood. Liberty in contemporary times, Wilson explained, meant the liberty of majorities to use the power of government as they see fit. Liberty thus has a history of evolving meaning, and the new meaning required an overturning of the old.[30] In his new conception of liberty as the right of majorities to rule unbounded by individual rights such as property, Wilson sketched an idea that would later be taken up by Theodore Roosevelt when he crusaded against anti-majoritarian judicial decisions. Too often, Roosevelt believed, progressives had been successful in enacting parts of their legislative agenda—workers' compensation or labor regulation, for instance—only to see those successes turned into defeats when overturned by courts.[31] Majority tyranny was no longer a problem that warranted concern, according to Roosevelt: "I have scant patience with this talk of the tyranny of the majority.... We are today suffering from the tyranny of minorities.... The only tyrannies from which men, women, and children are suffering in real life are the tyrannies of minorities."[32] This formulation demonstrates Roosevelt's

29 Woodrow Wilson, "From Wilson's Shorthand Diary," July 4, 1876, in *PWW*, 1:148–49.

30 Woodrow Wilson, *Constitutional Government in the United States* (New York: Columbia University Press), 4.

31 Prominent examples of cases that aggravated progressives are *Lochner v. New York*, 198 U.S. 45 (1905), and *Hammer v. Dagenhart*, 247 U.S. 251 (1918). Roosevelt was particularly sensitive about cases in New York, due to his tenure as governor there; see, for example, *Ives v. South Buffalo Railroad*, 201 N.Y. 271 (1911), where the New York Court of Appeals overturned the state's Workmen's Compensation Act of 1910.

32 Theodore Roosevelt, "The Right of the People to Rule," 251–52.

belief that notions of liberty must be taken from "real life"—life which had changed drastically from the days of the founding—and not from abstract doctrines about the natural rights of the individual.

Goodnow, like Roosevelt, was quite direct in his criticism of the natural conception of rights. He believed that "there was no justification in fact for this social contract theory and this doctrine of natural rights," since they came as a consequence of looking to universal principles as opposed to the conventions that emerge out of historical development. The conventional needs of American society had changed since the founding period, and the original protections for individual liberty and property now stood as obstacles to the expansion of government. Progressive Era Americans were thus being forced to accept political principles which had been contrived to confront very different historical circumstances. The old circumstances, Goodnow explained, "made men impatient of the restrictions on private initiative," and so they naturally "welcomed with eagerness a political philosophy which, owing to the emphasis it placed upon private rights, would if acted upon have the effect of freeing them from what they regarded as hampering limitations on individual initiative."[33] Progressive Era rights philosophy should continue to reflect the conventional needs of the day, Goodnow reasoned, and the extent of individual liberty—as well as private property—should be contingent upon prevailing social need. Indeed, as previously discussed, this is precisely the argument that Franklin Roosevelt would subsequently employ when drawing on progressive principles in explicating his New Deal. When discussing the founding-era conception of fundamental rights, for example, in his "Campaign Address on Progressive Government," Roosevelt contended that "the task of statesmanship has always been the redefinition of these rights in terms of a changing and growing social order."[34]

THE PROGRESSIVE REJECTION OF PROPERTY RIGHTS—IN PRACTICE

The progressive critique of the principles underlying the original American understanding of rights paved the way for an attack on those

33 Goodnow, "American Conception of Liberty," 56.

34 Franklin D. Roosevelt, "Campaign Address on Progressive Government," 753.

rights in practice. Progressives called for significant changes both to political institutions and to national policy that were animated by their new conception of rights. Having argued that rights such as property should no longer be understood as grounded in nature, progressives were liberated to seek changes to institutional arrangements that had originally been predicated on the old liberalism's privileging of natural rights. While it is impossible here to treat the numerous and varied ways in which the progressive movement affected the development of American political institutions, it is especially instructive to look at how progressives conceived of the judiciary. The progressive treatment of the judiciary is particularly relevant because it demonstrates how the meaning and relevance of property rights were transformed in the Progressive Era. As discussed above, both Goodnow and Wilson saw it as a critical (but not felicitous) difference between America and England that fundamental rights in America were regarded as natural as opposed to conventional, and that they were thus distinct from and above the ordinary positive law. Such a construction, they knew, implied a role for the judiciary as the guardian of fundamental rights[35]—a role which could put it at odds with the organic development of legislation if such legislation was deemed a threat to the original meaning of rights.

For Theodore Roosevelt, this is exactly what had happened, and he became the lead progressive antagonist to a judiciary that he believed was upholding the old theory of natural property rights at the expense of progressive majorities. This even led him to advocate, in his unsuccessful third-party campaign to recapture the presidency in 1912, what can best be described as popular referenda on judicial decisions—or, to put it in the language found in the Progressive Party Platform of 1912: "That when an Act, passed under the police power of the State, is held unconstitutional under the State Constitution, by the courts, the people, after an ample interval for deliberation, shall have an opportunity to vote on the question whether they desire the Act to become law, notwithstanding such decision."[36] When judges defied the will of the people in the name

35 I am well aware that the founders did not see the judiciary as the exclusive guardian of fundamental rights, and that there is much debate on how the founders understood judicial review and the role of the courts in invalidating legislation. That debate is well beyond the scope of this chapter, and probably beside the point. For us, what is relevant is that the progressives understood the original conception of the judiciary in this way.

36 "Progressive Party Platform of 1912," in Pestritto and Atto, eds., *American Progressivism*, 276.

of property rights, Roosevelt argued, this represented a corruption of democracy. "Democracy," he contended, "has a right to approach the sanctuary of the courts when a special interest has corruptly found sanctuary there."[37] Roosevelt almost always used the epithet "special interest" in cases where property rights had been employed as protection against majority will. "Special interest" seems to have meant, for Roosevelt, any non-majority entity asserting its natural property rights. It was the "special interests"—and their property rights in particular—that stood in the way of progressive social legislation. The courts, Roosevelt complained, "have construed the 'due process' clause[38] of the State Constitutions as if it prohibited the whole people of a State from adopting methods of regulating the use of property so that human life, particularly the lives of the working men, shall be safer, freer, and happier."[39] And whereas, under the old liberalism, property rights had been grounded in human nature and were understood as an integral part of the range of rights inherent in human personhood, Roosevelt conceived instead of "human rights" and "property rights" in opposition to one another. Judges who struck

37 Theodore Roosevelt, "The Right of the People to Rule," 254.

38 The Fifth Amendment to the U.S. Constitution stipulates that no person shall be "deprived of life, liberty, or property, without due process of law." The Fourteenth Amendment applies that exact language to the state governments, and most state constitutions have a similar provision. Roosevelt's complaint was that the "due process" clause had been employed by courts to protect the liberty interest of individuals against the exercise of regulatory or "police" power by state governments. In the *Lochner* case, for example, where the state legislature had enacted a law limiting the number of hours bakers could agree to work, the U.S. Supreme Court reasoned that "the general right to make a contract in relation to his business is part of the liberty of the individual protected by the Fourteenth Amendment of the Federal Constitution" and that "the right to purchase or to sell labor is part of the liberty protected by this amendment unless there are circumstances which exclude the right" [198 U.S. 45 (1905), at 53]. The Court continued: "There is a limit to the valid exercise of the police power by the State. There is no dispute concerning this general proposition. Otherwise the Fourteenth Amendment would have no efficacy, and the legislatures of the States would have unbounded power, and it would be enough to say that any piece of legislation was enacted to conserve the morals, the health or the safety of the people; such legislation would be valid no matter how absolutely without foundation the claim might be. The claim of the police power would be a mere pretext—become another and delusive name for the supreme sovereignty of the State to be exercised free from constitutional restraint" [198 U.S. 45 (1905), at 56]. With respect to the regulation of bakers' hours, the Court concluded that "there is, in our judgment, no reasonable foundation for holding this to be necessary or appropriate as a health law to safeguard the public health or the health of the individuals who are following the trade of a baker. If this statute be valid, and if, therefore, a proper case is made out in which to deny the right of an individual, *sui juris,* as employer or employee, to make contracts for the labor of the latter under the protection of the provisions of the Federal Constitution, there would seem to be no length to which legislation of this nature might not go" [198 U.S. 45 (1905), at 58].

39 Theodore Roosevelt, "The Right of the People to Rule," 254.

down laws due to a judgment that they contravened property rights were simply substituting a "political philosophy" for "the will of the majority."[40]

Roosevelt's strong reaction to courts that had employed the doctrine of property rights to thwart legislatures in "regulating the use of property" naturally raises the question of what kind of regulation he had in mind, and why it would have been considered as a threat to the rights of property. As had been the case in founding-era liberalism, Roosevelt recurs to the principle of equality. But equality for the founders, as outlined above, meant an equality of rights, and the equal protection of rights might often lead, as Madison explained, to an inequality of results or rewards, due to the "diversity in the faculties of men, from which the rights of property originate."[41] So equality and the protection of individual property rights were, for the founders, two sides of the same coin. Roosevelt, by contrast, spoke of an "equality of opportunity," and meant something very different, as becomes clear in his 1910 "New Nationalism" speech. Roosevelt's equality meant using the power of government to destroy the "special interests" or "special privilege"—defined, as explained above, as those asserting property rights against the will of the majority. These "special interests" had used the "rules of the game" to benefit themselves and not society as a whole; "I stand," Roosevelt proclaimed, "for having those rules

40 Theodore Roosevelt, "The Right of the People to Rule," 257. Roosevelt here echoes the argument of Supreme Court Justice Oliver Wendell Holmes—whom Roosevelt had appointed to the Court—that the Constitution was not built on any political theory and that courts ought not use a theory of the Constitution to strike down legislation. See Holmes's dissent in *Lochner v. New York*, 198 U.S. 45 (1905), at 75–76. It should also be noted that Wilson did not attack the judiciary in the way that Roosevelt did. In this respect Wilson had more foresight than Roosevelt, for he foresaw the potential for the judiciary to be an agent of progress. There could well come a time, Wilson reasoned, in which majority sentiment would lag behind the demands of progress, and that would be a time for judges to step up and take the lead. In any event Wilson's defense of the judiciary should not be misconstrued; it came not from an attachment to it as a protector of individuals against progressive majorities, but instead from a gratitude that the courts had often been willing to read the Constitution flexibly: "We can say without the least disparagement or even criticism of the Supreme Court of the United States that at its hands the Constitution has received an adaptation and an elaboration which would fill its framers of the simple days of 1787 with nothing less than amazement. The explicitly granted powers of the Constitution are what they always were; but the powers drawn from it by implication have grown and multiplied beyond all expectation, and each generation of statesmen looks to the Supreme Court to supply the interpretation which will serve the needs of the day" (Wilson, *Constitutional Government*, 157–58). Wilson, in other words, was able to see past the immediate sins of the Court during his own day, and understand (correctly, as it turns out) that the Court was fundamentally a progressive institution—that it had helped the country to escape the bonds of its original constitutionalism, and would likely be a force for a similar kind of progressive change in the future.

41 *Federalist* 10: 43.

changed so as to work for a more substantial equality of opportunity *and of reward*."[42] Unlike Madison, who accepted the fact that unequal rewards would result from the equal enforcement of individual property rights, Roosevelt seems to have called for the unequal enforcement of *rights* (changing the "rules of the game," to use his language) so as to produce more equal *results*.

Roosevelt justified changing the "rules of the game"—that is, abandoning the equal enforcement of natural property rights—because he subscribed to the progressive redefinition of rights themselves. One's right to property did not come, as it had in the eighteenth-century liberalism that influenced the founders, through an account of nature where individual labor gave title to property. Rather, one had a "right" to property, in Roosevelt's view, only insofar as it was socially beneficial for one to have it. Title to property became contingent upon its serving a social purpose. "We grudge no man a fortune which represents his own power and sagacity," Roosevelt explained, "when exercised with entire regard to the welfare of his fellows."[43] Property rights were no longer moored in nature, to be used as a trump against social action, but were instead, as Goodnow had urged they be, "conferred... by the society to which [an individual] belongs," and determined by "social expediency."[44] We know from Chapter One that Roosevelt was explicit about the contingency of property rights upon social utility, and about widening the scope of state power in order to accommodate his narrower conception of rights and vision for equalizing economic outcomes. Roosevelt was conscious that his vision for equalizing rewards—the "square deal," as he called it—was not compatible with the original American conception of property rights but was, instead, founded upon a new theory. "We are face to face with the new conceptions of the relations of property to human welfare," he proclaimed. In justifying this move from the old to the new, he once again employed the construction of property rights in opposition to human rights, where property is not an extension of the human person but serves instead to alienate man from his own welfare. We had been brought to this point, Roosevelt concluded, "because certain advocates

42 Theodore Roosevelt, "The New Nationalism," in Pestritto and Atto, eds., *American Progressivism*, 214–15. Emphasis added.

43 Theodore Roosevelt, "The New Nationalism," 217.

44 Goodnow, "American Conception of Liberty," 57.

of the rights of property as against the rights of men have been pushing their claims too far."[45]

This new conception of property rights undergirded a host of policies—advocated not only by Roosevelt but by progressives generally—that fulfilled the call for "far more active governmental interference with social and economic conditions." Progressives sought not only to have the federal government supervise the manner in which private wealth was earned, but also to redistribute private wealth in order to ensure that it would serve the common good. To this end, progressives pursued a graduated income tax and a substantial inheritance tax, both of which were called for in the planks of the 1912 Progressive Party Platform. Progressives also fought successfully for the ratification of the Sixteenth Amendment to the Constitution, which was written to overcome a Supreme Court decision denying to the federal government the power to tax certain forms of income.[46]

The dual aims of centralized regulation of economic activity and the redistribution of wealth comprised the heart of Theodore Roosevelt's "New Nationalism" campaign, the Progressive Party platform, and many other progressive enterprises. Progressive Era reforms thus helped to shape the future course of liberalism in the twentieth century. These reforms were grounded on a novel interpretation of the political theory of the American founding that was ultimately adopted, as explained above, by Franklin Roosevelt in his establishment of the New Deal order for American national government—reforms built upon a rejection of the rights of property, both in principle and in practice.

The new liberalism in America was built, in other words, upon a progressive transformation of the natural rights principles that had served as a foundation for the old liberalism. The two most prominent of America's national progressives—Woodrow Wilson and Theodore Roosevelt—were

45 Theodore Roosevelt, "The New Nationalism," 220.

46 Specifically, in 1895 the Supreme Court in *Pollock v. Farmers' Loan & Trust Co.* had ruled that federal taxes on income derived from interest, dividends, and rents were "direct" taxes and thus constitutionally required to be apportioned among the states on the basis of population [157 U.S. 429 (1895)]. Taxes on wages were still considered to be indirect, and thus not subject to the apportionment requirement. *Pollock* thus made the question hinge on the source of income. In order to nullify this point, the Sixteenth Amendment declared that taxes on income, "from whatever source derived," could be levied by the federal government "without apportionment among the several States, and without regard to any census or enumeration."

central to this transformation, both at the level of first principles and at the level of more concrete reforms to American institutions. The next chapter will treat these figures in greater depth.

CHAPTER THREE

★

ROOSEVELT, WILSON, AND THE DEMOCRATIC THEORY OF NATIONAL PROGRESSIVISM

While America's original progressives helped to usher in a robust, centralized system of national administration, they were even more well known for sounding the theme of democratic reform. The American Constitution, they contended, placed too much distance between the people and their government, due to an inordinate fear by the Constitution's framers of the factious tendencies of unfiltered public opinion. Because of this indirect and representative form of popular government, progressives complained that popular majorities of their own day were unable to direct the government to act effectively in response to the pressing social and economic crises of the nation.[1] Instead, a small but powerful minority, progressives argued, was taking advantage of the Constitution's limits on popular rule to benefit itself at the expense of

1 Progressives lamented, for example, the gap between rich and poor (see Jane Addams, "Subjective Necessity for Social Settlements," in Ronald J. Pestritto and William J. Atto, eds., *American Progressivism* [Lanham, MD: Lexington Books, 2008], 105), the effects on urban life of immigration (see Theodore Roosevelt, "State of the Union Message," December 3, 1901, in *State of the Union Addresses of Theodore Roosevelt* [Cirencester, Gloucestershire: Echo Library, 2007], 4–38), and the state of working conditions (see Theodore Roosevelt, "State of the Union Message," December 3, 1907, in *State of the Union Addresses*, 201–48).

the great mass of people.[2] It is for this reason that many of the reforms advocated by progressives involved reducing or eliminating the distance between majority opinion and governing at the federal, state, and local level. Progressives, regardless of certain important differences among them, universally supported movements toward more direct forms of democracy: the ballot initiative, recall, referendum, and direct primaries for elections. Democratization was, arguably, the most important theme of the progressive movement, as it sought to place more governing power in the hands of popular majorities.

The progressive push for democratization, however, is complicated by the fact that the movement was also the launching point for the modern administrative state, as Chapter Seven will show. It helped put into place a system whereby significant portions of government decision-making are performed not by the traditional branches of government that are accountable to the people through elections, but by unelected, bureaucratic agencies that regulate with substantial independence from political control. While progressives, on the one hand, sought to make the nation's traditional political institutions much more accountable to majority opinion, on the other hand they also believed that those institutions were not capable of managing all of the new activities in which progressives wanted the national government to become involved.[3] Under the progressive model, political institutions were to become both more democratic and less important. How democratic, then, was national progressivism? In what ways does its reliance upon expert governance complicate its democratic theory?

The relevance of these questions comes from the influence that this dual character of progressivism has had on contemporary American government. American politics today maintains a near obsession with public opinion; even minute movements in benchmarks such as the presidential approval rating are watched as intently as heart monitors on critical patients. And yet while public opinion occupies a place of tremendous importance, its authority is also deflected in ways that reflect progressive governing principles. In spite of the intense focus on national political debates, most real governing today is done by bureaucratic agencies. Often, these agencies govern in ways that defy public opinion. Most of

2 For a representative example of this argument, see Theodore Roosevelt, "The Right of the People to Rule," in Pestritto and Atto, eds., *American Progressivism*, 251–52.

3 For an enumeration of these aims, see "Progressive Party Platform of 1912," in Pestritto and Atto, eds., *American Progressivism*, 273–87.

the critical activity in Barack Obama's presidency took place in regulatory agencies as opposed to the national legislature, and the same is true thus far in the Trump presidency.

During the Obama Administration, for example, the Environmental Protection Agency (EPA) promulgated a series of rules regulating greenhouse gas emissions. Due mostly to concerns over the impact of such rules on the economy, a similar scheme of regulation faced strong, bipartisan opposition in 2010 and failed to pass Congress. (Many believe that Democratic Senate candidate Joe Manchin won election from West Virginia that year due in part to a television commercial which featured him shooting a copy of the proposed legislation with a high-powered rifle.) In spite of the legislative failure, these rules are now, for the most part, the law of the land. Such a maneuver was possible because when Congress enacted the Clean Air Act and its subsequent amendments,[4] it defined the EPA's power in such broad and vague terms that it amounted to a delegation of near-plenary legislative power.[5] The EPA has also been busy under the Trump Administration, this time in its attempts to scale back Obama-era policies. Again, in the absence of legislation from the elected representatives in Congress, the unelected personnel in the agency have taken the lead in policymaking. And this state of affairs goes back well beyond Trump and Obama. One of the most recent of such instances was the government's response to the economic downturn of 2008, when Congress considered, and voted against, a taxpayer-funded bailout of major American automobile manufacturers. Nonetheless, the national government proceeded to bail out both General Motors and Chrysler. It was able to do so because the previously enacted Troubled Asset Relief Program (TARP)[6]—drafted for the purpose of bailing out banks and

4 Per the website of the Environmental Protection Agency: "The legal authority for federal programs regarding air pollution control is based on the 1990 Clean Air Act Amendments (1990 CAAA). These are the latest in a series of amendments made to the Clean Air Act (CAA). This legislation modified and extended federal legal authority provided by the earlier Clean Air Acts of 1963 and 1970."

5 In *Massachusetts v. Environmental Protection Agency*, 549 U.S. 497 (2007), the U.S. Supreme Court ruled that the Clean Air Act not only granted the EPA the authority to regulate greenhouse gas emissions, but in fact obligated it to do so. Specifically, the Court held that, since such emissions fall under the Act's very broad definition of "air pollutant," the EPA was obligated to regulate the emissions unless it 1) found that the emissions did not contribute to global climate change, or 2) had a reasonable explanation for its unwillingness or inability to determine if the emissions contributed to global climate change. Subsequent rulings have, with some important exceptions, upheld the broad authority of the EPA to legislate on greenhouse gases. See Chapter Eight for a fuller treatment of this phenomenon.

6 For the language on the Treasury Department's authority, see 12 USCS § 5211 (a)(1). On

other financial service entities—had been written vaguely enough that the Treasury Department had ample discretion to divert funds to a wide array of entities having little to do with the financial services industry. Many such examples can be drawn from a variety of policy areas, as we will see in Chapters Seven and Eight. The point here is to establish that much governing today is done by expert agencies—sometimes with political support and sometimes without it.

The tension within today's administrative state—between democratic governance and governance by unelected experts—reflects a similar tension in the democratic theory of America's original progressives, especially in Theodore Roosevelt and Woodrow Wilson, the two most prominent progressives on the national political stage. This limits the scope of the inquiry in order to keep it at chapter length (among others, the progressive writer Herbert Croly would deserve attention in a fuller treatment of this question). Yet in Roosevelt and Wilson we find an important contrast which helps to illuminate the nature of progressive democratic theory. We have with Roosevelt the typical progressive critique of the republican constitutionalism of the Federalists, and the insistence upon very direct popular control over national government. Though it is almost impossible to believe, Roosevelt saw little or no tension between his strong democratic impulse and his call for the employment of expert commissions in the national regulation of business and property. Wilson, on the other hand, while equally convinced about the necessity of pushing democratic reforms, more readily acknowledged the tension he envisioned in the coexistence of an increasingly democratized politics with an increasingly expert and powerful administrative apparatus. The result was, in Wilson's case, a more nuanced and realistic democratic theory which has, as a consequence, a greater relevance for contemporary American government.

ROOSEVELT AND THE PEOPLE'S RIGHT TO RULE

For Theodore Roosevelt, the Constitution's Federalist framers had obsessed about majority tyranny and thus erected a system which

---

the extension of TARP authority beyond banks and ordinary financial institutions, see: *The Troubled Asset Relief Program: Report on Transactions through Jun 17, 2009*, http://www.cbo.gov/ftpdocs/100xx/doc10056/MainText.4.1.shtml#1094296, accessed February 5, 2011. See also *United States Department of the Treasury Section 105(a) Troubled Asset Relief Program Report to Congress for the Period December 1, 2008 to December 31, 2008*, http://www.treasury.gov/press-center/press-releases/Documents/0010508105_a_report.pdf, accessed February 5, 2011.

enshrined minority tyranny.[7] Worried that the many in a democracy would use their legislative power to vote themselves the wealth of the few, the framers had given pride of place to individual property rights which had turned, in Roosevelt's time, into a system of concentrated wealth and power. The courts—both state and federal—had become to Roosevelt the institutional enablers of this form of minority tyranny.[8] As we have already learned, Roosevelt crusaded against antimajoritarian judicial decisions, contending that majority tyranny was no longer a problem in America, and complaining that the founders had limited the power of popular majorities on the basis of an abstract theory of individual, natural rights. Fundamentally, Roosevelt believed any system that deliberately thwarted majority opinion in this way—or in any way—could not call itself popular. Such was the thrust of his crusade against the courts and his push for mechanisms of direct democracy. "How can the prevailing morality or a preponderant opinion," Roosevelt asked, "be better and more exactly ascertained than by a vote of the people?"[9]

Roosevelt believed that if the real will of the people was allowed to prevail, a fundamental recasting of the scope of national government would be in order. The existing concentrations of wealth, upheld by a theory of abstract equality, would have to give way to a system that regulated business and property in order to effect an actual "equality of opportunity" for the average man. Roosevelt's speech on the "New Nationalism," which he gave in 1910 and which became the foundation for his subsequent attempt to recapture the presidency, laid out a vision of national power that would spark progress toward real equality. The speech identifies the enemy as "special privilege" or "special interests," "who twist the methods of free government into machinery for defeating

---

7 For an example of the kind of thinking that Roosevelt complained about, see James Madison, *Federalist* 10, in *The Federalist*, ed. George W. Carey and James McClellan (Indianapolis, IN: Liberty Fund, 2001), 42: "Complaints are every where heard from our most considerate and virtuous citizens, equally the friends of public and private faith, and of public and personal liberty... that measures are too often decided, not according to the rules of justice, and the rights of the minor party; but by the superior force of an interested and overbearing majority."

8 See, for example, *Lochner v. New York*, 198 U.S. 45 (1905), where the U.S. Supreme Court overturned a state law limiting the number of hours bakers could agree to work; *Hammer v. Dagenhart*, 247 U.S. 251 (1918), where the U.S. Supreme Court upheld a lower court's ruling that a law preventing interstate commerce in products produced by child labor was unconstitutional; and *Ives v. South Buffalo Railroad*, 201 N.Y. 271 (1911), where the New York Court of Appeals overturned the state's Workmen's Compensation Act of 1910.

9 Roosevelt, "Right of the People to Rule," 256.

the popular will."[10] The way to defeat the special interests, Roosevelt argued, was to afford a "far more active" role to the federal government. Combinations of wealth could not be undone, Roosevelt reasoned, as they were "the result of an imperative economic law which cannot be repealed by political legislation." But their effects could be controlled—could even be transformed—for the benefit of all men. "The way out lies," Roosevelt concluded, "not in attempting to prevent such combinations, but in completely controlling them in the interest of the public welfare."[11]

How could such "complete control" be accomplished? Through the use of expert agencies. Among other tactics, Roosevelt emphasized in the New Nationalism the role of the Federal Bureau of Corporations and the Interstate Commerce Commission, the powers of which "should be largely increased."[12] When launching his run for the presidency in 1912, Roosevelt elaborated that the key to investing such agencies with regulatory power was their expert and non-partisan character. The problem had been that regulatory policy, to the extent it had been practiced at the national level, was overly subject to the influence of politics. Such influence led to unscientific policy. In order to remedy this problem, Roosevelt called for "administrative control of great corporations.... A national industrial commission," he contended, "should be created which should have complete power to regulate and control all the great industrial concerns engaged in interstate business."[13] Tariff policy, too, had suffered by having itself subject to the political process. Special interests were too influential in that process, leading again to "unscientific" regulatory policy. The remedy was to empower a "permanent commission of nonpartisan experts."[14]

In calling both for increased popular control over national government, and for removing economic policy from the political process

10 Theodore Roosevelt, "The New Nationalism," in Pestritto and Atto, eds., *American Progressivism*, 214.

11 Roosevelt, "The New Nationalism," 216. For a full treatment of Roosevelt's political principles, the best account is Jean M. Yarbrough's *Theodore Roosevelt and the American Political Tradition* (Lawrence, KS: University Press of Kansas, 2012). Yarbrough traces the origins of and influences on Roosevelt's thought, showing the connections between that thought and Roosevelt's various proposals for reform. Yarbrough also shows how Roosevelt's vision of state power was expansive, despite also being a more moderate alternative to the movement for state socialism that was spreading at that time.

12 Roosevelt, "The New Nationalism," 217.

13 Roosevelt, *Theodore Roosevelt's Confession of Faith before the Progressive National Convention, August 6, 1912* (New York: Roosevelt Memorial Association, 1943), 19.

14 Roosevelt, *Theodore Roosevelt's Confession of Faith*, 23.

and granting it to expert commissions, Roosevelt did not see a tension between the two aims. Nor did he seem to think that it called into any question "the right of the people to rule." The problem was not that democratic politics itself was corrupt and unscientific, but rather that *decentralized* politics—particularly as practiced by the national legislature—was corrupt. Thus the way to ensure objective and scientific regulation was not, as Wilson was arguing, through separating administration from politics altogether; it was instead to place ultimate accountability for expert regulating in the hands of the popular executive—the one political entity that could claim to embody the broad national will. Experts and commissions were to govern—this was the only way, Roosevelt acknowledged, for the national government to handle the many new tasks that progressives had in mind for it—but constantly with the understanding that they answered to the people. He explained in 1912 that "we, the people, rule ourselves, and what we really want from our representatives is that they shall manage the government for us along the lines we lay down.... We welcome leadership and advice, of course, and we are content to let experts do the expert business to which we assign them without fussy interference from us. But the expert must understand that he is carrying out our general purpose."[15] Policy could be managed by experts, Roosevelt later explained, but "it is for the people themselves finally to decide all questions of public policy and to have their decision made effective."[16]

Again, policymaking by commission did not threaten popular rule, as Roosevelt conceived of it. Expert commissions could be given great power, could be shielded from the influence of special interests by insulating them from the legislature, all while being held strictly accountable to democratic opinion. The key, Roosevelt explained, was centralization. In his 1908 State of the Union message, he argued that

> the danger to American democracy lies not in the least in the concentration of administrative power in responsible and accountable hands. It lies in having the power insufficiently concentrated, so that no one can be held responsible to the people for its use. Concentrated power is palpable, visible, responsible, easily reached, quickly held to account.

15 Theodore Roosevelt, "The Meaning of Free Government," in *Social Justice and Popular Rule* (New York: Charles Scribner's Sons, 1925), 236–37.

16 Roosevelt, "The Purpose of the Progressive Party," in *Social Justice and Popular Rule*, 460.

> Power scattered through many administrators, many legislators, many men who work behind and through legislators and administrators is impalpable, is unseen, is irresponsible, cannot be reached, cannot be held to account.[17]

Roosevelt clearly meant that the national government's new powers of economic control could be made democratic by concentrating ultimate responsibility for them in the president—that is to say, in himself. In looking to the presidential leader as the key to balancing democracy and expert governance, Roosevelt would have something in common with Woodrow Wilson.

WILSON AND ADMINISTRATION

Like Roosevelt, Wilson believed that the American system of government was too undemocratic and, also like Roosevelt, he pinned blame on the framers' obsession with a highly individualized and abstract notion of liberty. Fear of majority tyranny, or faction, had led the framers to restrict too severely the powers of the national government by means of mechanistic checks and balances, thereby impeding the people from using the government as an instrument of their will. While Roosevelt frequently railed against the courts for their anti-majoritarian decisions, Wilson criticized the separation of powers system as a whole. Wilson was an Anglophile and had, from his earliest years of thinking seriously about government, been an admirer of the British parliamentary model. The parliamentary model stood for democracy and efficiency, providing for the smooth translation of democratic will into public policy through the overlapping of and cooperation between legislative and executive functions. The American separation of powers system, by contrast, with its intentional antagonism between the legislative and executive branches, was designed to protect the people from themselves, purposely throwing up as many obstacles as possible to the people getting their way.

While Roosevelt's favored remedy for the undemocratic character of America's original system of government was to advocate direct popular means of circumventing institutions altogether (the ballot initiative, referendum, etc.), Wilson preferred to reform the institutions themselves.

---

17 Theodore Roosevelt, "State of the Union Message," December 8, 1908, in *State of the Union Messages*, 6–7.

He suggested new ways of conceiving of American political institutions that would facilitate the functional, if not formal, demise of the separation of powers system.[18] The point of these reforms was to make the system responsible. Wilson explained the challenge in his book *Congressional Government*:

> It is... manifestly a radical defect in our federal system that it parcels out power and confuses responsibility as it does. The main purpose of the Convention of 1787 seems to have been to accomplish this grievous mistake. The 'literary theory' of checks and balances is simply a consistent account of what our constitution-makers tried to do; and those checks and balances have proved mischievous just to the extent which they have succeeded in establishing themselves as realities. It is quite safe to say that were it possible to call together again the members of that wonderful Convention to view the work of their hands in the light of the century that has tested it, they would be the first to admit that the only fruit of dividing power had been to make it irresponsible.[19]

The criticism of separation of powers from the perspective of responsibility is a consistent feature of Wilson's writings, from the earliest to the most mature. He called repeatedly for America to be made more democratic by instituting some form of cabinet or parliamentary government—where the national legislature depends closely upon majority public opinion and the executive branch exists by virtue of sustained support in the legislature. The only means of bringing genuine democracy to American government, Wilson made clear, were "certainly none other than those rejected by the Constitutional Convention."[20]

Wilson's criticism of the Constitution for its undemocratic institutional arrangements was grounded in a democratic theory sharply distinct from that of the founding generation. The political theory of the founding is the subject of much debate, which I have addressed in Chapter Two at greater length. Wilson's democratic theory departs from the founders principally by its rejection of the idea of social compact. Wilson and other progressives identified this social compact principle, with

18 See Pestritto, *Woodrow Wilson and the Roots of Modern Liberalism* (Lanham, MD: Rowman & Littlefield, 2005), 123–27.

19 Woodrow Wilson, *Congressional Government* (1885; reprint, New York: Meridian Books, 1956), 187.

20 Wilson, "Cabinet Government in the United States, August, 1879," in *PWW*, 1:497.

its corresponding natural rights doctrine, as the heart of the American founding, and it was the point of departure for their own very different democratic theory.

Wilson criticized natural rights theory as contrary to the reality of historical development. It relied upon a fixed and speculative picture of man which, Wilson argued in his 1889 book *The State*, "simply has no historical foundation."[21] Instead, rights ought to be viewed through the lens of history, where their nature and extent depend upon social circumstance. Wilson offered his evolving understanding of human liberty as "destructive dissolvent" to the social compact principles of John Locke and others who had influenced the American founding generation. Locke and other social compact thinkers, Wilson claimed, put forth an unrealistic and static account of nature that served as the foundation for keeping government permanently limited and unresponsive to the evolving historical spirit. The true foundation of government, Wilson countered, could only be uncovered by looking to the actual history of its development, where one would see that the individual never had any primary or special existence that preceded or transcended society.[22]

Wilson took his democratic theory not from an autonomous conception of the individual, but from what he said was the true historical origin of government: the patriarchal family or tribe. Yet if such a rejection of the pre-political, abstract individual sounds certain Aristotelian themes, we should not mistake Wilson's democratic theory for a call to return to the classical model. Wilson rejected classical democratic theory just as thoroughly as he rejected the modern social compact. The classical conception of democracy, Wilson proclaimed, "exaggerates the part played by human choice."[23] He rejected the classical notion of prudence, according to which statesmen possess wisdom with respect to what is good universally and employ it as best they can in particular historical situations.[24] Such a conception gives too much credit to the ability of human choice to affect the course of history. Great individuals, Wilson countered, cannot transcend their environments but are instead the products of the great historical forces.[25]

---

21 Woodrow Wilson, *The State* (Boston: D.C. Heath, 1889), 13–14.

22 Wilson, *The State*, 11.

23 Wilson, *The State*, 14.

24 Aristotle, *Nicomachean Ethics*, 1134a23–1135a5, 1141b10-1145a10.

25 For more on the differences between classical and modern democracy, see Wilson, "The Real

Wilson rejected classical democratic theory not only because it falsely exalted the prudence of great men over the power of history, but also because it adhered to a "cycle" of regimes.[26] The problem with the Aristotelian cycle was that it failed to conceive of democracy as a permanent condition of man. While Aristotle had suggested a continuous cycle of regime change based both upon fortune and the wise or imprudent choices made by individuals, Wilson countered that history leads to the *permanent* victory of the modern democratic state. History is not cyclical, but linear; and the historical conditions were such, or were in the process of becoming such, that democracy was here to stay. Earlier periods of democratic activity were fleeting, Wilson reasoned, because history had not then adequately prepared a permanent home for democracy. He explained that "the cardinal difference between all the ancient forms of government and all the modern" is that "the *democratic idea* has penetrated more or less deeply all the advanced systems of government."[27] In an 1885 essay on "The Modern Democratic State," Wilson argued that modern democracy (as contradistinguished from both classical democracy and founding-era, rights-based democracy) is the permanent and most advanced form of government. "Democracy is the fullest form of state life: it is the completest possible realization of corporate, cooperative state life for a whole people."[28] The classical world had not been ready for genuine democracy. Neither had America been ready for it during the founding era. This is why the framers were fearful of popular majorities and had structured the Constitution so as to limit their influence. "Democracy is poison to the infant," Wilson wrote, "but tonic to the man." It "is a form of state life which is possible for a nation only in the adult stage of its political development."[29] The nation, Wilson argued, had matured to adulthood, but strict adherence to the Constitution would keep it bound to a form of government suited for infancy.

The critical ingredient for modern democracy—the historical condition that had been missing from earlier attempts—was unity in the mind of the public. The old fear of faction, which Madison had surmised was

---

Idea of Democracy, August 31, 1901," in *PWW*, 12:177–78.

26 See Aristotle, *The Politics*, Book V, esp. 1301a20–1301b30.

27 Wilson, *The State*, 600, 603–5. Emphasis original; hereafter all emphasis is in the original unless stated otherwise.

28 Wilson, "The Modern Democratic State, December, 1885," in *PWW*, 5:92.

29 Wilson, "Modern Democratic State," 5:71.

a permanent condition "sown in the nature of man,"[30] no longer applied. That the many might abuse their democratic power and rule only for their own advantage at the expense of the few was one of the "childish fears" about democracy that "have been outgrown." The difference was that "this democracy—this modern democracy—is not the rule of the many, but the rule of the *whole*."[31]

With the people thus unified in mind, the power of popular sentiment could be unleashed without fear of tyranny, in spite of the fact, Wilson argued, that "many theoretical politicians the world over confidently expect modern democracies to throw themselves at the feet of some Caesar."[32] The course of America's own history, as Wilson understood it, demonstrated the advance of the permanent democratic idea. In spite of the rigid and mechanistic structure of the Constitution, America had overcome its decentralized and individualistic origins to evolve into a true nation. Wilson brought up the presidency of Andrew Jackson to make his point. Jackson had tried to turn the clock back on national progress through his autocratic attack on the national bank. Jackson's "childish arrogance and ignorant arbitrariness" in seeking to retard the growth of national power proved futile; history was on the side of national growth and America had marched steadily from primitive to modern democracy.[33]

While Wilson's work reveals several intellectual influences—from that of Walter Bagehot on Wilson's love for the British constitution to that of social Darwinism on Wilson's concept of the American constitution as "living" organism—his idea of modern democracy as the permanent endpoint of history shows his profound debt to the German philosopher Georg Hegel.[34] Wilson believed that the modern democratic state was the preordained end of history, and that the history of regimes had not been mere random adaptation, as a Darwinian analysis might suggest, but had instead been leading up to the permanent victory of modern democratic ideas. In early essays such as "The Art of Governing," Wilson commented

30 Madison, *Federalist* 10, 43.

31 Wilson, "Modern Democratic State," 5:76, 79.

32 Wilson, "Modern Democratic State," 5:81.

33 Wilson, "Modern Democratic State," 5:81.

34 For more on the influence of Hegel on Wilson, see Pestritto, *Wilson and the Roots of Modern Liberalism*, 14–19, 34–40, 213–16. See also Scot J. Zentner, "President and Party in the Thought of Woodrow Wilson," *Presidential Studies Quarterly* 26, no. 3 (Summer 1996): 666–77; Zentner, "Liberalism and Executive Power: Woodrow Wilson and the American Founders," *Polity* 26, no. 4 (Summer 1994): 579–99.

that history points to the development of a single kind of human government.[35] And in later works such as *The New Freedom*, Wilson put forth a vision of modern democracy as the end-state of historical progress.

With history having thus prepared the ground, Wilson described his New Freedom as "A Call for the Emancipation of the Generous Energies of a People." He spoke on the 1912 campaign trail of the founding-era antipathy toward democracy and contrasted it to the progressive embrace of democracy. He spoke of these as "two theories of government" and identified the founding-era plan with the Federalist thought of Alexander Hamilton—"a great man," claimed Wilson, "but, in my judgment, not a great American." Hamilton and his fellow Federalists had constructed the Constitution on the principle of "guardianship"—a fear of what the people would do if they were given the freedom to govern themselves.[36] "I believe," Wilson countered, "in the average integrity and the average intelligence of the American people." He employed this argument to attack Roosevelt, connecting the old, Hamiltonian, guardianship theory with Roosevelt's plan to grant regulatory power to expert commissions. "I do not believe," he explained, "that the intelligence of America can be put into commission anywhere. I do not believe that there is any group of men of any kind to whom we can afford to give that kind of trusteeship. I will not live under trustees if I can help it." He proclaimed in the same speech that "I don't want a smug lot of experts to sit down behind closed doors in Washington and play Providence to me."[37]

Wilson used this kind of democratic, anti-expert rhetoric effectively against Roosevelt on the campaign trail. Yet when he won and assumed office, most of Wilson's major domestic initiatives involved the very kind of regulation by commission that Roosevelt had advocated in the New Nationalism.[38] In fact, Wilson's agenda looked so much like that on which Roosevelt had campaigned that one Roosevelt scholar has remarked that it was "exceedingly embarrassing to the Progressive Party. Wilson had stolen its thunder and much of its excuse for being."[39] As much as Wilson's domestic agenda as president was a sharp departure from the

35 Woodrow Wilson, "The Art of Governing, November 15, 1885," in *PWW*, 5:53.

36 Wilson, "Art of Governing," 55–56.

37 Wilson, "Art of Governing," 60, 64.

38 Among other key pieces of regulatory legislation, Wilson signed the Federal Trade Commission Act and the Clayton Antitrust Act in 1914.

39 George E. Mowry, *Theodore Roosevelt and the Progressive Movement* (New York: Hill and Wang, 1960), 287.

attacks on commission government he had made while campaigning, President Wilson was not actually setting off on a new direction. Instead, he was reverting to an embrace of expert administration which he had developed and endorsed throughout his voluminous writings on government, and from which his presidential campaign had been an expedient and temporary diversion.

For as long as Wilson had been writing about the theory and practice of government, he anticipated, as has been shown, that the increasing unity of the public mind would facilitate a final and permanent democratic state. And as intense as his democratic rhetoric could get, he did not think that democratic politics would be of the greatest importance in the modern democratic state. Since, instead, the people were already agreed—at least implicitly—on what they wanted, once their will was emancipated the real task of modern government would be administration. Once history had overcome factiousness and established the "rule of the whole," the vital question became one of means, not of ends. In the "Study of Administration," Wilson wrote: "The trouble in early times was almost altogether about the constitution of government; and consequently that was what engrossed men's thought.... The weightier debates of constitutional principle are even yet by no means concluded; but they are no longer of more immediate practical moment than questions of administration. It is getting harder to *run* a constitution than to frame one."[40] In spite of his attacks on Roosevelt's regulatory proposals in the 1912 campaign, Wilson had been saying since the mid-1880s that the wide scope of governmental responsibility that progressives advocated would require a system in which the particulars of policymaking were delegated to expert administrators. In attacking commissions as undemocratic in 1912, Wilson was actually attacking proposals that were largely consistent with his own, long-stated views. That he almost immediately turned to expert agencies upon assuming the presidency should surprise no one who read just about anything he wrote prior to coming on the national political stage.

Since the mid-1880s, Wilson's writings reflect a strong apprehension about the influence of politics on administration. He insisted that if progressives wanted to entrust the national government with significantly

40 Woodrow Wilson, "The Study of Administration," in Pestritto and Atto, eds., *American Progressivism,* 193–4.

increased supervision of private business and property, they could not do so until they had found a way for expert administrators to make decisions on the basis of objectivity and science as opposed to political considerations. In an 1887 essay "Socialism and Democracy," Wilson embraced socialism in principle, explaining that it is perfectly consistent with genuine democratic theory. Genuine democracy, like socialism, would not allow individual rights to be a barrier to unfettered state action. But, Wilson explained, democrats could not quite accept the socialist agenda in practice, because socialists wanted the government to act in areas where it was not then capable of doing so competently.[41] In order to remedy this practical obstacle to the adoption of the socialist agenda by progressive democrats, a new science of administration first had to be developed.[42] Administration had always been a part of American national government, of course, but it had been administration within the confines of the republican executive, and thus subject to political control. In order to move forward with modern democracy, administrative entities would, Wilson concluded, have to be shielded, to some considerable degree at least, from traditional political accountability.

It was in his landmark essay "The Study of Administration," written just around the same time (1886), that Wilson directed his most sustained thoughts to this new kind of administration and advocated—at least to some degree—the separation of administrative governance from politics. As such, it was an essay that would come to have a profound influence on the birth and development of the public administration discipline in the United States. Administration, Wilson wrote in the essay, could be freed from the control of politics because it differed from politics in fundamental ways. "Administration," he argued, "lies outside the proper sphere of *politics*. Administrative questions are not political questions." Understood this way, it was questionable if administration could even be subject to constitutional definition. "The field of administration is a field of business," Wilson argued. "It is removed from the hurry and strife of politics; it at most points stands apart even from the debatable

41 See, for example, the Socialist Party Platform of 1912, http://www.academicamerican.com/progressive/docs/SocialistPlat1912.htm, accessed February 5, 2011. Michael McGerr argues that progressivism and socialism had more in common than the progressives let on. McGerr, *A Fierce Discontent: The Rise and Fall of the Progressive Movement in America, 1870–1920* (New York: Free Press, 2003).

42 Woodrow Wilson, "Socialism and Democracy," in Ronald J. Pestritto, ed., *Woodrow Wilson: The Essential Political Writings* (Lanham, MD: Lexington Books, 2005), 77–79.

ground of constitutional study."[43] In making this argument, Wilson was extending the line of reasoning from an even earlier essay—"Government by Debate" (written in 1882)—where he had contended that large parts of national administration could be immunized from political control because the nature of the policies they made were matters of science as opposed to matters of political contention. The administrative departments, wrote Wilson, "should be organized in strict accordance with recognized business principles. The greater part of their affairs is altogether outside of politics."[44]

Civil service reform had been a start to the neutral science of administration that Wilson sought to develop. Wilson believed that continuing down that path would allow the increasingly complex "business" of national government to be handled by a professional class of experts. The most important achievement of the civil service reform movement had been the establishment of the principle that it was desirable, at least in some cases, for politics to be kept out of administration. Wilson explained that "civil service reform is thus but a moral preparation for what is to follow. It is clearing the moral atmosphere of official life by establishing the sanctity of public office as public trust, and, by making the service unpartisan, it is opening the way for making it businesslike."[45] Perhaps most importantly, a civil service appointment, with its secure tenure and independence from politics, would allow an expert to disregard special interests and act on behalf of the general interest. For Wilson, the importance of this calling can be traced back to his earliest works, where as a young man he frequently expressed disgust with the dominance of politics by narrow, special interests. He said repeatedly that a career in politics was no longer a respectable or worthy goal for an educated young man who was interested in public service. He envisioned that the young and educated could, instead, form the foundation of a new, apolitical class of expert policymakers, trained in the emerging social sciences for service in a national government with greatly expanded responsibilities. "An intelligent nation cannot be led or ruled save by thoroughly-trained and completely-educated men," Wilson explained. "Only comprehensive information and entire mastery of principles and details can qualify for

43 Wilson, "Study of Administration," 5:370–71.

44 Wilson, "Government by Debate, December, 1882," in *PWW*, 2:224.

45 Wilson, "Study of Administration," 5:370.

command." He championed the power of expertise—of "special knowledge, and its importance to those who would lead."[46]

RECONCILING DEMOCRACY AND ADMINISTRATION?

The obvious question is how one squares Wilson's tendency to champion the importance of educated experts—of their independence from political influence, and of their being given, at least to some degree, a role in governing—with his fervently stated democratic principles. While Roosevelt seems not to have acknowledged this conundrum, Wilson understood that he needed to deal with the question of public opinion. "The problem," Wilson explained, "is to make public opinion efficient without suffering it to be meddlesome." Public opinion is a "clumsy nuisance" when it comes to the "oversight of the daily details and in the choice of the daily means of government." While Wilson called for introducing public opinion more directly into politics, he also believed that politics must confine itself to general superintendence—to the role of setting the broad goals of the nation.[47] In conceiving of the separation of politics and administration, Wilson sought to maintain the veneer of popular government while giving fairly wide berth to unelected administrators. The greatest obstacle to the necessary growth of apolitical administration, Wilson candidly acknowledged, is what Roosevelt would call the "right of the people to rule." "What then," Wilson asked, "is there to prevent" this "much-to-be-desired science of administration?" And he answered: "Well, principally, popular sovereignty."[48]

If progressive governance was to involve the exercise of at least some authority over policymaking by unelected experts, then, as Wilson acknowledged, expert governance would somehow have to be reconciled with progressive democratic theory. This was true for Roosevelt as well, even if he did not quite see the difficulty in the way that Wilson did. For both men, the key to this reconciliation seems to have come from their notions of leadership. Roosevelt's was much more populist in tone and in its actual character than Wilson's. It was also, arguably, more simplistic and self-serving. As explained above, Roosevelt believed that expert

46 Woodrow Wilson, "What Can Be Done for Constitutional Liberty: Letters from a Southern Young Man to Southern Young Men, March 21, 1881," in *PWW*, 2:34–36.

47 Wilson, "Study of Administration," 5:374–75.

48 Wilson, "Study of Administration," 5:368.

governance could be reconciled with democracy by centralizing power. While the legislative process had become corrupted due to the influence of special interests, the president represented the unified whole of public opinion. Expert administration, held accountable to the people through their popular president, could thus be unleashed to make policy on behalf of the general interest as opposed to the special interests.

Wilson, too, spoke to the necessity of a popular leader embodying the unified public mind.[49] Yet he had reflected much more thoroughly on the question, and his conception of democratic leadership included not only the president as a popular focal point, but an entire class of administrators as discerners of the public's objective will. It was because, in Wilson's mind, history had overcome the problem of faction and had brought about a unified public mind that the focus of modern government would be on expert administration. Having come together on the broad questions of political justice, the people could now entrust administrators to manage the complex details involved in regulating a modern economy. Empirically, of course, such a claim of political unity may seem to fly in the face of the fierce contention of interests that characterized the Progressive Era as much as any other era of American history. But beneath such contentiousness on the surface of American politics, Wilson argued, was a deeper, implicit will of the people as a whole. This implicit, objective will was one of which the people themselves might be unaware; hence the task of leadership was to see through the superficial clash of subjective interests and to discern the true popular mind. Such a task requires a leader to distinguish between mere majority opinion and the implicit, objective will of society as a whole. Wilson could reconcile expert or elite governance with democratic theory because, for him, elites are able to discern the public's objective mind better than the public itself. The key to the democratic legitimacy of elite governance is the elites' ability to discern what Wilson called the "general" or "objective" will: it is "an assumption, still more curious when subjected to analysis," that "the will

49 See Pestritto, *Wilson and the Roots of Modern Liberalism*, 167–72, 206–16. See also Paul Eidelberg, *A Discourse on Statesmanship: The Design and Transformation of the American Polity* (Urbana: University of Illinois Press, 1974), 4, 279, 286; Henry A. Turner, "Woodrow Wilson: Exponent of Executive Leadership," *The Western Political Quarterly* 4 (1951): 97–115; James W. Ceaser, Glen E. Thurow, Jeffrey K. Tulis, Joseph M. Bessette, "The Rise of the Rhetorical Presidency," *Presidential Studies Quarterly* 11 (Spring 1981): 159, 161, 163, 166; Robert Eden, "Opinion Leadership and the Problem of Executive Power: Woodrow Wilson's Original Position," *Review of Politics* 57 (Summer 1995): 483-503.

of majorities,—or rather, the concurrence of a majority in a vote,—is the same as the *general* will." He argued, further,

> that the will of majorities is *not* the same as the general will: that a nation is an *organic* thing, and that its will dwells with those who do the *practical* thinking and organize *the best concert of action*: those who hit upon opinions *fit to be made prevalent*, and have *the capacity to make them so.*[50]

Under this construction, democratic rule is cast in terms of expert or elite governance. The example Wilson used to illustrate his vision of democratic rule confirms the point: the civil service. While administrative agencies might not comport with traditional notions of democracy (their agents are unelected and are drawn from the educated classes), Wilson believed administration was democratic in a much deeper sense: civil service experts would not be distracted by special interest contentions in ordinary politics, and would be free instead to discern the true and implicit will of the public as a whole. Administrators would be in the best position to adjust governmental policy to the general will.

In thinking about administration in this way—as a means of reconciling democratization with expert governance—Wilson thought in terms that have proved to be more relevant to contemporary American government than Roosevelt's ideas did. Popular presidential leadership, championed by both Wilson and Roosevelt, has proved to be a central feature of American politics. But the delegation of significant policymaking authority to expert administrative agencies, which has also become a staple of American government, was thought through much more comprehensively by Wilson. This is not to suggest that today's administrative governance is fully or even mostly Wilsonian (legislators are still far too involved in agency decision-making, and politics is still far too dominant, to have satisfied Wilson's model), but that contemporary American governance seems to reflect the dilemma between the democratic impulse and the deference to expertise that Wilson identified and thought it necessary to confront.

---

50 Woodrow Wilson, "Democracy, December 5, 1891," in *PWW*, 7:355.

PART II

★

PROGRESSIVISM IN AMERICAN POLITICAL DEVELOPMENT

CHAPTER FOUR

★

AMERICAN PROGRESSIVISM AND THE LEGACY OF ABRAHAM LINCOLN

with Jason R. Jividen

As Part I has shown, the first principles of progressivism manifested themselves in an agenda to remake American institutions—in particular, to democratize political institutions while empowering a bureaucracy that was to be largely insulated from those same political institutions. This transformative agenda did not take place in a vacuum, nor was it merely a theoretical exercise; it was shaped by the principal events and figures of the Progressive Era and of the history that preceded it. Part II seeks to illuminate the connection between key figures and developments in American history and the important pieces of the progressive program. And no historical event was more significant to American progressivism than the Civil War; no figure played a bigger part in the progressive narrative than Abraham Lincoln.

Lincoln's place in shaping the self-understanding of both original and contemporary progressivism is difficult to overstate, as a recent book by Jason R. Jividen has demonstrated.[1] Progressives at all stages in modern American history have laid claim to Lincoln's legacy. This has not gone

1 Jason R. Jividen, *Claiming Lincoln* (DeKalb: Northern Illinois University Press, 2011). The present chapter is Ronald J. Pestritto's revision of an essay originally co-authored with Jividen. While all parts of the chapter represent the work of both authors, the parts on Croly are most attributable to Jividen and the parts on Wilson are most attributable to Pestritto. Those seeking a

unnoticed by a segment of American conservatives. While American conservatives largely agree that the ideas and policies of the original progressives served as a springboard for the liberalism of our own time, they disagree as to whether the progressives introduced big government into the American political tradition or merely capitalized on something that had been smuggled into the American tradition much earlier.[2] While some conservatives contend that it was the progressives who imported a foreign philosophy of government into the American tradition and used it to pursue a fundamentally new direction in American politics, a rather eclectic alliance of libertarians and paleoconservatives has emerged to point the finger not only at the progressives themselves, but at Abraham Lincoln.

The nature of the libertarian-paleoconservative critique of Lincoln has been explored in a book by Thomas L. Krannawitter, who summarizes the essence of it this way:

> The major premise is that the Confederate South was fighting for limited government, trying to protect the states' rights from an overbearing national government. The minor premise is that Lincoln opposed the Confederacy by opposing secession. The conclusion, therefore, is that Lincoln opposed limited government. And by so opposing the rights of states, which served as powerful checks against an intrusive national government, Lincoln effectively paved the way for the big government we have today.[3]

This argument that the transformation to unlimited national government came with Lincoln, and was then seized upon by opportunistic liberals in the twentieth century, has been buttressed by the fact that liberals today like to portray Lincoln as a champion of their cause. Krannawitter provides the example of Barack Obama, who wrote in 2006 that "Lincoln's 'basic insight' was 'that the resources and power of the national government can facilitate, rather than supplant, a vibrant free market.'" As

broader treatment of the claim on Lincoln's legacy made by liberals at various stages of American history are directed to Jividen's monograph.

2 Among the many examples that might be cited is Patrick Deneen's *Why Liberalism Failed* (New Haven: Yale University Press, 2018), which was addressed in the Introduction and contends that today's liberalism came out of America's founding itself.

3 Thomas L. Krannawitter, *Vindicating Lincoln: Defending the Politics of Our Greatest President* (Lanham, MD: Rowman & Littlefield, 2008), 290.

Obama saw it, however, this "insight" had to wait for the opportunity of the Great Depression to find an outlet for expression. Krannawitter explains that, "according to Obama, Lincoln first envisioned the principles of New Deal liberalism, while Franklin Roosevelt put them into practice."[4] These assumptions about Lincoln as the originator of progressive liberalism underlie much of Thomas DiLorenzo's libertarian–neo-Confederate attack on Lincoln[5] and have given rise to comments such as this from the economist Walter Williams: "Abraham Lincoln opened the door to the kind of unconstrained, despotic, arrogant government we have today, something the framers of the Constitution could not have possibly imagined."[6]

Finally, to the list of those who see Lincoln as a source of progressivism and subsequent iterations of liberalism in American political development, we can add the progressives themselves. It is a common feature of Progressive Era writings to point to Lincoln as a guide and inspiration. Theodore Roosevelt proclaimed, for example, in his 1913 address "The Heirs of Abraham Lincoln," that "we progressives and we alone are to-day the representatives of the men of Lincoln's day who upheld the hands of Lincoln;" he claimed that "Lincoln and Lincoln's supporters were emphatically the progressives of their day."[7] In order to understand how and why progressives claimed Lincoln's legacy, we must bear in mind the general aims of the national progressive movement; as detailed in Chapter One, these aims were grounded in an appeal to move beyond the principles of the American founding.

Most relevant here is the progressive critique of the Declaration of Independence on the basis of its universal account of individual rights and of the purpose of legitimate government. Prior chapters have pointed to John Dewey's lament over the "crisis" in modern liberalism that came from the founding generation's lack of "historic sense."[8] Woodrow Wilson

---

4 Krannawitter, *Vindicating Lincoln*, 293.

5 See, for example, DiLorenzo's defense of the Confederacy as the model of limited government in *The Real Lincoln: A New Look at Abraham Lincoln, His Agenda, and an Unnecessary War* (Roseville, CA: Prima Publishing, 2002), 273–74.

6 Walter Williams, "Why the Civil War," syndicated column published December 2, 1998. http://economics.gmu.edu/wew/articles/98/civil-war.htm. Accessed May 14, 2009.

7 Theodore Roosevelt, "The Heirs of Abraham Lincoln," Speech at the Lincoln Day Banquet, New York City, February 12, 1913, in *The Works of Theodore Roosevelt*, National Edition, ed. Hermann Hagedorn, 20 Volumes (New York: Charles Scribner's Sons, 1926): 17:359–60.

8 See John Dewey, *Liberalism and Social Action* (1935; reprint, Amherst, NY: Prometheus Books, 2000), 37–60, esp. 40–43.

attempted to discredit the Declaration by exaggerating its abstractness and equating its natural rights doctrine with that of the French Revolution, notwithstanding the revulsion of most of the founders at that Revolution or the decisive differences between its principles and America's own. This was a sleight of hand for which Wilson engaged not only Lincoln, but Edmund Burke, as I shall soon show. Progressives also understood the important relationship between the Declaration and the Constitution, seeing that the institutional arrangement contained in the Constitution was made necessary by the natural rights doctrine of the Declaration.[9] Given the proposition that the permanent end of government is to secure the citizens' natural rights, the greatest threat in democratic government is faction. The political science of the Constitution was designed to mitigate the problem of faction, and did so, progressives believed, in a manner that would forever prevent it from being used as a tool of progressive liberalism.

In terms of invoking Lincoln for the sake of overcoming the principles of the Constitution, the speeches of Theodore Roosevelt are more familiar than the scholarship of Wilson or Dewey. In making his claim on Lincoln, Roosevelt was deeply influenced by having read Herbert Croly's *The Promise of American Life*. Thus I will begin with Croly's understanding and use of the Lincoln legacy, which will point the way to Roosevelt's reliance on Lincoln as a champion of the progressive cause. The final part of the chapter will return to the argument of Wilson, whose firm reliance on Lincoln is less well known but particularly illuminating for those who would seek to understand both how progressivism serves as a foundation for modern American liberalism and how Lincoln has justly or unjustly been caught up in the development of modern liberalism.

9 Put another way, the founders were careful to be guided not only by ideas but by the experience of political development, as can be seen in *Federalist* 9 with its dependence upon the historical "improvements" in the science of politics, as well as in *Federalist* 85 with reference to David Hume's exhortation to rely upon experience. And the founders also understood that experience would allow continued improvement to the institutional means by which the fixed ends of American government could be achieved, writing as they did in *Federalist* 82: "'Tis time only that can mature and perfect so sound a system." This argument of *The Federalist* is why, in part, Harvey Mansfield has written that the universal ideas of the Declaration are made particularly American through the prudence of the Constitution, which turns Americans into a "constitutional people." It is in this way that the Americans distinguish themselves from the "revolutionary" people of France. See Harvey C. Mansfield, "The Unfinished Revolution," in *The Legacy of the French Revolution*, ed. Ralph C. Hancock and L. Gary Lambert (Lanham, MD: Rowman & Littlefield, 1996), 33; Harvey C. Mansfield, *America's Constitutional Soul* (Baltimore: The Johns Hopkins University Press, 1991), 1–17.

HERBERT CROLY'S LINCOLN AND *THE PROMISE OF AMERICAN LIFE*

Among the several reasons for the progressives' adoption of Lincoln's legacy, the chief one is Lincoln's role in the Civil War. The progressive narrative here accords very closely with today's libertarian–neo-Confederate critics of Lincoln: that the founding established a decentralized form of government which exalted individuals and states over the central government, that Lincoln was a great champion of centralization as an end in itself, and that the post-Civil War government was a transformation of and departure from the original. This "new" conception of government, necessitated by history and championed by Lincoln, represented a paradigm shift in the American political tradition and served as the springboard for progressivism in subsequent decades.

In *The Promise of American Life*, Croly attempted to articulate and defend the ends of progressivism; his account of Lincoln's place in American political history was crucial to this effort. For Croly, Lincoln served as an enduring example of leadership that transcended merely local and individualistic politics for the sake of a living national idea. Lincoln was the first legitimate politician, Croly claimed, to reveal fully the promise of American national life.

According to Croly, the Jeffersonian, "democratic" tradition of local government and individual rights and the Hamiltonian, "nationalist" tradition of efficient central government and leadership had always been the most common reference points in American political discourse. Croly contended that the political problem throughout American history had been the persistent failure to bring these principles together.[10] Traditionally, Croly argued, Americans had embraced the Jeffersonian tradition of individualism, equal rights, and local self-government, at the expense of a coherent national idea. In a predominantly agrarian economy, where individual effort was more likely to reward one with prosperity, the common, national interest and the individual interest

10 Herbert Croly, *The Promise of American Life* (1909; reprint, New York: Capricorn Books, 1964), 27–51. See David Alvis, "Herbert Croly's Transformation of the American Regime," Claremont Institute, 2003, http://www.claremont.org/publications/pubid.247/pub_detail.asp (accessed May 4, 2007). Croly's use of Lincoln is treated at length in David Alvis and Jason R. Jividen, "Distaining the Beaten Path: Herbert Croly and the 100th Anniversary of Lincoln's Birth" (paper presented at the Annual Meeting of the American Political Science Association, Toronto, Canada, September 3, 2009).

often coincided. With the rise of modern industry and the increase of economic specialization, however, the average American could no longer achieve political, economic, and spiritual satisfaction merely through the sweat of his own brow. The Jeffersonian tradition, more applicable to a predominantly agrarian existence, had proven inadequate to address the problems facing Americans in a new, industrial economy where individual social and economic mobility were hampered by changing conditions.[11] American democracy would now need a model of leadership that would show reformers and average citizens how to transcend local and particular interests in favor of coherent national policy. Croly offered Lincoln as the best model for this purpose, suggesting that all of Lincoln's thoughts ultimately "looked in the direction of a higher level of human association."[12] Croly continued:

> It is this characteristic which makes him a better and, be it hoped, a more prophetic democrat than any other national American leader. His peculiar distinction does not consist in the fact that he was a "Man of the People" . . . Lincoln's peculiar and permanent distinction as a democrat will depend rather upon the fact that his thoughts and his actions looked towards the realization of the highest and most edifying democratic ideal. *Whatever his theories were*, he showed by his *general outlook and behavior* that democracy meant to him more than anything else the *spirit and principle of brotherhood.*[13]

According to Croly, the "Union might well have been saved and slavery extinguished without [Lincoln's] assistance; but the life of no other American has revealed with anything like the same completeness the peculiar moral promise of genuine democracy." Croly thus promoted the promise of a democracy dedicated not to the security of individual natural rights but to the realization of human brotherhood in the nation as a whole.[14]

---

11 Croly, *Promise*, 17, 100–05, 182–85. See David Levy, *Herbert Croly of the New Republic: The Life and Thought of an American Progressive* (Princeton, NJ: Princeton University Press, 1985), 99–101.

12 Croly, *Promise*, 93-94; cf. Herbert Croly, "The Paradox of Lincoln," *The New Republic*, February 18, 1920, 350–53.

13 Croly, *Promise*, 94. Emphasis added.

14 Croly, *Promise*, 89, 207.

CROLY'S LINCOLN AS "MORE THAN AN AMERICAN"

Lincoln had the kind of character, Croly argued, that made him a truly national man, and it was Lincoln's character that mattered to Croly much more than his words or deeds. He described Lincoln as "more than an American," asserting that Lincoln was not merely a pioneer democrat and man of the people, but also an embodiment of the coming national identity.[15]

Lincoln's role in the slavery dispute was a manifestation, Croly argued, of his national character. When Lincoln confronted the problem of slavery, he made it "plain that a democratic nation could not make local and individual rights an excuse for national irresponsibility." Lincoln, Croly reasoned, "began to emancipate the American national idea from an obscurantist individualism and provincialism." Even though the Constitution had tolerated slavery, Croly argued that the institution had been a threat to the American nation. Antebellum political parties had failed to address adequately the slavery crisis because they were far too willing to sacrifice the national, common good for mere self-interest. The Democrats believed the slavery question to be merely a matter of local or state importance; and the Whigs, despite their Hamiltonian roots and professed sympathy for the national ideal, were all too willing to compromise away their principles for political gain.[16] According to Croly, Lincoln's leadership offered the solution to this failure. The institution of slavery had to be gradually reduced to insignificance or it would tear the nation apart. By proclaiming that a house divided against itself cannot stand, Lincoln suggested that slavery was a national problem that required a truly national solution. For the first time, Croly argued, an American politician had publicly claimed that the American nation was a "living principle" rather than a mere "legal bond."[17]

And it was Lincoln's character that mattered most. Croly conceded, as mentioned above, that the Union might well have been saved and slavery extinguished without Lincoln. For Croly, what Lincoln really offered was an example of human excellence, of the qualities necessary for disinterested leadership to transcend the self-interested, local concerns

---

15 Croly, *Promise*, 89–99. See Alvis and Jividen, "Distaining the Beaten Path," 7–24.

16 Croly, *Promise*, 86.

17 Croly, *Promise*, 86–88.

of the average American in favor of a complete national vision. Yet for Croly to offer Lincoln as a model for progressive reformers, he needed to recast Lincoln in the progressive mold. Croly had to offer a discussion of Lincoln that diverted attention from Lincoln's own political principles.

CROLY'S MISUSE OF LINCOLN

One particularly clear example of Croly's propensity to invoke Lincoln in a manner contrary to Lincoln's own principles comes in Croly's discussion of human nature. Croly believed that the average American's hope for better things to come, his faith in the promise of American life, was rooted in his shared desire for social amelioration, something which could only be realized through a stronger, more focused, more efficient national government. Such a government "would not be dedicated either to liberty or to equality in their abstract expressions, but to liberty and equality, in so far as they made for human brotherhood." He assumed that human nature could be shaped in such a way that individuals might routinely sacrifice self-interest for the sake of the common good. In contradistinction to *The Federalist*, which thought men capable of self-government but carefully circumscribed the scope of popular government due to the permanent inclination to factiousness within man's nature, Croly made a more utopian assumption about the perfectibility of human nature. He thus had faith that human government could be entrusted with the achievement of actual material equality, as opposed to securing a merely "abstract" equality of rights. While Croly admitted that the extent to which human nature could be "modified by social and political institutions of any kind is, at least, extremely small," he concluded that democracy nevertheless "must stand or fall on a platform of human perfectibility," and "cannot be disentangled from an aspiration toward human perfectibility, and hence from the adoption of measures looking in the direction of realizing such an aspiration." For Croly, progressive reform and the pursuit of human brotherhood as the end of American democracy simply assumes—indeed it must assume—a malleable human nature that can be improved through social planning.[18]

Despite Croly's attempt to incorporate the Lincoln example into this progressive vision of man, Lincoln held a very different understanding of

18 Croly, *Promise*, 207, 399–400, 454.

human nature, perhaps best expressed in his 1864 "Response to Serenade." Reflecting upon the difficulty of holding elections during the war, Lincoln suggested:

> The strife of the election is but human-nature practically applied to the facts of the case. What has occurred in this case, must ever recur in similar cases. *Human-nature will not change. In any future great national trial, compared with the men of this, we shall have as weak, and as strong; as silly and as wise; as bad and good.* Let us, therefore, study the incidents of this, as philosophy to learn wisdom from, and none of them as wrongs to be revenged.[19]

In Lincoln's thought, there is no overcoming man's nature to advance to new heights of civic association. There is no assumption that history will culminate in the perfection of human nature through social planning. The enduring problems of political life are rooted in our enduring and necessarily imperfect human nature, and like the American founders, Lincoln understood that limited, constitutional government is structured in light of this observation. For Croly, however, Lincoln exemplified the promise of American life through his "general outlook and behavior," "whatever his theories were." That is to say, whatever Lincoln might have identified as his own political principles and reasoning is of no real consequence. Ultimately, in light of the progress of history, Croly claimed to understand Lincoln better than Lincoln understood himself and sought to appropriate the Lincoln image while rejecting Lincoln's principles.[20]

This rejection of Lincoln's principles is also evident in Croly's discussion of natural rights. Despite his attempt to invoke the Lincoln image, Croly explicitly turned away from the natural rights principles that served as the foundation of Lincoln's political thought. "The ideal of a constructive relation between American nationality and American democracy," Croly wrote, "is in truth equivalent to a new Declaration of Independence.... There comes a time in the history of every nation, when its independence of spirit vanishes, unless it emancipates itself

19 Abraham Lincoln, "Response to Serenade," November 10, 1864, in *The Collected Works of Abraham Lincoln*, ed. Roy P. Basler, 9 Volumes (New Brunswick, NJ: Rutgers University Press, 1953), 8:101. Emphasis added.

20 See Alvis and Jividen, "Distaining the Beaten Path," 31.

in some measure from its traditional illusions."[21] Croly called for a re-founding of our fundamental moral and political ends, contending that American democracy must free itself from the illusory notion that its purpose is to secure the natural and equal rights of individuals. "Belief in the principle of equal rights," Croly argued, "does not bind, heal, and unify public opinion. Its effect is rather confusing, distracting, and at worst, disintegrating."[22] Yet Lincoln, Croly's ideal statesman, claimed the opposite view. Responding to the Southern slave interest's denial of the principles of the Declaration, Lincoln suggested: "Public opinion, on any subject, always has a '*central idea*' from which all its minor thoughts radiate. That 'central idea' in our political tradition, at the beginning was, and until recently has continued to be, 'the equality of men.'" For Lincoln, the self-evident truth that all men are created equal—that is, that they are equally endowed with natural and inalienable rights—is "the electric cord that links the hearts of patriotic and liberty-loving men together."[23]

While Lincoln and Croly would agree that the equality of all men had served as the central idea informing American public opinion, they profoundly disagreed as to the real meaning of equality.[24] For Croly, if the purpose of American government is merely to secure our equal natural rights, then "democracy becomes an invitation to local, factional, and individual ambitions and purposes." According to Croly, "of all perverted conceptions of democracy, one of the most perverted and dangerous is that which identifies it exclusively with a system of natural rights. Such a conception of democracy is in its effect inevitably revolutionary, and merely loosens the social and national bond." For Croly, the notion of natural rights necessarily places undesirable limitations on the power of national government to address social problems.[25] Public opinion must be redirected toward a new understanding of democracy, based not upon the idea that the purpose of government is to secure natural rights, but

21 Croly, *Promise*, 278–79.

22 Croly, *Promise*, 185.

23 Abraham Lincoln, "Speech at a Republican Banquet, Chicago, Illinois," December 10, 1856, in *Collected Works*, 2:385; Abraham Lincoln, "Speech at Chicago, Illinois," July 10, 1858, in *Collected Works*, 2:500.

24 Alvis and Jividen, "Distaining the Beaten Path," 30.

25 Croly, *Promise*, 80–81. See Edward A. Stettner, *Shaping Modern Liberalism: Herbert Croly and Progressive Thought* (Lawrence: University Press of Kansas, 1993), 48–49; David K. Nichols, "The Promise of Progressivism: Herbert Croly and the Progressive Rejection of Individual Rights," *Publius: The Journal of Federalism* 17:2 (Spring 1987): 31; Alvis and Jividen, "Distaining the Beaten Path," 30–33.

rather upon the idea that "genuine democracy" must necessarily be dedicated to securing human brotherhood. Croly's effort to seize the Lincoln image is frustrated by the fact that Lincoln's moral and political reasoning is fundamentally rooted in the very natural rights principles that Croly himself rejects. For Croly to offer up Lincoln as a model for contemporary progressive reform, he had to recast Lincoln's example in terms of a progressive unfolding of American history and an abandonment of the very foundations of Lincoln's own understanding of free government and democratic statesmanship.

THEODORE ROOSEVELT'S ABRAHAM LINCOLN

After reading Croly's *The Promise of American Life* in 1909, Theodore Roosevelt was convinced that the founders' political science had become obsolete in light of changing historical and economic circumstances. The progress of history had led to the necessity of a stronger, more efficient national government, unhampered by institutional mechanisms like federalism and separation of powers. The new aim of government, Roosevelt believed, was not to secure the natural and inalienable rights of individuals, but rather the material and spiritual well-being of the entire community.[26] Roosevelt thus sought to transform the American polity into what he described as a "real" or "genuine" democracy.

There can be no real democracy without "economic democracy," wrote Roosevelt—that is, a democracy in which men are afforded the equal opportunity to become intellectually, morally, and materially fit to be their own masters.[27] In modern, industrial America, where men were increasingly tied not to the land but to the factory, Roosevelt contended that equality of opportunity could not be secured without an increase in the role of the national government in providing that security through social and economic legislation aimed at reigning in powerful special interests. Moreover, Roosevelt suggested, this object could not be attained

26 Jean M. Yarbrough, "Theodore Roosevelt and the Stewardship of the American Presidency," in *History of American Political Thought*, eds. Bryan-Paul Frost and Jeffrey Sikkenga (Lanham, MD: Lexington Books, 2003), 537, 542. See Theodore Roosevelt, "The New Nationalism," Speech at Osawatomie, Kansas, August 31, 1910, in *Works*, 17:5-22; Theodore Roosevelt, "Limitation of Governmental Power," Address at the Coliseum, San Francisco, September 14, 1912, in *Works*, 17:306–14.

27 Theodore Roosevelt, "Progressive Democracy," A review of Herbert Croly's *Progressive Democracy* and Walter Lippmann's *Drift and Mastery*, November 18, 1914, in *Works*, 12:232–39.

without a corresponding increase in the people's direct control over their elected representatives, court decisions, and the Constitution itself. In his political rhetoric, Roosevelt frequently appealed to Lincoln as a "pure democrat" who would have supported increased legislation for social and industrial justice on the principle that the people are the rightful masters of their public servants and the Constitution.

"EQUALITY OF OPPORTUNITY"

In his debates with Stephen Douglas, Lincoln claimed that the slavery question was a manifestation of "the eternal struggle between . . . two principles—right and wrong—throughout the world." One, Lincoln claimed, "is the common right of humanity, and the other is the divine right of kings. It is the same principle in whatever shape it develops itself. It is the same spirit that says: 'You toil and work and earn bread, and I'll eat it.'" In his 1913 address, "The Heirs of Abraham Lincoln," Roosevelt suggested that the progressive platform "is but an amplification of this statement of Lincoln's."[28]

Roosevelt sought to connect Lincoln's expression of equal natural rights with his own vision of "equality of opportunity." In his "New Nationalism" speech, Roosevelt claimed that, in "every wise struggle for human betterment one of the main objects, and often the only object, has been to achieve in large measure equality of opportunity." The "essence of the struggle" is always "to equalize opportunity, destroy privilege and give to the life and citizenship of every individual the highest possible value both to himself and to the commonwealth. That is nothing new." Roosevelt suggested that, while we might not achieve perfect equality in this struggle, we could achieve a "practical equality of opportunity," which promises that "every man will have a fair chance to make of himself all that lies in him . . . unassisted by special privilege of his own and unhampered by the special privilege of others." This "equality of opportunity means that the commonwealth will get from every citizen the highest service of which he is capable."[29] In "The Heirs of Abraham Lincoln," Roosevelt explained how Lincoln could be a source for this vision of equality. He claimed that the purpose of the Progressive Party was none

28 Abraham Lincoln, "Reply: Seventh Debate with Stephen A. Douglas at Alton, Illinois," October 15, 1858, in *Collected Works*, 3:315; Theodore Roosevelt, "The Heirs of Abraham Lincoln," 363.

29 Roosevelt, "New Nationalism," 8–10.

other than Lincoln's purpose, declared in Lincoln's July 4, 1861, Message to Congress in Special Session, to "elevate the condition of men," to "lift artificial weights from all shoulders," to "clear the paths of laudable pursuit for all," and to "afford all, an unfettered start, and a fair chance, in the race of life."[30] For Lincoln, the artificial weights of chattel slavery were to be lifted by emancipation and the free labor system. For Roosevelt, government must lift the artificial weights as they existed in his day in the form of "wage slavery" practiced by modern industry. But, Roosevelt argued, the "real issue" confronting the Progressive Party was the same basic issue that confronted Lincoln: the struggle between the rights of man and the tyrannical principle that it is one man's duty to labor and another man's right to enjoy the fruits of that labor.[31]

Yet the "New Nationalism" speech illustrates how far Roosevelt actually departed from Lincoln's principles. We know from Chapter One's explication of the speech that government, for Roosevelt, must determine the acceptable use of property and must respect property rights if, and only if, it is deemed socially useful to do so. Specifically, Roosevelt's effort to claim the Lincoln inheritance for his "practical equality of opportunity" departs from Lincoln's principles. For Lincoln, the principles of the Declaration suggest that all human beings are equally endowed with natural and inalienable rights. To whatever extent one man is superior to another in accidental characteristics or talents, he may indeed fare better in securing his advantage in the world, but no one can claim a right by nature to rule over another without the other's consent. In everyday practice this equality means that a man should be able to eat the bread that he has earned. Lincoln's understanding of natural equality is central to his defense of free labor, in that the origin of private property consists in the natural and equal right that each human being has to his body, to the labor of that body, and to the fruits of that labor.[32] Lincoln consistently

---

30 Abraham Lincoln, "Message to Congress in Special Session," July 4, 1861, in *Collected Works*, 4:438.

31 Roosevelt, "Heirs of Abraham Lincoln," 362-66; cf. Theodore Roosevelt, "Washington and Lincoln: The Great Examples," in *Works*, 19:56–58; Abraham Lincoln, "Address before the Wisconsin State Agricultural Society, Milwaukee, Wisconsin," September 30, 1859, in *Collected Works*, 3:478–81; Abraham Lincoln, "Speech at New Haven, Connecticut," March 6, 1860, in *Collected Works*, 4:24; Abraham Lincoln, "Annual Message to Congress," December 3, 1861, in *Collected Works*, 5:52.

32 See George Anastaplo, *Abraham Lincoln: A Constitutional Biography* (Lanham, MD: Rowman and Littlefield Publishers, 1999), 234, 330–473; Harry V. Jaffa, *How to Think About the American Revolution: A Bicentennial Celebration* (Durham, NC: Carolina Academic Press, 1978), 45.

maintained this Lockean understanding that all men are equally entitled, so far as it is possible, to eat the bread that they earn by the sweat of their own brow.[33]

Far from implying the redistribution Roosevelt advocated in the "New Nationalism," Lincoln's pursuit of equality suggests the justice of an equality of rights, but not an equality of rewards. For Lincoln, free labor ensures that all have an equal right to pursue happiness under the rule of law, while understanding that unequal rewards will necessarily result—the same point made by Madison in *Federalist* 10. Lincoln's understanding of equality accords directly with the Madisonian principle, and thus diverges sharply from Roosevelt's redistributionism. This is why Lincoln could suggest to the New York Workingmen's Association in 1864 that

> property is the fruit of labor—property is desirable—it is a positive good in the world. That some should become rich, shows that others may become rich, and hence is just encouragement to industry and enterprise. Let not him who is houseless pull down the house of another; but let him labor diligently and build one for himself, thus by example assuring that his own house shall be safe from violence when built.[34]

Roosevelt obscured the distinction between equality of rights and equality of rewards that was so crucial to Lincoln's understanding of equality. He also denied the very foundation of Lincoln's views on free labor—that by nature, nothing should come between a man's hand and his mouth.

Harry V. Jaffa, *A New Birth of Freedom: Abraham Lincoln and the Coming of the Civil War* (Lanham, MD: Rowman and Littlefield, 2000), 300.

33 See, for example, Abraham Lincoln, "Speech at Springfield, Illinois," June 26, 1857, in *Collected Works*, 2:405–06; Abraham Lincoln, "Speech at Springfield, Illinois," July 17, 1858, in *Collected Works*, 2:520; Abraham Lincoln, "Reply: First Debate with Stephen A. Douglas at Ottawa, Illinois," August 21, 1858, in *Collected Works*, 3:16; cf. John Locke, *The Second Treatise of Government: An Essay Concerning the True Original, Extent, and End of Civil Government* in *Two Treatises of Government*, ed. Peter Laslett (Cambridge: Cambridge University Press, 1988); see esp. §54.

34 Abraham Lincoln, "Reply to New York Workingmen's Democratic Republican Association," March 21, 1864, in *Collected Works*, 7:259–60. In one of the few works to critically examine the progressive claim to Lincoln, Steven Hayward suggests that, despite their claim to Lincoln's legacy, the Progressives rejected Lincoln's understanding of natural rights and equality. See Steven Hayward, "The Children of Abraham," *Reason* 23 (May 1991): 26, 29. Also see Jaffa, *How to Think*, 45.

For Lincoln, this meant that, insofar as it is possible, government should exalt and protect the rights of private property.

"DIRECT DEMOCRACY"

For Roosevelt, if government is to secure "practical equality of opportunity," the people must have increased and more direct control over the power of government. Roosevelt's opponents had criticized the progressives for seeking to incorporate elements of direct democracy into American republicanism. Roosevelt responded by pointing to Lincoln:

> Our opponents have especially objected to our doctrine that the people have the right to control all their servants, judicial, executive, and legislative alike. Well, listen to Abraham Lincoln. He assailed his opponents because they "made war upon the first principle of popular government, the rights of the people," because they "boldly advocated" "the denial to the people of the right to participate in the selection of public officers except the legislative," and because they argued "that large control by the people in government" is the "source of all political evil." Mind you, I am quoting from Lincoln's words uttered over fifty years ago. They are applicable in letter and in spirit to our opponents to-day. They apply without the change of a word to those critics who assail us because we advocate the initiative and the referendum and, when necessary, the recall, and because we stand for the right of the people to control all their public servants, including the judges when they exercise a legislative function.[35]

Roosevelt referred here to Lincoln's December, 1861 Annual Message to Congress. Lincoln did indeed suggest in this address that the Confederate "insurrection is largely, if not exclusively, a war upon the first principle of popular government—the rights of the people." According to Lincoln, in "the most grave and maturely considered public documents" of the Confederacy "we find the abridgment of the existing right of suffrage and the denial to the people of all right to participate in the selection of public officers except the legislative boldly advocated, with labored arguments to prove that large control

35 Roosevelt, "Heirs of Abraham Lincoln," 364–65.

of the people in government is the source of all political evil. Monarchy itself is sometimes hinted at as a possible refuge from the power of the people."[36] But nothing in this address suggests that Lincoln's support for the sovereignty of the people prefigured the initiative, referendum, or the right of the people to recall public officials. Rather, Lincoln was speaking of elections, and he understood the right of people to control all their public servants to consist in their right to exercise their voice through established, constitutionally structured modes of consent. Consider the following from Lincoln's First Inaugural Address:

> By the frame of the Government under which we live... [the] people have wisely given their public servants but little power for mischief; and have, with equal wisdom, provided for the return of that little to their hands at very short intervals. While the people retain their virtue and vigilance, no administration, by any extreme of wickedness or folly, can very seriously injure the Government in the short space of four years.[37]

Put another way, extra-constitutional mechanisms such as the recall were unnecessary in Lincoln's view of government because, unlike the progressives, Lincoln conceived of the ends of government in limited terms. Lincoln spoke here of the executive, yet the principle could clearly apply to other elected officials. According to Lincoln (who does not mention impeachment here), elected officials may be "recalled" in the usual constitutional way: through elections coming at fixed intervals.[38]

Drawing on Lincoln, Roosevelt took particular issue with his critics' opposition to the progressive call for "the people to control all their public servants, *including the judges* when they exercise a legislative function."[39] Although Roosevelt did not support proposals for the recall of judges in New York, he did suggest that such measures might be necessary in some states and he claimed that progressives took a Lincolnian "attitude" when they supported the recall of judges.[40] Lincoln, however, never said

---

36 Lincoln, "Annual Message to Congress," December 3, 1861, 51.

37 Abraham Lincoln, "First Inaugural Address," March 4, 1861, in *Collected Works* 4:270.

38 See Judd Stewart, "Abraham Lincoln on Present-Day Problems and Abraham Lincoln as Represented by Theodore Roosevelt," Letter to the Members of the Ohio State Constitutional Convention, Columbus, Ohio, February, 1912 (Springfield: Illinois State Historical Society), 8.

39 Roosevelt, "Heirs of Abraham Lincoln," 364–65. Emphasis added.

40 See Roosevelt, "Heirs of Abraham Lincoln," 373–74, cf. Theodore Roosevelt, "The Right of the People to Rule," Address at Carnegie Hall, New York City, March 20, 1912, in *Works*, 17:164.

anything about the "return" of unelected officials, nor did anything in his speeches and writings suggest that he thought that the "right" to *recall* public servants, including judges, was a necessary inference from the idea that the people have the right to *control* those servants. Yet Roosevelt went further than merely to suggest that Lincolnian principles would require the popular recall of judges. He also suggested that Lincolnian principles required the popular recall of judicial decisions. Critics of the progressive Party, Roosevelt claimed, were "especially fond of denouncing our attitude toward the courts, and above all, our demand that the people shall be made the masters of the courts as regards constitutional questions." In response, Roosevelt reminded us that Lincoln had once suggested, in an 1859 speech at Cincinnati, that "the people of these United States are the rightful masters both of Congresses and courts, not to overthrow the Constitution, but to overthrow the men who pervert the Constitution." According to Roosevelt, this was the progressive position.[41]

Lincoln did assert in Cincinnati that the people are the "rightful masters of both Congresses and courts." However, if we consider Lincoln's statement in its fuller context, we find that Roosevelt failed to convey Lincoln's thoughts accurately:

> I say that we must not interfere with the institution of slavery in the states where it exists, because the constitution forbids it, and the general welfare does not require us to do so. We must not withhold an efficient fugitive slave law because the constitution requires us, as I understand it, not to withhold such a law. But we must prevent the outspreading of the institution, because neither the constitution nor general welfare requires us to extend it. We must prevent the revival of the African slave trade and the enacting by Congress of a territorial slave code. We must prevent each of these things being done by either Congresses or courts. The people of these United States are the rightful masters of both Congresses and courts not to overthrow the constitution, but to overthrow the men who pervert that constitution. *To do these things we must employ instrumentalities. We must hold conventions; we must adopt platforms if we conform to ordinary custom; we must nominate candidates, and we must carry elections.*[42]

41 Roosevelt, "Heirs of Abraham Lincoln," 367; cf. Abraham Lincoln, "Speech at Cincinnati, Ohio," September 19, 1859, in *Collected Works*, 3:460.

42 Lincoln, "Speech at Cincinnati, Ohio," September 19, 1859, 460-61. Emphasis added.

Roosevelt obscured, in other words, the fact that Lincoln sought to address the slavery problem *through established constitutional and political means*. Nothing in Lincoln's remarks at Cincinnati, nor in the whole of his statements on slavery extension (pertaining, e.g., to *Dred Scott*, the African slave trade, the fugitive slave law, or a national slave code) suggests that a right to recall judges or judicial decisions by popular vote ought to follow from Lincoln's principles. In order to address unwise policies or erroneous decisions made by congresses or the courts, and to demonstrate that the people are the rightful masters of both, Lincoln urged that the people must speak through the established electoral process and established, constitutionally structured, representative institutions.

Nevertheless, Roosevelt contended that there was an "exact parallelism" between Lincoln's attitude toward the courts and the progressive support for the recall of judicial decisions by popular referendum. This argument became the dominating theme in "The Heirs of Abraham Lincoln" and was voiced frequently by Roosevelt during the 1912 presidential campaign. In "The Recall of Judicial Decisions," Roosevelt defended his opposition to several New York State Court of Appeals decisions that he believed had frustrated the ability of legislatures to foster social and industrial justice. Roosevelt asserted that the recall of judicial decisions by popular referendum was "*precisely and exactly* in line with Lincoln's attitude toward the Supreme Court in the Dred Scott case and with the doctrines he laid down for the rule of the people in his first inaugural as President," and that his position differed "in *no essential way*... from the principles laid down and acted upon by Lincoln in this matter."[43] But Roosevelt and Lincoln really did differ in an "essential way" on this question, in that they fundamentally disagreed about the means by which erroneous or irresponsible judicial decisions could be addressed. This concrete disagreement may be why Roosevelt focused on Lincoln's "attitude" toward the Court rather than the specific details of his opinions on *Dred Scott*.

Roosevelt did correctly claim that Lincoln "would not have the citizen conform his vote" to the "decision of the Supreme Court [in *Dred Scott*] nor the member of Congress his," and that Lincoln would oppose

43 Theodore Roosevelt, "The Recall of Judicial Decisions," Address at Philadelphia, Pennsylvania, April 10, 1912, in *Works*, 17:195. Emphasis added. Also see Roosevelt, "Right of the People to Rule," 163–64.

making it a "rule of political action for the people."[44] But this, of course, does not suggest anything close to "judicial recall," as much as Roosevelt tried to conflate the two in his 1912 Speech to the Ohio Constitutional Convention:

> It was Lincoln who appealed to the people against the judges when the judges went wrong, who advocated and secured what was practically the recall of the Dred Scott decision... Lincoln actually applied in successful terms the principle of the recall in the Dred Scott case. He denounced the Supreme Court for that decision... and appealed to the people to recall the decision—the word "recall" in this connection was not known then, but the phrase exactly describes what he advocated. He was successful, the people took his view, and the decision was practically recalled. It became a dead letter without the need of any constitutional amendment.[45]

Roosevelt conflated the "exact" conception of judicial recall with its "practical" equivalent, illustrating the inherent difficulty in his appeal to Lincoln in support of this mechanism of direct democracy. To assert that Lincoln appealed to the people when the judges went wrong is not accurate in the sense that Roosevelt suggested. Lincoln appealed to the people insofar as he appealed to established constitutional and political means to deal with a decision he judged to be erroneous and irresponsible. He did this, above all, by urging the people to elect more Republicans to office, to change the makeup of the Court, and to convince the Court itself to reverse the *Dred Scott* decision.[46]

Roosevelt's claim that *Dred Scott* became a dead letter, with no need of constitutional amendment to overcome it, would also have us forget Lincoln's unwavering belief that emancipation would ultimately require constitutional amendment. For Roosevelt, judicial recall, "practical" or otherwise, was simply a quick and easy method of controlling and amending the Constitution. Roosevelt's reliance upon institutions of direct democracy was predicated upon his belief, characteristic of

44 Roosevelt, "Heirs of Abraham Lincoln," 369. See Abraham Lincoln, "Speech at Springfield, Illinois," July 17, 1858, 516.

45 Theodore Roosevelt, "A Charter of Democracy," Address before the Ohio State Constitutional Convention at Columbus, Ohio, February 21, 1912, in *Works*, 17:121, 139.

46 See, for example, Abraham Lincoln, "Speech at Chicago, Illinois," July 10, 1858, 495.

progressivism generally, that the problem of faction had been overcome by historical development and changing economic conditions. Roosevelt suggested that

> there are sincere and well-meaning men of timid nature who are frightened by the talk of tyranny of the majority. These worthy gentlemen are nearly a century behind the times. It is true that De Tocqueville, writing about eighty years ago, said that in this country there was great tyranny by the majority. His statement may have been true then, although not to the degree he insisted, but it is not true now.[47]

Constitutional and political institutions that had originally been designed to moderate and structure democratic rule were thus deemed obsolete in light of the progress of history.

On the question of majority tyranny, Roosevelt compared his contemporary opponents to Lincoln's opponent, Stephen Douglas. Roosevelt claimed that, just as Douglas had denounced Lincoln for publicly disagreeing with the *Dred Scott* decision, contemporary opponents of judicial recall were denouncing the progressives for resisting the courts.[48] Yet Roosevelt had far more in common with Douglas than with Lincoln. Like Roosevelt's vision of direct democracy, Douglas' doctrine of "Popular Sovereignty" was premised on the idea that majority tyranny was impossible. "Popular Sovereignty" illustrates the dangers of unmitigated majority rule in which there are no longer any overarching moral or constitutional limits placed upon the objects to which a majority might consent. Lincoln's devastating critique of "Popular Sovereignty" in his debates with Douglas suggests that, despite Roosevelt's attempt to adopt Lincoln as the precursor to progressive reform, there is no better critic of Roosevelt's dismissal of majority tyranny than Lincoln himself.

Roosevelt's dismissal of the concept of majority tyranny is fundamental to his attempt to redefine the ends and means of American

47 Roosevelt praised Bryce's statement that the "once dreaded danger" of majority tyranny had disappeared from American life. See James Bryce, *The American Commonwealth*, 3 Volumes (London: MacMillan and Company, 1888), 3:143. For Roosevelt, it is not that the problem of tyranny as such had disappeared, but rather that the tyrannies from which men, women, and children were suffering in "real life," were tyrannies by the minority of wealthy special interests. See Roosevelt, "The Recall of Judicial Decisions," 202.

48 Roosevelt, "Heirs of Abraham Lincoln," 367–68.

democracy. Breaking sharply with the political theory of the American founding, Roosevelt came to believe that any interest that did not actively and consciously serve the common good as defined by the government was necessarily a "special interest" that must be "driven out of politics."[49] For Roosevelt, direct democracy offered an efficient means of doing so and he sought to connect the Lincoln image with his call for progressive reform. But Lincoln had more in common with the American founders than he did with Theodore Roosevelt. As previously explained, the founders' political science was based upon the idea that the problem of faction could not be driven out of political life.[50] Likewise, although Lincoln certainly believed that self-interest could not serve as the sole standard of right action, he understood that our natural selfishness and our natural love of justice stand in "eternal antagonism."[51] Thus, institutional arrangements designed to temper and moderate the demands of factious majorities were both necessary and desirable, and always would be. In order to argue that such institutional restraints were no longer necessary, progressives relied on a rather peculiar account of American history and of Lincoln's role in it. This is where Woodrow Wilson's vision of American political development becomes crucial to understanding the progressive reliance on Lincoln's legacy.

WILSON'S USE OF LINCOLN

Wilson employed a narrative of Lincoln's role in American history as part of his effort to recast the Constitution in progressive terms. Wilson's many writings on American history, often overlooked by scholars, provide the clearest picture of this narrative. To understand American constitutionalism properly, Wilson contended that the single most important historical lesson to learn was that American history represented a triumph over the narrow individualism of the founding. America, he claimed, had evolved into a genuine nation. He elaborated:

> Our life has undergone radical changes since 1787, and almost every change has operated to draw the nation together, to give it the common

49 Yarbrough, "Theodore Roosevelt," 548. See Roosevelt, "New Nationalism," 5–22.

50 See Madison, *Federalist* 10, 58–59.

51 Abraham Lincoln, "Speech at Peoria, Illinois," October 16, 1854, in *Collected Works*, 2:271; cf. Lincoln, "Response to a Serenade," November 10, 1864, 101.

consciousness, the common interests, the common standards of conduct, the habit of concerted action, which will eventually impart to it in many more respects the character of a single community.[52]

Wilson urged that the Constitution be read in light of these centralizing developments, and that the power of the central government be expanded accordingly. His hope for America's future rested in his confidence that America would change its principles to fit new conditions, as it had done in the past. "No one who comprehends the essential soundness of our people's life can mistrust the future of the nation," Wilson reasoned. "He may confidently expect a safe nationalization of interest and policy in the end, whatever folly of experiment and fitful change he may fear in the meanwhile." We could have the confidence that history would bring about a true and complete nation, Wilson explained, because one could see how far the country had come toward this end in spite of an ill-designed, fractured government with little or no energetic leadership. He proclaimed: "Unquestionably we believe in a guardian destiny! No other race could have accomplished so much with such a system."[53] Without Lincoln and the Civil War, this old order would have continued and America could not have taken the steps necessary to mature. As Wilson summarized in *The State*, the "Civil War completes the Union,"[54] by which he meant that the last vestiges of the old order, which had stood in the way of progress, were swept away by the conflict.

That the Civil War was a decisive step forward in America's progress as a nation is an important theme of Wilson's five-volume work, *A History of the American People*. The significance of the change that Wilson attributed to the War cannot be overstated. The following passage captures the sense of the War's importance to Wilson:

The nation, shaken by those four never to be forgotten years of awful war, could not return to the thoughts or to the life that had gone before them. An old age had passed away, a new age had come in, with the sweep of that stupendous storm. Everything was touched with the

52 Woodrow Wilson, *Constitutional Government in the United States* (New York: Columbia University Press, 1908), 46–47.

53 Woodrow Wilson, "The Making of the Nation," April 15, 1897, in *PWW*, 10:231, 235. See also "A Commemorative Address," April 30, 1889, in *PWW*, 6:177.

54 Wilson, *The State*, 480.

> change it had wrought. Nothing could be again as it had been. The national consciousness, disguised, uncertain, latent until that day of sudden rally and call to arms, had been cried wide awake by the voices of battle, and acted like a passion now in the conduct of affairs. All things took their hue and subtle transformation from it: the motives of politics, the whole theory of political action, the character of the government, the sentiment of duty, the very ethics of private conduct were altered as no half century of slow peace could have altered them.[55]

Several things are worth noting about this characterization of the War's significance. In particular, once the old historical spirit—"the national consciousness"—has been replaced by a new one, everything changes. Politics, political theory, government, duty, ethics are all contingent upon the historical spirit and become transformed when that spirit advances. Wilson's five-volume history goes on to portray the post-war American spirit as truly national. This new national spirit especially manifested itself in the new mode of understanding the Constitution. Modern America had moved beyond the narrow, legalistic constitutionalism characteristic of the founding generation. Wilson explained that in the new era, the forms of the Constitution cease to be the main focus of national life. Instead, what really matters is the unity of will in the nation, and the government's reflection of that new will. In this regard, the War had "disclosed the real foundations of the Union; had shown them to be laid, not in the Constitution, its mere formal structure, but upon deep beds of conviction and sentiment." What became most important, then, in national politics, was not the Constitution's protection of individuals, but rather its ability to put into action "the passionate beliefs of an efficient majority of the nation." The War helped to overcome an excessive fixation on the forms of the Constitution because the prosecution of the War itself often required that those forms be disregarded. Once the fighting stopped, the nation had been conditioned out of its slavish reliance on the legalisms of the Constitution, and there was no looking back. In this way, the legal formula of federalism gave way to a national spirit that invigorated central government.[56]

55 Woodrow Wilson, *A History of the American People*, 5 vols. (New York: Harper & Brothers, 1902), 4:265.

56 Wilson, *History of the American People*, 5:128–9. For a discussion of Wilson's vision of the Civil War as necessary for progress, see the following: Niels Aage Thorsen, *The Political Thought of*

Wilson saw American development in the first half of the nineteenth century as a struggle between the forces of originalism, which wanted to keep the country fragmented, and the forces of union, led by Abraham Lincoln, which were on the side of progress. These two main forces contended for decades in a conflict that led up to, and was decisively resolved by, the Civil War. Wilson saw John Marshall and Daniel Webster as forerunners of Lincoln, and he called them the first true "American" statesmen. They were true Americans because they fought for national unity, which was in accord with the future for which America was destined. In his "Calendar of Great Americans," Wilson reserved some of his strongest praise for Marshall and Webster, particularly because they did not feel constrained by an overly legalistic interpretation of the Constitution. Instead, Wilson contended, they were gifted at taking the written Constitution and reading into it whatever the times required, which Wilson characterized as the ability to find "life" in the Constitution. Marshall and Webster "viewed the fundamental law as a great organic product, a vehicle of life as well as a charter of authority; in disclosing its life they did not damage its tissue; and in thus expanding the law without impairing its structure or authority they made great contributions alike to statesmanship and to jurisprudence."[57] Marshall and Webster were uniquely American, Wilson explained, because they had to practice a form of statesmanship that formulated broad national policies within the tight framework of a written constitution. His praise for Marshall and Webster is in contrast to his sharp criticism of figures like John C. Calhoun. Calhoun did not represent the American spirit of national unity, instead fighting against union by refusing to abandon the originalism of fragmented power and weak national government. So while Marshall, Webster, and Lincoln were genuine Americans who were on the side of historical progress, Calhoun was reactionary and "provincial."[58]

To understand the significance of Lincoln and the union issue to Wilson's conception of American politics, and to understand why Wilson was no southern partisan, it is vital to know that, for Wilson, it was the

---

Woodrow Wilson, 1875–1910 (Princeton, NJ: Princeton University Press, 1988), 15; David Steigerwald, "The Synthetic Politics of Woodrow Wilson," *Journal of the History of Ideas* 50 (July/September 1989): 476; Anthony Gaughan, "Woodrow Wilson and the Legacy of the Civil War," *Civil War History* 43:3 (1977): 227–38.

57 Woodrow Wilson, "A Calendar of Great Americans," September 15, 1893, in *PWW*, 8:371.

58 Wilson, "Calendar of Great Americans," 372.

southerners who were the constitutional originalists. Wilson foreshadowed today's libertarian–neo-Confederates: the forces of states' rights and secession, as Wilson understood them, represented the founders' constitution as it was originally intended to be—one that placed strict limits on the sphere of federal authority. Those who favored national unity and the cause of the North, then, were the progressives. Lincoln and the progressive, pro-union forces advocated a departure from the original constitutional understanding and an embrace of national unity and expanded national government. The pro-union forces were progressive because they wanted to adjust political principles to the advances and new circumstances brought about by history. They understood that America was growing and evolving, and they wanted to read the Constitution accordingly. The southerners, according to this narrative, had the correct view of the original Constitution, and they wanted the country to stick to it. Secession, therefore, was not an attack on the Constitution, but rather a movement of reactionary forces who wanted to restore original constitutionalism in a fight against progress.

In *Division and Reunion*, Wilson expressed his approval of Webster's pro-union argument—"that the Constitution had created, not a dissoluble, illusory partnership between the States, but a single federal state, complete in itself." But he made clear that this interpretation, however much he embraced it, was probably *not* the view of those who framed the Constitution: "It may, nevertheless, be doubted whether this was the doctrine upon which the Union had been founded." While the states' rights view of the southerners may have been the one that most accurately reflected original intent, it was inferior historically and contrary to the march of progress, since "Webster's position was one toward which the greater part of the nation was steadily advancing."[59] Wilson explained in a subsequent essay that, in spite of its inferiority, Calhoun's "doctrine of the ultimate sovereignty of the States was not new. It had once been commonplace to say that the Union was experimental, to speak of circumstances in which the contracting States might deem it best to withdraw." The historically inferior understanding of federal power that animated the founding generation was simply a reflection of the particular historical environment in which it grew up—one where

59 Woodrow Wilson, *Division and Reunion: 1829–1889* (1893; reprint, New York: Longmans, Green, 1901), 44–7.

it was simply more common for the focus to be on the states and their primacy.[60] In the face of this undue attachment to original forms, those who favored a national union adopted what might be called today a "living constitution" understanding of government. Wilson explained: "The legal theory upon which [secession] was taken was one which would hardly have been questioned in the early years of the government.... But constitutions are not mere legal documents: they are the skeleton frame of a living organism; and in this case the course of events had nationalized the government once deemed confederate."[61] In the dialectical contest between the forces of the old order and those of the new, history inevitably and necessarily decided things in favor of the side representing progress. Wilson commented in a letter on the War that "*I think the North was wholly right then*, and that the South paid the inevitable penalty for lagging behind the national development, stopping the normal growth of the national constitution."[62]

STATESMANSHIP AND LEADERSHIP

Lincoln, according to this Wilsonian narrative, was the agent of historical progress; he helped the country shed its original principles by acting as a man of his times—by his willingness to embrace the new spirit of a new age. It was for this very reason that Wilson put Lincoln in the same category as Edmund Burke, whom Wilson considered to be the best model for statesmanship. In a view of Burke that was too exclusively influenced by the *Reflections on the Revolution in France*, Wilson considered Burke's greatest virtue to be his historical pragmatism—that Burke was guided in his statesmanship, as Wilson saw it, by whichever way the historical winds seemed to be blowing at the time. Like Wilson's Lincoln, Wilson's Burke did not theorize about what politics ought to be in form; he did not conjure up abstract principles of political justice to serve as guides to political action. Instead, he constantly adjusted to fit changing circumstances. In his 1893 essay on Burke, Wilson identified a series of key issues that Burke confronted during his career. Wilson contended that Burke approached each of these issues in a consistent

60 Woodrow Wilson, "State Rights," December 20, 1899, in *PWW*, 11:311–12.
61 Wilson, *Division and Reunion*, 211.
62 Wilson, "To Hermann Eduard von Holst," June 29, 1893, in *PWW*, 8:271–2.

manner: he "had no system of political philosophy" but was guided instead by the circumstances of each case.[63]

In addition to his alleged Burkean antipathy to abstract principles in politics, Lincoln represented to Wilson the ideal model of presidential leadership. This was a model in which the president was to tap directly into the people's opinion and thus circumvent the Constitution as the principal source of presidential power and the separation of powers system as the principal means of checking that power. Wilson's criticism of the separation of powers has been detailed earlier and will not be repeated here. As it pertains to presidential leadership, the problem with the original separation of powers system for Wilson was that it cast the president merely as leader of a single branch of government, thus denying singular, energetic leadership to the government as a whole. In *Constitutional Government in the United States*, Wilson urged that "leadership and control must be lodged somewhere," and that the president use his direct connection to the people as a means of navigating around constitutional restraints on government.[64] It was in this way that Wilson saw presidential leadership as a means of energizing the kind of active national government that the progressive agenda required, but which the Constitution seemed always to thwart.[65]

This Wilsonian notion of presidential leadership rested upon the leader's connection to public opinion and his ability to interpret it and move it. As explained most thoroughly in the essay "Leaders of Men," Wilson conceived of "leadership" as "interpretation."[66] The leader embodies, or "reads up" from the people their will, their spirit. But the leader is

---

63 Woodrow Wilson, "Edmund Burke: The Man and His Times," August 31, 1893, in *PWW*, 8:334–36.

64 See Wilson's chapter on "The President of the United States," from *Constitutional Government*, 54–81. See especially 54, 66–67.

65 Whether or not, in seeing presidential leadership this way, Wilson actually promoted something new in the American tradition or simply tapped into something that had been there all along is the subject of debate among scholars. While scholars such as James Ceaser, Glen E. Thurow, Jeffrey Tulis, Joseph M. Bessette, Paul Eidelberg, and Robert Eden see Wilson as the founder of the modern presidency, others, such as David K. Nichols, question the very idea that there is a "modern presidency" and suggest that Wilson was mistaken if he thought that his vision of presidential leadership could be achieved only by transcending the Constitution. This debate is referenced in Chapter One, in the context of Roosevelt's stewardship theory. We see here its relevance for Wilson as well. While avoiding a fuller treatment of that debate, in this chapter I endeavor only to show how Wilson relied upon Lincoln as a model for his view of the presidency, and how such a reliance defies the facts of both Lincoln's words and deeds.

66 Woodrow Wilson, "Leaders of Men," June 17, 1890, in *PWW*, 6:659.

not merely an empty vessel, responding to whatever direction the public's opinion happens to give him. This is because the leader, in interpreting, often reads the implicit will of the public better than the public itself does. Therefore the leader must have the ability to persuade the people that his understanding of their will—his vision of their future—is, in fact, their will and their future. "The leader of men," Wilson explained, "must have such sympathetic and penetrative insight as shall enable him to discern quite unerringly the motives which move other men *in the mass*."[67] Wilson most frequently named Abraham Lincoln as this kind of popular leader—at least among American presidents.

For Wilson, Lincoln contrasted very favorably with several earlier presidents, especially Thomas Jefferson, whom Wilson believed did not sufficiently seek out a close connection to public opinion.[68] Wilson praised Lincoln, by contrast, for serving as a man of the people, for embodying the spirit of the masses. Yet he also praised Lincoln for standing out in front of the masses, for seeing their own will more clearly than they were able to see it themselves:

> A great nation is not led by a man who simply repeats the talk of the street-corners or the opinions of the newspapers. A nation is led by a man who hears more than those things; or who, rather, hearing those things, understands them better, unites them, puts them into a common meaning; speaks, not the rumors of the street, but a new principle for a new age; a man in whose ears the voices of the nation do not sound like the accidental and discordant notes that come from the voice of a mob, but concurrent and concordant like the united voices of a chorus, whose many meanings, spoken by melodious tongues, unite in his understanding in a single meaning and reveal to him a single vision, so that he can speak what no man else knows, the common meaning of the common voice. Such is the man who leads a great, free, democratic nation.[69]

Much in the same terms that Croly would later employ in *The Promise of American Life*, Wilson described Lincoln as the perfect American.

---

67 Wilson, "Leaders of Men," 649. Emphasis original.

68 Wilson, "An Address on Thomas Jefferson," April 16, 1906, in *PWW*, 16:363.

69 Wilson, "Abraham Lincoln: A Man of the People," February 12, 1909, in *PWW*, 19:42.

Like Andrew Jackson, he was a man of the people, and came from the frontier. But unlike Jackson, Lincoln was able to interpret the true spirit of the American people and to understand that the American future was one of nationalization. In this respect, Lincoln was the leader for whom the time was ripe. He was the agent of change that the progress of history required. "To the Eastern politicians," wrote Wilson, Lincoln "seemed like an accident; but to history he must seem like a providence."[70] Displaying the qualities necessary for any modern leader, Lincoln used popular rhetoric to affect the people, to pull them in the direction of his vision for their future. "He was vastly above [the people] in intellectual and moral stature," Wilson wrote of Lincoln. "He gained an easy mastery over them, too, by cultivating, as he did, the directer [*sic*] and more potent forms of speech."[71]

WILSON AND THE PROGRESSIVE ABUSE OF LINCOLN

In sum, progressives painted a picture of Lincoln that depicted him as an icon for their movement: as a new man for new times who seized on the circumstances of the day as a justification for abandoning constitutional government, as a visionary centralizer who used public opinion leadership to redefine the scope of government, and as a man who would not be guided by theories or principles—who refused to hold the nation back or be bound by a stubborn adherence to the outmoded doctrines of the Declaration and Constitution. The picture of Lincoln painted by Wilson, Croly, and Roosevelt is, in other words, very much like the one painted of him by the libertarians and neo-Confederates of our own day. And in both cases, the picture is almost entirely at odds with the reality of Lincoln's words and deeds. The progressive characterization of Lincoln—particularly Wilson's narrative of Lincoln as a man unconcerned with the original theory of American government—is at a sharp variance with the reality that even a cursory review of Lincoln's speeches would have revealed. This variance is so sharp that one is initially at a loss for an explanation. More closely examined, however, the progressives' encounter with Lincoln fits a pattern they employed when celebrating the key figures of America's political tradition: their celebrations are almost

70 Wilson, "Calendar of Great Americans," 378–79.
71 Wilson, *Division and Reunion*, 216.

exclusively historical and biographical, and carefully avoid any reference to—or commemoration of—ideas or principles.

In this respect, progressive accounts of the founders are remarkably different from Lincoln's own accounts. If progressive accounts can be identified by their avoidance of the founders' principles, Lincoln's primary reason for calling to mind the founders was to recover their principles and bring them to bear on the debates of his own day. In attacking the doctrine of popular sovereignty in the Kansas-Nebraska law, and in contending against the denial of black citizenship in *Dred Scott*, Lincoln's mode was to call to mind the founders for the purpose of calling to mind the principles of the Declaration and Constitution.[72] It was Justice Roger Taney's view, after all, that the founders had merely been men of their time—that their principles merely reflected the racial animus prevalent in the latter part of the eighteenth century. In refuting this assertion, Lincoln talked not so much about the founders as representatives of their age, as about the abstract equality doctrine of the founding, paying careful attention to what it meant and what it did not mean, and bringing it to bear on the central questions of the 1850s. As Lincoln explained in his speech on the *Dred Scott* case, the value of the Declaration's equality doctrine did *not* come from its relevance at the time of its having been written, but precisely from its applicability across generations: "The assertion that 'all men are created equal' was of no practical use in effecting our separation from Great Britain; and it was placed in the Declaration, not for that, but for future use."[73]

It was in emphasizing the historical and biographical approaches that progressives could write romantically of men of the founding era, or of Lincoln, while at the same time offering consistently sharp criticisms of the actual principles espoused by the founders or by Lincoln. Wilson, for example, devoted a significant portion of his scholarly career—about ten years—to writing histories and biographies, and it is no accident that these are the works where the key figures of America's past are most celebrated and held up for admiration. When it comes to the other categories of Wilson's scholarly work—his writings on the principles of government and administration or his various treatments of American political institutions—there is no celebrating of past figures, documents, or ideas. In

72 Lincoln, "Speech at Peoria, Illinois," October 16, 1854, 247–83.
73 Lincoln, "Speech at Springfield, Illinois," June 26, 1857, 406.

fact, any references to the critical figures or documents of American history in these works is normally for the purpose of showing how they are outmoded and how they are inadequate when measured against the more historically advanced ideas and systems of Europe. It was in this way that Wilson wrote an entire biography of George Washington which says very little, if anything, about Washington's conception of government. And it was in the same way that several progressive commentators on Lincoln could celebrate his leadership of the union during the Civil War, without once attempting to come to terms with Lincoln's own explanation of that leadership or Lincoln's own understanding of the war's causes and aims. Coming to terms with these things would, of course, have led progressives to uncover much about Lincoln that would have cast him not as an iconic progressive, but—to use the progressive vocabulary—as a reactionary.

LINCOLN AS BURKE

Wilson's understanding of Lincoln as a model Burkean statesman serves as an excellent illustration of how Lincoln was adopted for the progressive cause. By this characterization of Lincoln as Burke, Wilson meant, as explained above, that Lincoln's greatest virtue was his liberation from any overarching set of principles—his willingness to go in the new direction for the country that history was bringing about, unbounded or unlimited by any abstract notions of constitutionalism or natural right. Leaving aside the problematic reading of Burke inherent in Wilson's view, the relevant point for us is that Wilson simply denied that Lincoln was guided by abstract principles: "What commends Mr. Lincoln's studiousness to me," wrote Wilson, "is that the result of it was he did not have any theories at all.... Lincoln was one of those delightful students who do not seek to tie you up in the meshes of any theory."[74] In reality, of course, Lincoln's statesmanship is characterized by the quality exactly opposite to the one which Wilson asserts here. Lincoln's 1859 letter to Henry Pierce immediately comes to mind, pointing as it did to "an abstract truth, applicable to all men and all times."[75] To show that Lincoln, contrary to Wilson's assertion, was indeed guided by a certain abstract theory of politics does not suggest that he was a kind of ideologue, after the fashion

74 Wilson, "Abraham Lincoln," 39.

75 Abraham Lincoln, "Letter to H.L. Pierce and Others," April 6, 1859, in *Collected Works*, 3:376.

of the French revolutionaries who carried out their atrocities in the name of some demented version of natural justice. Rather, Lincoln's model of statesmanship relied upon prudence, as his Temperance Address from 1842 shows. The accomplishment of moral reform in politics requires, as Lincoln explained, both a commitment to a "theory" or moral principle, and an understanding of and appeal to the prevailing tradition and popular conventions.[76] Wilson's objection to this understanding of statesmanship was its mooring in any kind of principle that might transcend history; such a mooring stood as an obstacle to the progressive agenda to remake American government not just in its means but in its ends.

HISTORICAL CONTINGENCY

Both in Lincoln's celebration of the "abstract" quality of Jefferson's Declaration, and in his remark from the *Dred Scott* speech that the principles of the Declaration were "for future use," we see a quality that pervades his major speeches and writings: a rejection of the historical contingency that infused the political philosophy of Wilson, Croly, Roosevelt, and other progressives. Recalling Wilson's admonition, previously mentioned, to "not repeat the preface" of the Declaration, we see that Lincoln celebrated precisely that part of the document that Wilson wished had never been written, and which Wilson denigrated as a mere "rhetorical introduction." It was this mere "rhetorical introduction" from which Wilson wanted to free American government, whereas Lincoln put it at the heart of the most pressing political disputes of his own time. In contending against the doctrine of popular sovereignty espoused by Stephen Douglas and implemented in the Kansas-Nebraska law, the crux of Lincoln's argument was that the doctrine contradicts the "spirit of seventy-six," which spirit is enshrined in that part of the Declaration that Wilson would have us disregard. In fact, Lincoln took the passage of Kansas-Nebraska as sad evidence that many Americans had already gone down the path that Wilson would later urge them to take—to disregard the equality and natural rights principles of the Declaration and deny their applicability beyond their own age. Lincoln lamented that "we have been giving up the old for the new faith."[77] Yet Wilson championed

76 Lincoln, "Temperance Address Delivered Before the Springfield Washington Temperance Society," February 22, 1842, in *Collected Works*, 1:271–79.

77 Lincoln, "Speech at Peoria, Illinois," October 16, 1854, 275

Lincoln precisely because Lincoln was a man, according to Wilson, who happily gave up the old for the new faith—who promoted "a new principle for a new age."[78] In the Kansas-Nebraska speech, however, Lincoln famously drew on the old principles of the old age, and made fairly clear what ought to befall those who would replace the old with the new faith:

> When Pettit, in connection with his support of the Nebraska bill, called the Declaration of Independence "a self-evident lie," he only did what consistency and candor require all other Nebraska men to do. Of the forty odd Nebraska Senators who sat present and heard him, no one rebuked him.... If this had been said among Marion's men, Southerners though they were, what would have become of the man who said it? If this had been said to the men who captured Andre, the man who said it, would probably have been hung sooner than Andre was. If it had been said in old Independence Hall, seventy-eight years ago, the very door-keeper would have throttled the man, and thrust him into the street.[79]

The contrast could not be clearer. While Wilson urged us to disregard the Declaration, Lincoln urged a return to it: "Let us re-adopt the Declaration of Independence, and with it, the practices, and policy, which harmonize with it." While Wilson's solution for the imperfections of American republicanism was to bury the principles of the Revolution, Lincoln's was to resurrect them: "Our republican robe is soiled," he wrote, "and trailed in the dust. Let us re-purify it. Let us turn and wash it white, in the spirit, if not the blood, of the Revolution."[80]

THE PURPOSE OF STATESMANSHIP

Such a contrast also helps bring to light the broader problem with the progressive characterization of Lincoln's statesmanship. As Wilson understood it, Lincoln embraced the cause of union as a consequence of having

78 Wilson, "Abraham Lincoln," 42.

79 Lincoln, "Speech at Peoria, Illinois," October 16, 1854, 275.

80 Lincoln, "Speech at Peoria, Illinois," October 16, 1854, 276. See also Abraham Lincoln, "Speech in Independence Hall, Philadelphia, Pennsylvania," February 22, 1861, in *Collected Works*, 4:240, where Lincoln suggested: "[A]ll the political sentiments I entertain have been drawn, so far as I have been able to draw them, from the sentiments which originated and were given to the world from this hall. I have never had a feeling politically that did not spring from the sentiments embodied in the Declaration of Independence."

perceptively read the trends of history. The cause of the union in the Civil War represented, in the eyes of progressives, the historical triumph of nationalization and centralization over originalism. The essence of Lincoln's statesmanship, for them, was his keen vision of where history was going and the fact that he did not let adherence to outdated principle interfere with his steering the nation down the historically appointed path. A key quality of Lincolnian statesmanship, according to progressives, seems to have been that Lincoln did not take the principles of the Declaration and the law of the Constitution too seriously, or at least that he was willing to read them flexibly or organically. Not only does such an estimation fly in the face of Lincoln's actual dedication to the principles and law of the founding, as demonstrated above, but it also misunderstands what Lincoln himself saw as the task of statesmanship. What most disturbed Lincoln in the 1850s was not the actual practice of slavery in those states where it already existed (while he abhorred this, he said repeatedly that nothing could be done about it at the time as a matter of law),[81] but the notion that it could be extended into new territories without doing violence to the principles of the founding. It was what Lincoln referred to as the principle of "indifference" in his Kansas-Nebraska speech—the idea that the establishment of slavery through popular sovereignty was a matter on which our founding principles were neutral—that clearly caused Lincoln the greatest consternation. He would, therefore, certainly have been appalled to see Roosevelt champion the purely majoritarian principles of popular sovereignty, to attribute them to Lincoln, and to confuse them with those of America's founders.

The state of affairs in the 1850s indicated to Lincoln that many Americans had ceased both to understand their fundamental law and to practice an attachment to it. The goal of his statesmanship, then, seems not to have been—as progressives suggested—the liberation of America from its fundamental law, but rather a reintroduction of America to this law and an encouragement to renew devotion to it. This is why Lincoln called for Americans to "re-adopt the Declaration of Independence." He worried not that Americans would be held back by a commitment to this old document, but rather that they had become corrupted by abandoning

81 See, for example, Lincoln, "Reply: First Debate with Stephen A. Douglas," 16. This statement was repeated in Lincoln's First Inaugural Address. See Lincoln, "First Inaugural Address," March 4, 1861, 262–63.

it. The principle of "indifference" represented, for Lincoln, "a dangerous dalliance for a free people—a sad evidence that, feeling prosperity, we forget right—that liberty, as a principle, we have ceased to revere."[82] The task of the statesman under such circumstances—where the people have detached themselves from their fundamental law—is not to go with the historical trends, as progressives urged, but to do as the young Lincoln did in his Lyceum Speech in 1838. In that speech Lincoln called not for a progressive remaking of our political institutions, but for a perpetuation of them. Such a perpetuation was to be effected by encouraging a devotion to the law—both to the ordinary civil and criminal law, and to the fundamental law of the Constitution:

> Let every American, every lover of liberty, every well wisher to his posterity, swear by the blood of the Revolution, never to violate in the least particular, the laws of the country; and never to tolerate their violation by others. As the patriots of seventy-six did to the support of the Declaration of Independence, so to the support of the Constitution and Laws, let every American pledge his life, his property, and his sacred honor;—let every man remember that to violate the law, is to trample on the blood of his father, and to tear the character of his own, and his children's liberty.[83]

Lincoln saw it as a task of statesmanship to encourage a devotion to the fundamental law, and this devotion took on a religious tone, encouraging a kind of worship of the law and of the great men who had promulgated it. As Lincoln went on to exhort: "Let it become the *political religion* of the nation, and let the old and the young, the rich and the poor, the grave and the gay, of all sexes and tongues, and colors and conditions, sacrifice unceasingly upon its altars." The old images of the founders and the founding had served as "pillars of the temple of liberty," but as time had passed they had come in need of being reestablished through this political religion.[84] The contrast between this Lincolnian exhortation for political religion and Wilson's own reflections on American independence speak directly to the essential difference between the two. Recall, in particular,

82 Lincoln, "Speech at Peoria, Illinois," October 16, 1854, 274.
83 Lincoln, "The Perpetuation of Our Political Institutions: Address before the Young Men's Lyceum of Springfield, Illinois," January 27, 1838, in *Collected Works*, 1:112.
84 Lincoln, "The Perpetuation of Our Political Institutions," 112, 115. Emphasis original.

Wilson's 1907 remarks on the Fourth of July that were detailed in Chapter One:

> We are not bound to adhere to the doctrines held by the signers of the Declaration of Independence.... We are not here to worship men or a document.... Neither are we here to indulge in a mere rhetorical and uncritical eulogy. Every Fourth of July should be a time for examining our standards, our purposes, for determining afresh what principles, what forms of power we think most likely to effect our safety and happiness.[85]

Much of the difference at work here comes from the starkly different accounts of American history that underlie the progressives' as opposed to Lincoln's political thought. In one important respect, the two sides agreed in their assessments of mid nineteenth-century America: Americans had indeed distanced themselves from the principles of the founding. Yet the similarity ends there. For the progressives, this state of affairs was a positive development, proof that history was a force for progress. Under this narrative the losing side in the conflict—the South—stood for the old principles of the founding, and Lincoln, as the leader of the victorious North, was to be celebrated precisely for his role in overcoming America's origins. For Lincoln, on the other hand, the events of the 1850s were sad evidence that America had lost sight of its founding. His speech on the *Dred Scott* decision makes this very point, taking Taney to task for assuming a moral superiority in the prevailing sentiments of the 1850s as opposed to those of the founding era. Taney had made a progressive assumption about the course of American history—suggesting that it was the founding generation that had had a less just and historically inferior conception of human freedom, and concluding that the founders, consequently, had not intended to include blacks in their vision of natural or civil rights. Lincoln, by contrast, held up the principles of the founding as the standard of justice from which America had strayed. "In those days," said Lincoln, "our Declaration of Independence was held sacred by all, and thought to include all; but now, to aid in making the bondage of the negro universal and eternal, it

85 Woodrow Wilson, "The Author and Signers of the Declaration of Independence," July 4, 1907, in *PWW*, 17:251.

is assailed, and sneered at, and construed, and hawked at, and torn, till, if its framers could rise from their graves, they could not at all recognize it."[86] Both *Dred Scott* and the Kansas-Nebraska law were evidence of a growing ignorance of the political theory of the founding.[87] This move away from the founding was not progress to Lincoln. The South did not, as progressives contended, represent to Lincoln the founding order that had to be overcome; rather, the conflict between North and South was the result of a house that had become divided over its founding principles and the question of whether or not the nation should, as Lincoln believed, return to them.

PRESIDENTIAL LEADERSHIP AND LINCOLN'S LEGACY

This difference between the progressives' Lincoln, who was an integral part in America's *move away* from its original constitutionalism, and the real Lincoln, whose statesmanship was animated by a drive to *return* the country to its original ideas, emerges clearly in the debate over Lincoln's conception of presidential leadership. While the debate over the propriety of Lincoln's actions during the Civil War is beyond the scope of this chapter, Lincoln's own understanding of those actions offers a useful contrast to the Wilsonian vision for presidential leadership (previously explained). For Wilson, the great promise of presidential leadership was in its prospects for transcending the Constitution. Because Wilson worried that the Constitution's separation of powers system would stand as a barrier to the expansive government favored by progressives, he looked to the presidency—and especially to the president's popularity—as the means of surmounting the barrier. The whole point of presidential leadership, for Wilson, was to move the country beyond the Constitution. This is exactly the charge leveled against Lincoln by today's libertarian–neo-Confederate critics, and it is one of the reasons they characterize Lincoln as a founder of American progressivism. Yet while Wilson saw the president's popularity as a mode of overcoming the Constitution (he contrasted the "political" and "constitutional" aspects of the presidency, as previously explained), Lincoln saw popular rhetoric—or an appeal to fashion, as he

86 Lincoln, "Speech at Springfield, Illinois," June 26, 1857, 404.
87 Lincoln, "'A House Divided': Speech at Springfield, Illinois," June 16, 1858, in *Collected Works*, 2:461–69.

termed it in his Temperance Address[88]—as a means of pointing the people back to their fundamental principles. All of Lincoln's great speeches have this quality. Furthermore, Lincoln understood preservation of the Constitution as the primary aim of his presidential statesmanship, even in those cases where his actions may arguably have violated the letter of the Constitution's law. As he explained in an 1864 letter to Albert Hodges:

> By general law, life and limb must be protected; yet often a limb must be amputated to save a life; but a life is never wisely given to save a limb. I felt that measures, otherwise unconstitutional, might become lawful, by becoming indispensable to the preservation of the Constitution, through the preservation of the Nation.[89]

For Lincoln, the cause of the nation and the cause of the Constitution were indistinguishable. For Wilson, and for his progressive brethren generally, the vitality of the nation required moving beyond the Constitution. This is the fundamental difference between the two camps, and it is why the progressive claim to Lincoln's legacy ought seriously to be questioned.

88 Lincoln, "Temperance Address," 277.
89 Lincoln, "Letter to Albert G. Hodges," April 4, 1864, in *Collected Works*, 7:281.

CHAPTER FIVE

★

MAKING THE STATE INTO A GOD

American Progressivism and the Social Gospel

Having shown that the connection of progressivism to the legacy of Abraham Lincoln and the cause of emancipation is not as strong as the progressives themselves claimed, there are connections to other important historical developments of the nineteenth century. The religious movements of the time are particularly important to understanding progressive thought and policies, none more so than Social Gospel.[1]

The relevance of the Social Gospel movement to American progressivism may be curious to some, since it is not uncommon to be asked whether or not America's original progressives relied on anti-religious arguments to promote their agenda. Strong attachment to religious faith is associated far more strongly with the Right than with the Left in America, and thus it is often assumed that liberal political ideology—progressivism, in this case—grew out of, or was accompanied by, some kind of atheism or anti-religious animus. In the case of America's original progressives,

1 The work on the original version of this chapter of my former assistant—Erika Sabo—is gratefully acknowledged, as is the intellectual debt owed to my old friend Matthew Spalding, whose remarks on Social Gospel at a conference long ago helped to shape my initial thoughts on the topic.

however, this was far from the case. While there were certainly some progressive figures who were overtly hostile to revealed religion[2] (one thinks, for instance, of *The New Republic* founder and editor Herbert Croly, whose parents literally baptized him into the atheistic "church of humanity" devoted to the positivism of Auguste Comte), as a whole the movement was profoundly bound up with religious belief and many in it were driven by a sincere and fervent Christianity.

This chapter endeavors to address the connection between progressive political principles and the Social Gospel movement that was common among America's original adherents to progressivism.

THE RISE OF SOCIAL GOSPEL

To read the speeches of many of the most prominent progressives, pronouncing on the most important issues of that era, is to read the kind of religious language and fervor that would only be associated with the so-called "religious Right" of our own time. Recall these excerpts from two of the most renowned speeches of the Progressive Era:

> Our cause is based on the eternal principle of righteousness; and even though we who now lead may for the time fail, in the end the cause itself shall triumph.... We stand at Armageddon, and we battle for the Lord![3]

And:

---

2 This was particularly true of those associated with *The New Republic* and the more scientific wing of the movement, which was concerned with the effect of the orthodox variant of Christianity on education. Progressives of all stripes saw in traditional religious education an unhealthy encouragement of the young to focus on the private sphere, thus detracting from the undivided devotion to the state on which progressive democracy was to depend. *The New Republic* editorialized in 1916 that there should be a "change in the meaning of tolerance." Contrary to eighteenth-century liberalism, the editors explained, "twentieth-century democracy believes that the community has certain positive ends to achieve, and if they are to be achieved the community must control the education of the young." It editorialized that "freedom and tolerance mean the development of independent powers of judgment in the young, not the freedom of older people to impose their dogmas on the young." Modern democracy, it concluded, "insists that the plasticity of the child shall not be artificially and prematurely hardened into a philosophy of life." "Father Blakely States the Issue," unsigned editorial from *The New Republic*, July 29, 1916, 320.

3 Theodore Roosevelt, "A Confession of Faith: Address Before the National Convention of the Progressive Party in Chicago, August 6, 1912." In *Progressive Principles*, ed. Elmer H. Youngman. (New York: Progressive National Service, 1913), 173.

> You shall not press down upon the brow of labor this crown of thorns, you shall not crucify mankind upon a cross of gold![4]

As indicated in Chapter One, the first is the speech given by Theodore Roosevelt as he accepted the presidential nomination of the Progressive Party at its Chicago convention in 1912, and the second excerpt is from the "Cross of Gold" speech given by William Jennings Bryan to the Democratic National Convention in 1896.

Religious fervor was an important factor in the America of the late nineteenth century—a time which saw the rise of progressivism as a political force. Some of the religious sentiment of this time doubtless grew from the remnants of abolitionism and other social movements of the antebellum period that constituted the Second Great Awakening. The antebellum Awakening sought revival and the salvation of souls on the basis of eradicating social ills—not only slavery, but also drinking and prostitution. But the religious fervor of the latter part of the century was not simply a more communitarian variant of the Second Great Awakening. It gave rise, instead, to the Social Gospel movement, which at its core was quite radical. What was new about Social Gospel, among other things, was that it crossed the line into matters of economic justice. Whereas America's Protestant churches had solidly backed the free market system throughout most of the century, Social Gospel turned part of the Protestant church against capitalism, as ministers such as Washington Gladden began to advocate workers' rights to union organization.[5]

This new direction reflects the fact that the mainline denominations found themselves in the position of reacting to the great cultural and intellectual challenges that had arisen in the middle of the nineteenth century—especially the doctrine of evolution. Beginning in the 1880s and lasting through the First World War,[6] Social Gospel represented the

---

4 William Jennings Bryan, "In the Chicago Convention." In *Speeches of William Jennings Bryan, Vol. I*, ed. William Jennings Bryan. (New York: Funk & Wagnalls, 1909), 249.

5 See Bradley W. Bateman, "The Social Gospel and the Progressive Era," Driving America, TeacherServe. National Humanities Center, http://nationalhumanitiescenter.org/tserve/twenty/tkeyinfo/socgospel.htm (accessed May 27, 2011).

6 As a consequence of which the Movement became blamed, rightly or wrongly, for an excess of fervor which contributed to the massive human cost of the War. See Richard M. Gamble, *The War for Righteousness: Progressive Christianity, the Great War, and the Rise of the Messianic Nation* (ISI Books, 2003), esp. 233–39.

response of the liberal wing of evangelical Protestantism to this new doctrine, and this explains why Social Gospel was much more than a simple development out of the antebellum revival movement. The Protestant church responded in two very distinct ways to evolution. The orthodox response, generally speaking, was to oppose the new evolutionary science as atheistic and anti-religious, and to reassert the fundamentals of the orthodox faith. In fact, it is in this orthodox reaction that the origin of the term "fundamentalist" is found: a series of twelve pamphlets titled "The Fundamentals: A Testimony to the Truth" was widely circulated from 1910 to 1915 and emphasized the infallibility and literal meaning of the Bible, among many other orthodox tenets.[7]

The adherents of what would become the Social Gospel took a very different approach in response to the idea of evolution. They saw it as an opportunity to use historical progress as an argument for moving the church away from the conservative doctrines and moral teachings that had, in their view, been its greatest vulnerabilities. Orthodox religion was not adequate for the new conditions of new times, and so a set of new teachings, undergirded by historicism and Higher Criticism, came to the fore in some seminaries and churches.[8] Specifically, Social Gospel adherents questioned the literal inspiration of the Bible. An example of this skepticism can be found in Gladden's 1891 book, *Who Wrote the Bible*? Gladden (1836–1918) was a Congregationalist minister who spent most of his adult life in Columbus, Ohio, where he became involved in progressive politics and, as mentioned above, was among the first in the ministry to advocate laborers' right to organize into unions. In laying out the purpose of his book, he explained that "what I desire to show is, that the work of putting the Bible into its present form was not done in heaven, but on earth; that it was not done by angels, but by men."[9] Citing the

7 The twelve pamphlets contained ninety different essays, and were edited by A.C. Dixon, Louis Meyer, and Reuben Archer Torrey from 1910 to 1915.

8 And, as Bateman explains, many mainline Protestant denominations adopted a more social disposition, even if they did not adopt the more radical theology and politics of the Social Gospel. The Methodist church, for example, was the first to adopt the so-called "Social Creed" in 1907, with many other denominations soon to follow suit. Bateman, "The Social Gospel and the Progressive Era." The "Social Creed" of the United Methodist Church from the year 2000 still dedicates itself in this way, including belief in the right to "collective bargaining" and in "the elimination of economic and social distress." http://archives.umc.org/interior.asp?mid=1836 (accessed May 27, 2011).

9 Washington Gladden, *Who Wrote the Bible? A Book for the People* (Boston: Houghton, Mifflin, & Company, 1891), 4.

disagreements among the Apostles in St. Paul's epistle to the Galatians, Gladden reasoned that because the Apostles had erred in judgments with respect to administering the early church, they could not be counted on to be infallible when writing and organizing the Bible.[10] He pointed also to the different languages used in the books of the Bible, and hence the need for the words of Christ to be handed down not directly, but through translation. If, then, we don't have the literal words of Christ, how can we say that we have to take them as if they were literal? The only inspiration which those who wrote the Bible could have received was an inspiration to remember facts and avoid serious errors. That the Bible came to us, in part, from an obscure language—"consist[ing] only of consonants," Gladden observed—"is the conclusive and unanswerable evidence that God never designed to give us an infallible book."[11] Because it lacks infallibility, Gladden concluded, Christians are not bound by the Bible's moral teachings but are, instead, free to adopt doctrines more suitable for their own time.[12]

Instead of formal doctrinal creeds, the Social Gospel stressed ethical social behavior. Instead of a threat, it saw in evolution great opportunity for moving the church to a mission of Christian social action. This is not to suggest that Social Gospel swallowed evolution whole; like the Reform Darwinism of Lester Frank Ward,[13] it rejected the harsh, laissez-faire, survival-of-the-fittest Social Darwinism of figures such as Yale sociologist William Graham Sumner.[14] From evolutionary thinking, Social Gospel drew not a harsh determinism, but rather a divine plan for human liberation and advancement. In this respect its evolutionary foundations were of the historicist variety, which saw in human history not just random adaptation to endless change, but social development through the force of history that would ultimately culminate in a perfected social order. This is why Social Gospel can be understood as a fusion of liberal Protestantism and Hegelianism.

As I have argued in Chapter One, the progressive movement imported the principles of the philosophy of history and the

10 Gladden, *Who Wrote the Bible?*, 211.

11 Gladden, *Who Wrote the Bible?*, 248, 250–52, 331. He refers here to Hebrew.

12 Gladden, *Who Wrote the Bible?*, 352–53.

13 See Lester Frank Ward, *Dynamic Sociology* (New York: D. Appleton & Co., 1883).

14 For the clearest expression of what Social Gospel adherents would have rejected in Sumner's work, see his *What Social Classes Owe to Each Other* (New York: Harper Bros., 1883).

rational end-state into America from the German tradition of thought informed primarily by the philosopher Georg Hegel.[15] The influence of these same principles on Social Gospel is what accounts for the intertwining of the two movements in late nineteenth-century America.[16] Hegel's thought, which dominated nineteenth-century Germany, contended that history was not simply a record of random events but was, instead, a rational force used by God to bring about a perfected state. In that perfected state, which Hegel loosely associated with his own Prussian regime, God Himself was made present in its institutions, laws, and policies. Hegel called the state "the Divine Idea as it exists on earth" and encouraged the complete devotion of each citizen to the state because in it, God had become immanentized. "All the worth which the human being possesses," Hegel emphasized, "all spiritual reality, he possesses only through the State."[17] It has been well established that American progressives were taken with the argument about the forward progress of history culminating in a perfected social order, and that it became for them a means for arguing that historical advancement had made the Constitution's original limits on the national state outdated and unjust. For the Social Gospel adherents within the progressive movement, one's Christian identity became fused with one's devotion to the social action of the national state. The connection between the progressives' Hegelianism in general and the political theology of Social Gospel in particular comes into sharper focus when we bear in mind the point made in Chapter One about the German educational pedigree of many progressives. One of the most prominent among them—Richard T. Ely—was both a central figure in bringing the German influence into the American progressive movement, and easily the most important economic thinker of the Social Gospel movement.

15 In addition to Chapter One of this book, see Pestritto, *Woodrow Wilson and the Roots of Modern Liberalism* (Lanham, MD: Rowman & Littlefield, 2005), 33–43; see also Pestritto, "The German Stamp on Wilson's Administrative Progressivism," in *The American Mind* (https://americanmind.org/discourse/the-german-stamp-on-wilsons-administrative-progressivism/), accessed July 6, 2019.

16 On the historicist character of progressive religious principles—particularly those of Woodrow Wilson—see Gregory S. Butler, "Visions of a Nation Transformed: Modernity and Ideology in Wilson's Political Thought," *Journal of Church and State* 39 (Winter 1997): 40–45.

17 Georg Wilhelm Friedrich Hegel, *The Philosophy of History*, trans. J. Sibree (New York: Dover Publications, Inc., 1956), 39.

ELY, RAUSCHENBUSCH, AND SOCIAL GOSPEL'S NEW THEOLOGY

Ely (1854–1943) began his higher education at Dartmouth and Columbia, joining the Protestant Episcopal Church while in New York. He then undertook a three-year fellowship to study in Germany with the political economist Karl Knies at Heidelberg, where he received his Ph.D. in 1879. Upon his return to America he took up a teaching post at Johns Hopkins and helped to found the American Economic Association as an alternative association for those economists who dissented from the mainstream, classical principles of the discipline at that time. At both Hopkins and later at the University of Wisconsin, Ely influenced many graduate students who would go on to become important figures in both the intellectual and political circles of the progressive movement. With his publications, Ely had arguably become by the end of the nineteenth century the best known advocate of social Christianity and was nearly a household name.[18] As one historian of Social Gospel has put it, "previous to 1890 probably no other man did more to turn the attention of organized religion in the United States to the ethical implications of the industrial revolution and to the religious obligations in the field of economics than Richard T. Ely."[19]

While Ely played a vital role in bringing new economic thinking to the United States, it is his profound contributions to the progressive theology of Social Gospel that are of interest to us here. In one of his most influential works—*Social Aspects of Christianity* (1889)—he argued that the Christian church had become too otherworldly and preoccupied with doctrine, which had led to its neglect of the poverty problem here on earth. Instead of focusing so much on individual salvation in the next

18 For these details of Ely's career and influence I am indebted to the work of one of my former students, Luigi A. Bradizza. See Bradizza, *Richard T. Ely's Critique of Capitalism* (Palgrave Macmillan, 2013), 1–2. Bradizza goes on to show the impact of Ely's teaching and writing. He points to Ely's reputation for introducing new economic thinking into the United States, to the widespread use of his books (*An Introduction to Political Economy*; *Social Aspects of Christianity*; *The Social Law of Service*; *The Past and Present of Political Economy*), and to the prominence of so many of his students (John R. Commons, Davis R. Dewey, Edward W. Bemis, Thomas Nixon Carver, Edward A. Ross, Albion Small, David Kinley, Albert Shaw, John H. Finley, Newton D. Baker, Frederic C. Howe, Frederick Jackson Turner, J. Franklin Jameson, Charles Haskins, W.W. and W.F. Willoughby, and Woodrow Wilson). See Bradizza, *Ely's Critique of Capitalism*, 8-13.

19 James Dombrowski, *The Early Days of Christian Socialism* (Columbia University Press, 1936), 50. Quoted in Bradizza, *Ely's Critique of Capitalism*, 9.

life, Ely urged the church to take up the abolition of poverty as a central element of its earthly mission to establish a general social welfare. The old theology had failed to see how badly its emphasis on the self—on individual salvation—had detracted from the Christian duty of service to others. Ely blamed the church for becoming too bound up in the economic system of capitalism and private gain, which necessarily impedes the selfless thinking required by the Gospels. Wrote Ely: "The ruling motive of the one service—egotism, selfishness—is the opposite of the ruling motive of the other—altruism, devotion to others, consecration of heart, soul, and intellect to the service of others. Men are still quite willing to make long prayers on Sunday, if on weekdays they may devour widows' houses." The inescapable conclusion, Ely reasoned, was that the current economic system was not conducive to living a Christian life; "the arrangements of this world," he concluded, "are not in accord with the commandment given to love our neighbor as ourselves."[20]

What was the remedy for this conflict between worldly economic and political arrangements and the social duties of Christianity? Ely urged that the church cease to focus so much on the *next* life, and look instead to what he believed had been the neglected, central message of the Gospels: service to others in *this* life. Christians ought to pursue progressive social, political, and economic policies that would take up this mission of service—"things like temperance, righteous dealing, fair elections, the uprooting of crime and poverty, the elevation of the masses."[21] Ely wanted to redefine what was meant by the term "church militant." Orthodox Christianity had used the term to signify laboring and praying for the salvation of souls in the next life. Ely urged, instead, a militancy for social justice here on earth:

> Salvation means righteousness, in all the earth, and its establishment means hard warfare.... It means a never-ceasing attack on every wrong institution, until the earth becomes a new earth, and all its cities, cities of God. It is as truly a religious work to pass good laws, as it is to preach sermons; as holy a work to lead a crusade against filth, vice, and disease in slums of cities, and to seek the abolition of disgraceful

20 Richard T. Ely, *Social Aspects of Christianity and Other Essays* (Thomas Y. Crowell & Co., 1889), 5–8.

21 Ely, *Social Aspects of Christianity*, 23. See also 30–38, 63.

> tenement-houses of American cities, as it is to send missionaries to the heathen. Even to hoe potatoes and plant corn ought to be regarded, and must be regarded by true Christians, as religious acts; and all legislators, magistrates, and governors are as truly ministers in God's Church as any bishop or archbishop.[22]

As Ely moved to address the role of government in Christian social action, he had to redefine not only the term "church militant," but also what was meant by philanthropy. If Christian duty required philanthropy, he explained, we had to move away from the one-dimensional understanding of philanthropy as wholly voluntary. While the voluntary element of philanthropy was essential, we should also understand that some philanthropy could and must come from government coercion. Ely referred here to the Bible's praise of the social duties imposed by the law of ancient Israel. The Bible showed, he argued, that "coercive philanthropy must rest on voluntary philanthropy. Neither one alone is sufficient." And Ely emphasized the point by endorsing an author who had written that "we ought never trust to the justice and humanity of men whose interests are furthered by injustice and cruelty."[23] The attachment of Christian social obligations to the realm of government and economics necessitated, Ely argued, a move away from theology and toward sociology. With its preoccupation with theology, the orthodox church stood on moral prescriptions for salvation in the next life. Sociology, by contrast, would use modern social science to discover new methods of helping our fellows in this life through economics and government.[24] And so Ely aimed "to bring to pass *here* a kingdom of righteousness and to rescue from the evil one and redeem all our social relations."[25]

If Ely was concerned principally with the ways in which Social Gospel could be translated into a new vision for economics, it was the Baptist preacher Walter Rauschenbusch who dug even more deeply into the theological principles of Social Gospel and who became the most important clergyman of the movement. Rauschenbusch (1861–1918) was raised an orthodox Protestant by a father who taught at Rochester Theological Seminary, where the younger Rauschenbusch ultimately became a

22 Ely, *Social Aspects of Christianity*, 73.
23 Ely, *Social Aspects of Christianity*, 92–93.
24 Ely, *Social Aspects of Christianity*, 86.
25 Ely, *Social Aspects of Christianity*, 53. Emphasis added.

seminarian after spending some time as a student in Germany. It was at Rochester where he began to question the infallibility of the Bible and to see Christianity as a ground for social action. He also became one of the founders of the Brotherhood of the Kingdom, a group which sought to focus Christian social teaching on improving the conditions of men on earth.[26] In embracing social Christianity Rauschenbusch seems to have been profoundly influenced by his first pastoral experience in the Hell's Kitchen neighborhood of New York City in the mid-1880s. He would have encountered there the harshest conditions of poverty, malnutrition, and crime.[27] Rauschenbusch later concluded from these experiences, in his 1912 book *Christianizing the Social Order*, that America's social order needed to undergo a radical makeover, and that this makeover would require substantial reforms to the American capitalist system.

The problem with the capitalist system, Rauschenbusch argued, was that it exploited the labor of the working class, and was thus responsible for the reprehensible working conditions in major American cities. The only solution, he contended, was to democratize or "socialize" the rights of property, so that the uneven distribution of wealth which was at the heart of urban poverty could be remedied. He called, as we will see, for the public ownership of essential industries and what he called the "cooperative ownership" of other businesses. For these revolutionary economic policies, Rauschenbusch laid the foundation in a social Christianity which necessitated throwing off traditional theology and concentrating on the achievement of God's kingdom here on earth.

The old theology, Rauschenbusch explained, was grounded on the concept of original sin, and thus on the permanently fallen nature of man; it taught that man's permanently fallen nature could only be overcome by the grace offered in the Gospels and ministered by the church. The objective of the old theology was the next life, and particularly in saving individual souls for that next life; from this objective the traditional

26 Paul M. Minus, *Walter Rauschenbusch: American Reformer* (Macmillan Publishing Company, 1988), 1–18, 35–48, 85–93.

27 If the Social Gospel movement gained strength due to a revulsion in its adherents to the harsh conditions of urban life during the late decades of the nineteenth century, we should note the importance of the muckraking journalist Jacob Riis, who became known for exposing through photojournalism the conditions of the poor in America's cities. His book, *How the Other Half Lives* (Charles Scribner's Sons, 1890), was particularly influential. In addition to Rauschenbusch, Gladden's social Christianity seems also to have been influenced by his experiences visiting poor laborers. See Bateman, "The Social Gospel and the Progressive Era."

church took its role as the provider of doctrinal prescriptions which would lead to individual salvation. This old idea of original sin—of man's nature being permanently fallen—was the bedrock of orthodox Christian faith, and it was a problem. With man's nature permanently fallen, there is no way to attain paradise in this life. Human life and human works—including those of human government—were limited and circumscribed accordingly, incapable of perfection.

This older, limited view of man and the earthly life was the backbone of what Rauschenbusch called "other-worldly religion," which religion, he wrote in *Christianizing the Social Order*,

> was the full expression of the highest aspirations of ancient and medieval life. Contemporary philosophy supported it. The Ptolemaic astronomy made it easy to conceive of a heaven localized about the starry firmament, which was only a few miles up. But today the whole *Weltanschauung* which supported those religious conceptions has melted away irretrievably. Copernican astronomy, the conviction of the universal and majestic reign of law, the evolutionary conception of the history of this earth and of the race, have made the religious ideas that were the natural denizens of the old world of thought seem like antique survivals today, as if a company of Athenians should walk down Broadway in their ancient dress.[28]

Instead of the old, other-worldly religion based on original sin and man's permanent Fall, the theory of evolution offered the promise of man's improvement and even perfection here in this earthly life. Man no longer had to wait for the next life in order to achieve paradise; evolution offered the promise that he could achieve it here, in this life, and could do so through the social activities of the modern state. Sin itself came to be redefined too. Old-style sins came from weakness of the flesh and individual moral transgressions, whereas the new sins were social acts—working against progressive legislation, or participating in an economic system that perpetuated poor working conditions.

Rauschenbusch also explained that orthodox religion was too

28 Walter Rauschenbusch, *Christianizing the Social Order* (The Macmillan Company, 1912), as excerpted in Ronald J. Pestritto and William J. Atto, eds., *American Progressivism* (Lanham, MD: Lexington Books, 2008), 114.

"individualized"—that it focused insufficiently on social acts in this life, and too much on the salvation of the individual soul for the next life. In "religious individualism," as Rauschenbusch called it,

> there was a subtle twist of self-seeking which vitiated its Christlikeness. Thomas à Kempis' "Imitation of Christ," and Bunyan's "Pilgrim's Progress" are classical expressions of personal religion, the one Roman Catholic and monastic, the other Protestant and Puritan. In both, piety is self-centered. In both, we are taught to seek the highest good of the soul by turning away from the world of men.[29]

This focus on salvation in the next life, and the permanent limits of man in this life, were tremendous obstacles, Rauschenbusch complained, to man giving himself entirely to the social enterprises of the state here on earth. They had to be overturned if the state was to become the means for bringing about heaven on earth. In the new understanding, salvation comes from serving the worldly, social good and obtaining a secular heaven.[30] Sinfulness occurs when man seeks to establish a private kingdom and, distracted by the prospect of his own other-worldly reward or punishment, fails to work for the progress of all mankind.

THE CONNECTION BETWEEN SOCIAL GOSPEL AND PROGRESSIVISM

Social Gospel was intimately bound up with the progressive movement, and it is no accident that the most important Social Gospel figures were also prominent progressives. Understanding the connection between the two movements requires consideration of how the theological argument of Social Gospel parallels an important element of progressive political philosophy. In Social Gospel, as this chapter has maintained, the problem with the orthodox order is that it holds to a static

29 Rauschenbusch, *Christianizing the Social Order*, in Pestritto and Atto, *American Progressivism*, 113.

30 On Rauschenbusch's goal of bringing about the Kingdom of God on earth, see Steven Cassedy, "Walter Rauschenbusch, the Social Gospel Movement, and How Julius Wellhausen Unwittingly Helped Create American Progressivism in the Twentieth Century," in Shawna Dolansky, ed., *Sacred History, Sacred Literature: Essay on Ancient Israel, the Bible, and Religion in Honor of R.E. Friedman on His Sixtieth Birthday* (Winona Lake, IN: Eisenbrauns, 2008), 315–324.

conception of man—that is, due to original sin and his fallen nature, paradise for man will never be attained here in this earthly life. Such is the consequence men must suffer for the Fall. Bearing this theological conception in mind, consider what the book has already established about the political view that dominated the American founding: human nature is permanently flawed, thus government must be permanently limited. It was thought folly by America's founders to conceive of government as something perfectible, or to think that human government could ever be capable of solving every human problem. Bearing in mind this permanent, fallen nature, the founders designed a system of limited government, based upon Madison's warning in *Federalist* 51 that men, in this life at least, would never be angelic.[31]

Just as Social Gospel hoped for the perfection of human life here on earth, and thus urged a new devotion to a vastly empowered central state, so too in the progressive critique of founding-era constitutionalism we see the argument that history had solved the problem of faction, that man's nature was no longer a danger to his own good, and thus the restrictions put on human government could be removed for the purpose of achieving a fully just political order.

The Progressive Policies of Social Gospel

As a practical matter, what would a fully just political order look like? What was Social Gospel theology calling for when it contemplated the devotion of the individual to social action and to the common enterprise of the state? Principally, it called for dismantling the system of capitalism. Such a dismantling would require, as Rauschenbusch openly argued, an evisceration of the private rights of property, and turning private property into a resource for social use.

When speaking of all of the new central-government activity that would be required under his vision of social Christianity, Rauschenbusch stated the problem, and its solution, succinctly in *Christianizing the Social Order*: "Where is the money to come from for all of these new expenditures? . . . There is plenty of property, but it is not available for

---

31 James Madison, "Federalist No. 51," in George W. Carey and James McClellan, eds., *The Federalist* (Indianapolis: Liberty Fund, 2001), 269.

social purposes. If we want to conserve life, we shall have to resocialize property."[32] What does that mean, exactly? Rauschenbusch clarified:

> By "socializing property," we mean, then, that it is made to serve the public good, either by the service its uses render to the public welfare, or by the income it brings to the public treasury.... Socializing property will mean, therefore, that instead of serving the welfare of a small group directly, and the public welfare only indirectly, it will be made more directly available for the service of all.[33]

And if one were to inquire about the status of individual property rights, which the original constitutional limitations on government were principally designed to protect, Rauschenbusch agreed that the original understanding of rights in tension with state action would have to be undone. He complained that "the plain path of justice and good sense is blocked by the property rights brought down from a different past." And so, "property rights will have to be resocialized to bring them into accordance with our actual moral relations." The idea of government dedicated to securing the rights of the individual must give way to the dedication all must have to the enterprises of the state in Rauschenbusch's social Christianity. He explained: "The whole institution of private property exists because it is for the public good that it shall exist. If in any particular it becomes dangerous to the public welfare, it must cease. *Salus republicae summa lex.*"[34]

SOCIAL GOSPEL AND ROOSEVELT'S PROGRESSIVISM

The economic and political prescriptions of Social Gospel may sound rather radical, even for the Progressive Era, and at first blush it may be asked what relation such prescriptions have to "mainstream" progressivism. There is, however, little that has been described in this chapter's survey of Social Gospel that did not apply to the political ideology of most progressives. Theodore Roosevelt's vision of national government

32 Rauschenbusch, *Christianizing the Social Order*, in Pestritto and Atto, *American Progressivism*, 117.

33 Rauschenbusch, *Christianizing the Social Order*, in Pestritto and Atto, *American Progressivism*, 118.

34 Rauschenbusch, *Christianizing the Social Order*, in Pestritto and Atto, *American Progressivism*, 122. The Latin phrase can be loosely translated as "the welfare of the people is the highest law."

and critique of private property rights have been detailed in Part I, and are useful in seeing this connection.[35]

We should first recall that Roosevelt's attacks on the judiciary, as they provide a useful and representative way for reminding us of how many progressive political arguments fit well with the call of Social Gospel to "resocialize" property. Roosevelt was fixated on the judiciary because it had been in the practice at the time of occasionally overturning progressive legislation that impinged upon property rights in order to achieve some aim of social justice (labor regulations, for example, including child labor laws). Property rights, claimed Roosevelt, were the last defense of what he called the "special interests," and these special interests put forth their own individual advantage at the expense of the common good.[36] Roosevelt acknowledged that the American system of government had been designed with just such a protection of private property in mind, and so he called for "changing the rules of the game" to bring about "a more substantial equality of opportunity *and reward*."[37] Just as Rauschenbusch called for "resocializing" property in order to make it reflect the new social condition of man that had been brought about by history, Roosevelt subscribed to the progressive redefinition of property rights.

One's right to property did not come, as it had for the eighteenth-century liberalism that influenced the founders, through an account of nature where individual labor gave title to property. Rather, one had a "right" to property, in Roosevelt's view, only insofar as it was socially beneficial for one to have it. Title to property became contingent upon

35 It is worth noting Roosevelt was rather directly influenced by Ely, as Bradizza has shown. Roosevelt is once reported to have said that "I know Dr. Ely. He first introduced me to radicalism in economics and then he made me sane in my radicalism." (Ely, *Ground Under Our Feet: An Autobiography* [MacMillan, 1938], 278–79). Ely himself remarked that "I have felt that from things that he has said that I have had some influence upon the thought of Colonel Roosevelt." (Ely to Albert Shaw, January 9, 1919, in *Richard T. Ely Papers*, State Historical Society of Wisconsin, 1982, microfilm reel 65, frame 656). In a letter from E.A. Ross to Ely, Ross remarked as follows: "Referring to his talk with you Col. Roosevelt said: 'I could have fallen upon his neck—though I did not tell him so—and wept tears of joy at meeting at last with so much wisdom and common sense.' On leaving he said: 'Tell Ely that I lament that he is not nearer so that I could oftener take advantage of his wisdom and good judgment.'" Ross to Ely, January 12, 1915, in *Ely Papers*, reel 50, frame 865). All of these are quoted in Bradizza, *Ely's Critique of Capitalism*, 11.

36 Roosevelt, "The Right of the People to Rule," in *The Outlook* 100 (March 1912): 618–23, excerpted in Pestritto and Atto, *American Progressivism*, 251–60.

37 Roosevelt, "The New Nationalism" in *The New Nationalism* (The Outlook Company, 1910), 3–33, excerpted in Pestritto and Atto, *American Progressivism*, 211–23. See p. 215 (emphasis added).

its serving a social purpose.[38] Property rights were no longer moored in nature, to be used as a trump against social action, but were instead to be determined by social expediency. As shown in Chapter One, Roosevelt was explicit about the contingency of property rights upon social utility, and about the increased scope of state power which would correspond with such a conception of rights.[39]

Such a reconceiving of something as fundamental as the rights of property was central both to Roosevelt's political vision and to the agenda of Social Gospel. It is offered as one concise example of how progressivism and Social Gospel were deeply connected at the levels of both ideas and policy.[40] For Social Gospel and progressivism generally, the evolutionary power of history had brought a paradigm shift in what was possible in human nature and in human government. The power of the state came to be looked upon with new optimism, a vision that required the overturning of both the old theology and the old political philosophy.

---

38 Roosevelt, "New Nationalism," in Pestritto and Atto, *American Progressivism*, 217.

39 Roosevelt, "New Nationalism," in Pestritto and Atto, *American Progressivism*, 217. Emphasis added.

40 Additional examples, while beyond the scope of this chapter, can be found in Jean M. Yarbrough, *Theodore Roosevelt and the American Political Tradition* (University Press of Kansas, 2012), 159–161, 197–199, 211–220.

CHAPTER SIX

★

REALISM AND IDEALISM IN PROGRESSIVE FOREIGN POLICY

The Case of Woodrow Wilson

with William J. Atto

I have argued that the new political principles imported into the American tradition by the progressives reflected an amalgam of historical thinking that pervaded the nineteenth century—an amalgam in which the realism of the historical school and the idealism of the philosophy of history both had significant parts.[1] Looking to the actual context of events in the Progressive Era, there may be no better way to appreciate this mix than in the arena of foreign policy. Woodrow Wilson's is especially relevant because it is peculiar in its reliance on both realism and idealism, and because it is an approach to foreign policy that continues to resonate strongly in our own time.

Woodrow Wilson's status as the godfather of idealism in American foreign policy stands unquestioned.[2] In both academics and politics, among scholars and politicians of various persuasions, Wilson's

---

1 This chapter is Ronald J. Pestritto's revision of an essay originally co-authored with William J. Atto.

2 On the connection between Wilson's moral idealism and his foreign policy, see: Alan Dawley, *Changing the World: American Progressives in War and Revolution* (Princeton, NJ: Princeton University Press, 2003); Patricia O'Toole, *The Moralist: Woodrow Wilson and the World He Made* (New York: Simon & Schuster, 2018).

leadership of American involvement in World War I and the subsequent peace negotiations is pointed to as a founding moment for liberal internationalism, which from then on became a defining characteristic of American foreign policy. Boiled down, this liberal internationalism posits democracy as a universal ideal, understands America as its greatest or at least its most powerful example, and places on America a kind of moral duty to act in foreign policy in a way that will lead other nations down the same path to the democratic ideal. While "idealism" in foreign policy is a term so overused as to render it virtually meaningless, in the context of its Wilsonian roots it is relatively straightforward: an idealistic foreign policy is one where the nation serves the ideal, and that ideal transcends national boundaries and national interest. The motivations for a foreign policy of idealism, accordingly, come not from the goal of securing national self-interest, but from the goal of promoting democracy for all nations.

A century after Wilson's presidency, American presidents still cite him when articulating the idealism of American foreign policy. Even George W. Bush, as he spoke aggressively of American national interest in forging a post–9/11 foreign policy, did so by invoking the unselfish ends of Wilsonian idealism. In a major speech delivered in London in 2003, Bush pointed specifically to Wilson's words and example. He urged his audience to look beyond the strategic alliance between Britain and America, to their "alliance of values," which he grounded in Wilson's idealism: "The last president to stay at Buckingham Palace was an idealist, without question. At a dinner hosted by King George V, in 1918, Woodrow Wilson made a pledge; with typical American understatement, he vowed that right and justice would become the predominant and controlling force in the world." Bush invoked Wilson's Fourteen Points, and called for a recommitment of the alliance to "the global expansion of democracy."[3] In his Second Inaugural Address, Bush was even more ambitious in committing America to the aims of Wilsonian idealism, employing the very kind of Wilsonian pledges of which he had reminded his London audience in 2003. His Second Inaugural announced that it was "the policy of the United States to seek and support the growth of democratic movements

3 George W. Bush, "President Bush Discusses Iraq Policy at Whitehall Palace" (speech, London, England, November 19, 2003). Accessed by web, January 16, 2015. http://teachingamericanhistory.org/library/document/president-bush-discusses-iraq-policy-at-whitehall-palace/

and institutions in every nation and culture, with the ultimate goal of ending tyranny in our world." Such a foreign policy, Bush explained, came from America's faith in ideals that transcend its own interests, and its faith in the ultimate universal triumph of those ideals: "Because we have acted in the great liberating tradition of this nation, tens of millions have achieved their freedom. And as hope kindles hope, millions more will find it. By our efforts, we have lit a fire as well—a fire in the minds of men. It warms those who feel its power, it burns those who fight its progress, and one day this untamed fire of freedom will reach the darkest corners of our world."[4]

And while both the foreign-policy strategy and tactics of Bush's successor diverged from Bush's in several critical ways, President Obama continued to frame American foreign policy in the unselfish terms of Wilsonian idealism. In the first major foreign-policy speech of his presidency, Obama pointed to the shared ideals of America and the Muslim world: to the "common principles" of "justice," "progress," the "dignity of all human beings," and "tolerance." Obama explained that American foreign policy was "not simply about America's interests," and that while it would not seek to impose democracy outright, it would pursue a "commitment...to governments that reflect the will of the people." He pointed to his "unyielding belief that all people yearn for certain things: the ability to speak your mind and to have a say in how you are governed; confidence in the rule of law and the equal administration of justice; government that is transparent and doesn't steal from the people; the freedom to live as you choose. Those are not just American ideas, they are human rights."[5]

That presidents as politically diverse as Bush and Obama still felt a common need to frame their foreign policy in idealistic terms is a credit to the staying power of Wilson's paradigm, even if President Trump's foreign policy has, thus far, been framed in very different terms. It is also one reason why, presumably, Wilson's role as the godfather of liberal internationalism is as widely acknowledged in the scholarly

4 George W. Bush, "Second Inaugural Address" (speech, Washington, D.C., January 20, 2005). Accessed by web, January 16, 2015. http://teachingamericanhistory.org/library/document/second-inaugural-address-6/

5 Barack Obama, "Remarks by the President on a New Beginning" (speech, University of Cairo, Cairo, Egypt, June 4, 2009). Accessed by web, January 19, 2015. http://www.whitehouse.gov/the-press-office/remarks-president-cairo-university-6-04-09

literature as it is in the conduct of politics.[6] The historian H.W. Brands, for example, attributes to Wilson the idea that all peoples have the right of self-government, and contends that this Wilsonian idea remains at the core of international governing bodies. "The essential philosophy of the United Nations," he writes, "the conviction that peace was the responsibility of all countries, that collective action was the surest guarantee against aggression, that self-government was the right of every people, that the world must find a way beyond the old anarchy to a new cooperation—was pure Wilsonianism."[7] Lloyd Ambrosius is more concise: "Liberalism [in international relations] found its leading advocate in Wilson."[8] Moreover, as Kendrick A. Clements testifies, this sentiment was shared by a wide range of individuals in subsequent periods of American history: "Woodrow Wilson's long-term influence on the United States justifies the claim that he is one of the most important presidents of the twentieth century. Historians and policymakers alike still commonly refer to policies, especially foreign policies, as 'Wilsonian,' although they often disagree violently about whether that adjective is complimentary or insulting."[9] Even other presidents, who normally might be more interested in creating their own legacy, openly adopted the "Wilsonian" label—including presidents as diverse as Herbert Hoover, Franklin Roosevelt, and Richard Nixon.

This chapter does not aim to call into question the consensus on Wilson's role as godfather of liberal internationalism in foreign policy. It does seek to show, however, that the path Wilson took in arriving at his foreign-policy idealism was a most peculiar one, in light of the progressive principles that have been laid out in the book thus far. The political philosophy of American progressivism does not naturally give rise to the kind of idealism for which Wilson is most known in the wider world. This chapter will show that, while Wilson's reputation as a godfather of foreign-policy idealism is well deserved, this reputation comes in sharp contrast to the core political principles that he espoused during all but

6 For examples of this treatment of Wilson in the scholarly literature, see the following from some of the important historical accounts: Kendrick A. Clements, *Woodrow Wilson: World Statesman* (Chicago: Ivan R. Dee, 1999), ix-xi; Lloyd Ambrosius, "Democracy, Peace, and World Order," in *Reconsidering Woodrow Wilson: Progressivism, Internationalism, War, and Peace*, ed. John Milton Cooper, Jr. (Washington, D.C.: Woodrow Wilson Center Press, 2008), 225–249; H.W. Brands, *Woodrow Wilson* (New York: Times Books, 2003), 131–139.

7 Brands, *Woodrow Wilson*, 137.

8 Ambrosius, "Democracy, Peace, and World Order," 225.

9 Clements, *World Statesman*, ix.

the latest stages of his life. I will turn first to explaining the sources for Wilson's well-deserved reputation as an idealist, looking both to his own words and to his actions as war leader and peace negotiator. I will then move to bringing out the peculiarity of this idealism, when considered in the context of the liberal realism that had long been the anchor for Wilson's progressive political principles.

HOW WILSON EARNED HIS REPUTATION AS A FOREIGN-POLICY IDEALIST

It is unsurprising that Wilson is most known for his foreign-policy idealism when one bears in mind that, by far, his two most well-known speeches are the War Message to Congress from 1917, and the Fourteen Points address he made in 1918 as a roadmap for peace. Of course Wilson had been writing and speaking about government—both national and international—since the 1880s as part of a prolific career as a scholar and university president. He published many books and articles, some of which were well-known in their time and a few of which have, arguably, had a reach well beyond their own time. But any influence of the wider body of work has been dwarfed by the reputation of Wilson's War Message and Fourteen Points.

Just as contemporary American leaders routinely call for "ending tyranny in our world" or a worldwide commitment to our "common principles," Wilson called for America to enter World War I because "the world must be made safe for democracy." And America was "not simply about America's interests," as President Obama put it, but serving, as Wilson described it, as "one of the champions of the rights of mankind." Wilson explained that "we have no selfish ends to serve. We desire no conquest, no dominion. We seek no indemnities for ourselves, no material compensation for the sacrifices we shall freely make."[10] And Wilson underscored this policy of universal idealism when he outlined his program for peace, calling for "a general association of nations" founded on the "principle of justice" for "all peoples and nationalities, and their right to live on equal terms of liberty and safety with one another."[11]

---

10 Woodrow Wilson, "An Address to a Joint Session of Congress," April 2, 1917, in *The Papers of Woodrow Wilson*, ed. Arthur Link (Princeton: Princeton University Press, 1966), 41:525.

11 Woodrow Wilson, "An Address to a Joint Session of Congress," January 8, 1918, in *PWW*, 45:538–39.

In addition to his words, Wilson's actions as war leader and peace negotiator also reflected a commitment to liberal internationalism—even if, initially, he hastened to proclaim American neutrality at the outbreak of hostilities in Europe in August 1914. A steady stream of memorable phrases followed, urging Americans to resist the temptations to war and to remain "impartial in thought as well as in action." "We are at peace with all the world," he announced in his Annual Message to Congress in 1914, "We never have had, and while we retain our present principles and ideals we never shall have, a large standing army." [12] There was such a thing, Wilson would later intone in his Peace Note of 1916, as "being too proud to fight," an idea he had already sounded out in response to the *Lusitania* disaster the year before.[13] These phrases, and many others like them, undergirded Wilson's reputation as an idealist who "kept us out of war" and would continue to protect America's sons from the carnage of trench warfare. He appealed to the ethnic plurality of America, with her rich tradition of immigrants from many lands, as the example to be emulated. He rejected the bellicose language of Theodore Roosevelt and others who clamored for war with "Kaiser Bill" even as Roosevelt essentially accused him of cowardice.

Impartiality in action obtained, at least for a time, but impartiality in thought was another matter. Clearly the majority of Americans, though they wanted no part of the bloodletting in Europe, favored the Allies. Germany's tromp across neutral Belgium and the reports (embellished by the British press) of German atrocities there convinced many that the war was the result of the Prussian militarism that had plagued Europe throughout much of the eighteenth and nineteenth centuries. And Wilson's impartiality did not prevent him from allowing the House of Morgan and other banks to loan upwards of $2 billion to the Allies before the United States had entered the war.

The most pressing cause for America's entry in the war, however, was the question of neutral rights. In this, the Wilson administration had difficulties with both the British and German governments. For their part, the British pressed the issue of neutral rights by declaring a blockade of

12 Woodrow Wilson, "Annual Message to Congress," December 8, 1914. Quoted in A. Scott Berg, *Wilson* (New York: Putnam Publishing Group, 2013), 352.

13 Woodrow Wilson, "Peace Note," December 20, 1916. Quoted in Martin Gilbert, *A History of the Twentieth Century, Vol I: 1900–1933* (New York: William Morrow, 1997), 422.

Germany, but then enforced it by means contrary to international law, namely, by their refusal to close German ports, relying instead upon a more fluid interpretation whereby the British navy roamed the North Sea searching for contraband, which they defined strictly to their own advantage. Such feeble protests as the Wilson administration lodged were politely ignored by the British. The German blockade of the British Isles, however, was established by virtue of the submarine, which sank merchant and naval ships alike. With the German surface fleet drastically out-gunned by the British navy, submarines represented the best hope Germany had for blockading Britain. However, all advantage was lost if the U-boats surfaced to give warning, running the risk of being sunk by British warships disguised as merchant vessels. These "Q ships" often concealed guns, shrouded on the deck and unleashed on the hapless U-boat that surfaced to warn the ship of an impending attack. Consequently, Germany warned neutrals that, if their ships entered the war zone around the British Isles, they incurred a grave risk of being sunk. Wilson's angry protest to the German government was of no avail. However, the German embassy in Washington did publish dozens of warnings in American newspapers not to sail on British ships and those of her allies. Nonetheless, on May 7, 1915, the British passenger ship *Lusitania* was sunk by a U-boat in the Irish Sea, killing 1,198 passengers, including 128 Americans. Wilson was unmoved by German protests that the ship was carrying contraband (ammunition), which was in fact true. Rather, he sternly rebuked the German government, maintaining that what was at stake was "something much greater than mere rights of property," namely, "nothing less high and sacred than the rights of humanity."[14] He consistently and stubbornly insisted on the right of Americans to travel on merchant vessels of belligerent nations. Secretary of State William Jennings Bryan's protest that Wilson's policy must be changed, as it was clearly non-neutral and favored the British, went unheeded, resulting in Bryan's resignation. Three days after the *Lusitania* was sunk, Wilson spoke to a crowd in Philadelphia, lecturing his audience that "there is such a thing as a nation being so right that it does not need to convince others by force that it is right."[15] However, subsequent American casualties due

14 Woodrow Wilson quoted in John Morton Blum, *The Progressive Presidents: Theodore Roosevelt, Woodrow Wilson, Franklin D. Roosevelt, Lyndon B. Johnson* (New York: Norton, 1980), 89.

15 Quoted in Berg, *Wilson,* 364.

to German attacks on British and French passenger ships in 1915 and early 1916 led Wilson to demand, via the *Arabic* and *Sussex* pledges, that Germany virtually abandon submarine warfare, a demand to which the Germans reluctantly agreed.

Nineteen sixteen was an election year and confidence in Wilsonian idealism was manifest in St. Louis at the Democratic Convention where the ubiquitous slogan "He kept us out of war!" was proudly proclaimed.[16] Privately, Wilson was not so confident as the convention delegates, confiding to Navy Secretary Josephus Daniels: "I can't keep the country out of war. They talk of me as though I were a god. Any little German lieutenant can put us into the war at any time by some calculated outrage."[17] Wilson narrowly defeated his Republican challenger, Charles Evans Hughes, but he was right: he could not prevent America's entry into the Great War. Within a matter of months after his election, Wilson went before Congress to ask for a declaration of war against Germany.

In early January, 1917, the German high command made the fateful decision to declare unrestricted submarine warfare effective February 1, so notifying Secretary of State Robert Lansing on January 31. Wilson's earlier call for both Germany and Great Britain to state their war aims as a means to facilitate peace negotiations failed—with Britain making demands Germany could not conceivably accept, and Germany refusing to state its aims at all. Wilson immediately broke diplomatic relations with the German government and sought Congressional authorization to arm U.S. merchant ships. With impeccable timing, Britain released a recently-intercepted communiqué on March 1 between the German Foreign Secretary, Arthur Zimmerman, and the German ambassador in Mexico. It proposed an alliance with Mexico should the U.S. enter the war against Germany. The Zimmerman Telegram provoked American outrage, but the mounting loss of American lives due to Germany's U-boat attacks guaranteed America's entry into the war. Wilson went before Congress and asked for a war declaration on April 2.

---

16 In addition to its relevance to the War, Lewis L. Gould argues that the election was consequential for the principles of American domestic politics. Gould, *The First Modern Clash over Federal Power: Wilson versus Hughes in the Presidential Election of 1916* (Lawrence, KS: University Press of Kansas, 2016).

17 Ray Stannard Baker, *Facing War, 1915–1917,* vol. 6 of *Woodrow Wilson: Life and Letters* (Garden City, N.Y.: Doubleday, Page, and Co., 1937), 258.

While Wilson repeated, in his war message, the idealistic theme of a "peace without victory" that he had issued to Congress in January, such rhetoric was lost on Allied leaders. Both the British and the French resented Wilson's elevated rhetoric about being "too proud to fight" in his Peace Note of 1916—a statement which made no sense in the face of their losses in the field.[18] Nor did the Allies entertain notions of fighting a war for democracy. It was mid-1918 before America's doughboys entered the war in significant numbers and the Allies were pushed to the limit of their endurance—fighting a mere forty miles from Paris. Nonetheless, as German Chancellor Theobold von Bethmann Hollweg had feared, America's rapid, massive mobilization tipped the scales in favor of the Allies, and by October Germany asked Wilson to secure an armistice based on his Fourteen Points.

Wilson had announced his Fourteen Points to Congress nearly a year earlier. Included among them were calls for open diplomacy among nations, freedom of the seas, and disarmament. The victors must not engage in a land grab nor seek to extend their colonial holdings. These results must be achieved through "open covenants, openly arrived at." The means of enforcing the peace would be Wilson's cherished League of Nations, an international organization dedicated to universal peace. As president, Wilson took the unprecedented action of traveling to Europe to participate in the Paris peace conference. Great cheering crowds greeted him as the savior of Europe and Wilson's hopes for a just and lasting peace soared as he arrived at Versailles. Awaiting him, however, were British Prime Minister David Lloyd George and French Premier Georges Clemenceau. Neither shared Wilson's messianic vision for a peace among equals; both sought and secured a punitive peace that substantially weakened Germany and the rest of the Central Powers while securing territorial concessions for their respective nations. With the exception of the League, which the Allies agreed to support, Wilson's Fourteen Points were effectively abandoned at Versailles. The pain of Wilson's failure to secure his principles in the peace agreements only intensified upon his return to the United States, where Senator Henry Cabot Lodge, an adamant opponent of the League as Wilson devised it, was preparing to hand him a humiliating defeat.

Though Lodge, a Boston Brahmin, is often represented as a

18 Gilbert, *A History of the Twentieth Century*, 422.

reactionary isolationist, he was, in fact, a nationalist who stood for an aggressive American acceptance of its place as a world power, placing him clearly in the company of Theodore Roosevelt. His undeserved reputation as an isolationist is undoubtedly due not only to his opposition to Wilson's version of the League, but also to his historic and staunch support for immigration restriction. Lodge was a leader among the sponsors of immigration restriction, and his actions included a critical role in the formation of the Immigration Restriction League in 1894. He subsequently supported literacy tests for immigrants in 1896 that, he candidly admitted, were designed substantially to reduce immigration from southern and eastern Europe in favor of English-speaking peoples. Yet Lodge also advocated for a strong military, territorial expansion, and U.S. entry into World War I "as early as 1915."[19]

Not surprisingly, Wilson had taken plenty of intellectuals with him to Paris. However, he unwisely refused to take any Republicans, who held a majority in the Senate. Thus the controlling party in the Senate, which would ultimately ratify the treaty or not, had no say in the proceedings at Versailles. On his return, Wilson found that Lodge had organized a "Republican Round Robin" which was sufficient, along with the opposition of the so-called Irreconcilables (fourteen Republican and two Democrats who steadfastly opposed the League regardless of whether it was Wilson's or some other version), to ensure the defeat of both the League and the treaty.

Clearly a majority of Americans initially supported U.S. participation in some kind of collective security arrangement based on principles of national self-determination and universal justice. However, Lodge and a considerable number of his fellow senators were concerned that America not sacrifice its sovereignty in choosing if and when to commit troops to wars which may or may not be related to American national interest. Accordingly, Lodge, who headed the Senate Foreign Relations Committee, attached fourteen "reservations" to the League which, contrary to popular belief, were not obstacles to foreign support for the League as amended by the Republicans.[20] They reflected, at least in part, concerns expressed even by the editors of *The New Republic*, surely a

19 Eric A. Nordlinger, *Isolationism Reconfigured: An American Foreign Policy for a New Century* (Princeton, N.J.: Princeton University Press, 1995), 55.

20 See, for example, Paul Johnson's discussion of foreign support with Lodge's Reservations in *A History of the American People* (New York: Harper Collins, 1997), 652–654.

journal not unsympathetic to Wilson's initial goals at Paris.[21] Though Wilson was advised by many, including his adviser, Colonel House, and a number of Democratic supporters of the League, to compromise with Lodge, the president would have none of it. Wilson stubbornly refused to consider amending his demands. "The Senate must take its medicine," Wilson said, and he launched a dramatic speaking tour to rouse public support and force the League's passage.[22] The crusade failed and Wilson collapsed in exhaustion—suffering a stroke shortly after returning to Washington.

WILSON'S LONG-HELD PHILOSOPHY OF LIBERAL REALISM

For a president who understood America's role in the post-war order as leader of a group of nations all commonly committed to a set of universal ideas about self-government, it would be natural to assume that Wilson would have found the opening passages of the American Declaration of Independence to be of particular relevance. It is in these passages, after all, where America commits itself to a set of principles that apply equally to all human beings, regardless of time or place, grounded in their common human nature. Thomas Jefferson's appeal not to the rights of Englishmen in North America but to the rights of nature inherent in "all men" was intended specifically to appeal to the "opinions of mankind" about the single best form of government for human beings—a form of government requiring consent of the governed. Such a framework seems to be teed up perfectly for the kind of idealism that Wilson pursued at the close of World War I, where he sought to proceed not on the basis of national interest but on a commitment to the transcendent principles of democracy. As we know from Chapter One, however, Wilson had grounded his thinking about government in open hostility to the Declaration for the vast majority of his life. We need only recall his 1911 address, where Wilson proclaimed: "If you want to understand the real

21 See, for example, "This is Not Peace," *The New Republic,* May 24, 1919, 1.

22 Wilson's medicinal prescription was nonetheless refused, for, as historian Walter McDougall noted, the Senate "refused the spoon." See Walter A. McDougall, *Promised Land, Crusader State: The American Encounter with the World Since 1776* (New York: Houghton Mifflin, 1997), 142.

Declaration of Independence, do not repeat the preface."[23] Do not repeat, in other words, the very part of the Declaration with all of the universalistic language about self-government—the part of it that would seem a perfect launching point for the foreign-policy idealism for which Wilson is most well-known.

Yet at this point in the book we know that Wilson, like almost all of the most influential Progressive Era intellectuals, found it necessary to discredit the political principles of the Declaration of Independence, and to posit, instead, the historical argument that the ends, scope, and role of just government must be defined by the different principles of different epochs. We know that he believed it impossible to speak—as the Declaration does—of a single form of just government for men of all ages. It is for this reason that for most of his adult life Wilson is known *not* as an idealist, but quite the opposite: he was one of the most important expositors in America of late nineteenth-century liberal *realism*.

Without diverting into the many complexities of realism's development in the United States, it came ashore as part of the general influence of the European historical school—a school that reacted to the abstract radicalism of the French Revolution by rejecting talk of universal ideas and focusing instead on the concrete particulars of history. Realism was thus a natural ally for American progressives who were searching for ways to move beyond the permanent, universal principles of government enshrined in the Declaration of Independence. It was also a mainstay of Wilson's many writings in the 1880s and 90s, as he championed historical contingency in the development of the new discipline of political science that was emerging in the American Academy at the turn of the twentieth century.[24] Wilson was, after all, probably the most prominent American

23 Woodrow Wilson, "Address to the Jefferson Club of Los Angeles," May 12, 1911, in *PWW*, 23:33.

24 The best examples of Wilson's realism, especially as it applies to the development of the political science discipline in the United States, are often found in draft sections for a textbook he worked on in fits and starts throughout the 1880s and into the 1890s: Wilson, "Of the Study of Politics," November 25, 1886, in *PWW*, 5:395–406; Wilson, "The Study of Politics," September 1891, in *PWW*, 7:278–83. See also a selection Wilson drafted for his teacher Richard T. Ely's never-published textbook on political economy: Wilson, "Wilson's Selection for a 'History of Political Economy in the United States,'" May 25, 1885, in *PWW*, 4:630–63. And see his address to the American Political Science Association in 1910, where he calls for adjusting the principles of government to fit the facts of the current historical period: Wilson, "The Law and the Facts," December 27, 1910, in *PWW*, 22:264–71.

devotee of the British liberal realist Walter Bagehot, whose works *The English Constitution* and *Physics and Politics* Wilson quoted extensively in his own writings and speeches.[25] Wilson, through Bagehot's realism, developed a deep admiration for the British constitution as an example of the best approach to government—with nothing permanent, universal, or written, the British constitution simply evolved in response to the reality of changes brought about by history. This was, for Wilson, the way the American Constitution ought to be read and understood, and it was here that the language of a "living constitution" seems to have entered the American lexicon.

WILSON AS FOREIGN-POLICY REALIST

No realist would speak of a single, best form of government for all human beings, as the champions of democracy did at the conclusion of World War I. Instead, the best form of government for a particular people would depend on the realities of their own circumstances. Democracy might thus be a fit for some peoples, but not for others. And this is exactly the view that Wilson held in foreign policy for most instances where we have any record of it prior to the second term of his presidency. The best example of this is probably Wilson's set of observations on the conclusion of the Spanish-American War, where he used a speech titled "The Ideals of America" to comment on American policy toward Cuba and the Philippines in 1901, and to show how he diverged from the idealists of that time.

The United States ostensibly went to war with Spain in 1898 to support Cuban independence and thus free it from the clutches of a crumbling, autocratic power. And the Congress made clear, via the Teller Amendment, that the United States had no designs on Cuba. However, the origins of the war were rather more complicated than that, and involved a considerable dose of progressive imperialism. For expansionists like Assistant Secretary of the Navy Theodore Roosevelt, Admiral Alfred Thayer Mahan, and Senators Albert Beveridge and Henry Cabot Lodge, the path to America's rise as a superpower was clear and necessitated both the growth of foreign markets secured by a first-rate navy, as

25 On Bagehot's realism and its influence, see David Easton, "Walter Bagehot and Liberal Realism," *American Political Science Review* 43 (1949): 17–37.

well as the export of American civilization epitomized by political democracy and Christianity. That such expansionist thought was imbued with a heavy dose of Anglo-Saxonism and, not infrequently, Social Darwinism, is evident from even a cursory examination of its supporters. As progressive Senator Beveridge wrote in 1898, "We are Anglo-Saxons, and must obey our blood and occupy new markets, and, if necessary, new lands.... We go forth to fight for humanity.[26]

Aided by the sensationalist yellow press of William Randolph Hearst and Joseph Pulitzer as well as the deadly explosion of the *USS Maine* in Havana harbor, America entered the ranks of the imperial powers as it declared war on Spain in April of 1898. No sooner had war been declared than the U.S. Pacific Fleet, under the command of Admiral George Dewey, engaged and crushed the Spanish fleet in the Philippines. In fewer than six months the U.S. army wrapped up the "splendid little war" with a victory over the courageous but hapless Spanish army in Cuba. America acquired territorial concessions from Spain, including the Philippines, Puerto Rico, and Guam. However, the price for empire was yet to be fully paid. Filipinos who had fought alongside Americans as they sought to oust their Spanish overlords were now given to understand they had simply traded one master for another. The result was the "Filipino Insurrection" led by Emilio Aguinaldo, which proved far bloodier than the war to defeat Spain had been, lasting more than two years and taking thousands of American and Filipino lives.

Wilson took the opportunity in 1901 presented by the 125th anniversary of the Battle of Trenton to lay out his own view of the Philippines conflict. He began by reminding Americans of how it was that they came to acquire the practice of self-government. His remarks were grounded firmly in the realist tradition, arguing that Americans had not acquired democratic government by simply declaring their independence and setting up a legal framework in the Constitution of 1787. Real democratic government in America had, instead, developed gradually over more than 100 years of history; democratic government had become perfected in America not by the imposition of a form or idea, but by the gradual process of historical development. This is what made democracy in America different from attempts at democracy in France, and he used

26 Quoted in Richard W. Leopold, Arthur S. Link, and Stanley Coben, eds., *Problems in American History* (Englewood Cliffs, N.J.: Prentice, 1966), 2: 139–140.

this contrast to warn those who were too ready to impose the American model on the Philippines:

> Have they, then, forgot that tragic contrast upon which the world gazed in the days when our Washington was President: on the one side of the sea, in America, peace [and] ordered government,...on the other, in France, a nation frenzied, distempered, seeking it knew not what....[27]

The historical conditions among the Americans were such that they had been prepared for self-government, Wilson contended. He cited Edmund Burke's defense of the American colonies to this effect, and used Burke's words to make his general point that "the general character and situation of a people must determine what sort of government is fit for them"[28]—a point perfectly consistent with the realism of Wilson's progressive principles.

As always, Wilson brought a realist perspective on the American founding to bear on his analysis. Insofar as self-government was not something for which the American people had grasped but was, instead, something for which history had prepared them, the American Revolution had not been, strictly speaking, a revolution at all. The English Crown had been denying to the Americans that kind of government for which the time was ripe, and so the founders, Wilson explained, were "a generation, not of revolutionists, but of statesmen. They fought, not to pull down, but to preserve,—not for some fair and far-off thing they wished for, but for a familiar thing they had and meant to keep."[29] In colonial practice the Americans had gradually established a tradition of self-governing institutions, and the British Crown sought to turn back the clock and to deny Americans the self-government that was historically inevitable. Just as America would soon become the beacon for democracy around the world, Wilson explained that revolutionary America had really been a beacon for democratic development in all of England. "It turned out," he reasoned, "that the long struggle in America had been the first act in the drama whose end and culmination should be the final establishment of constitutional government for England and for English

27 Woodrow Wilson, "The Ideals of America," December 26, 1901, in *PWW*, 12:217.
28 Wilson, "Ideals of America," 211–12.
29 Wilson, "Ideals of America," 218.

communities everywhere."[30] The English people as a whole—including the Americans—had been prepared by history for self-government. America was simply leading the way for all of England toward that for which the time was ripe. So here, as later, Wilson sees America as a beacon for democracy, but only insofar as history has brought about the proper conditions for democratic government.

This understanding of the origins of American democracy served as the foundation for the policy Wilson advocated with respect to Cuba and the Philippines. Both nations, he explained, deserved America's assistance in developing self-government, when "they are ready."[31] The Filipinos had to undertake the slow process of historical development before America could grant self-government—"they can have liberty no cheaper than we got it," as Wilson put it. "They are children and we are men in these deep matters of government and justice." Being further along in the process of democracy's development, the wise policy for America was to wait for the proper historical conditions in the Philippines. Wilson warned against any policy that would attempt to impose democracy too soon:

> There are, unhappily, some indications that we have ourselves yet to learn the things we would teach. You have but to think of the large number of persons of your own kith and acquaintance who have for the past two years been demanding . . . that we give the Philippines independence and self-government now, at once, out of hand. It were easy enough to give them independence, if by independence you mean only disconnection with any government outside the islands, the independence of a rudderless boat adrift. But self-government? How is that "given"? *Can* it be given? Is it not gained, earned, graduated into from the hard school of life?[32]

And so if America was to serve as a beacon of democracy for other nations, it must be as an example of the kind of historical conditions that must be in place in order for self-government to function properly and in lasting fashion.

30 Wilson, "Ideals of America," 212.
31 Wilson, "Ideals of America," 217.
32 Wilson, "Ideals of America," 222–223.

There are certain elements of this more concrete approach in Wilson's later foreign policy as president. When he railed against autocracy in his war speech to Congress in 1917, Wilson suggested that the practice of any government must be consistent with the current historical spirit of its people: "the menace to peace and freedom," he explained, "lies in the existence of autocratic governments backed by organized force which is controlled wholly by their will, not by the will of their people."[33] Russia served as Wilson's example here. There was, at the time, heightened domestic discord in Russia and growing opposition to the autocratic rule of Czar Nicholas II. Provoked by Russian participation in World War I, members of the Duma were, by late 1916, voicing outrage at the imbecility of the existing regime. By 1917 bread riots and strikes had broken out while pleas to the Czar to appoint a popular government went unheeded. Nicholas II was subsequently arrested, along with his family, and replaced by a Provisional Government drawn from the middle class and headed by Prince Lvov. It was believed that this was a temporary arrangement and that Lvov would rule only until a new government could be formed with a constituent assembly and a written constitution, although this was not accomplished while the Provisional Government ruled from March–November, 1917. Wilson welcomed the end of the Romanov autocracy and the abdication by Nicholas II, since, in the words of historian A. Scott Berg, it "clearly defined this war as one between Democracy and Absolutism."[34]

As strange as it may seem in hindsight, Wilson in 1917 rejoiced at developments in Russia because he saw in them democracy coming to a people who had been historically prepared for it:

> Russia was known by those who knew it best to have been always in fact democratic at heart, in all the vital habits of her thought, in all the intimate relationships of her people that spoke their mutual instinct, their habitual attitude towards life. The autocracy that crowned the summit of her political structure, long as it had stood and terrible as was the reality of its power, was not in fact Russian in origin, character, or purpose.[35]

---

33 Woodrow Wilson, "Address to Congress," April 2, 1917, in *PWW*, 41:523.
34 Berg, *Wilson*, 430.
35 "Address to Congress," April 2, 1917, in *PWW*, 41:524.

As was the case with his 1901 remarks on the history of colonial America, Wilson here endorsed democratic "revolution" as the arrival of something for which the time was ripe—as history matching up democratic government with the right set of conditions.

CAN WILSON'S REALISM AND IDEALISM BE RECONCILED?

Can Wilson's long-held realism be reconciled to the idealistic foreign-policy principles for which he is most well-known? At first glance, it would seem difficult to square Wilson's earlier admonitions that peoples cannot be "given" democracy with the postwar policies he pursued. And surely there is something to the fact that Wilson was tremendously inexperienced in foreign affairs when he took office and was thus quite unprepared for the role world events would thrust upon him. Wilson himself once confided, to his friend E.G. Conklin, that "it would be an irony of fate if my administration had to deal chiefly with foreign affairs."[36] Given all of the thinking and writing that Wilson had done as a political scientist about American institutions and domestic policy, that he made his legacy in foreign policy is certainly an irony. There may even be something to the notion that a certain amount of the tragedy resulting from Wilson's unsuccessful efforts to ratify the League of Nations can be explained by the departure in his postwar diplomacy from his long-held realist principles.

But there are also some important threads of continuity that can be traced from Wilson's earlier liberal realism to his later brand of internationalism. These threads are helpful in showing how a sensible, almost-conservative view of regime change through gradual historical development gave way to a more utopian philosophy of history. While it is the case that Wilson's understanding of government operated on historical contingency—that is, the idea that principles of government are contingent upon historical circumstances—it is also the case that Wilson understood history to be moving all of government in a single direction. In other words, Wilson coupled the realism of historical contingency with the idealism of a deep faith in progress.

36 Wilson to E.G. Conklin, cited in Ray Stannard Baker, *President, 1913–1914*, vol. 4 of *Woodrow Wilson: Life and Letters* (Garden City, N.Y.: Doubleday, Page, and Co., 1931), 55.

Democracy might not have been the best form of government for everybody, according to Wilson's long-held realism, but he was also quite confident that one day *it would be*. History determines what kind of government is best for particular peoples at particular times and places, but history, as Wilson understood it, was not random—it brought about conditions that would ultimately give rise to democratic government. This movement happened much more quickly for some peoples as opposed to others, of course, but at the end of the day it was bound to happen for all.[37] Even in Wilson's seemingly hard-nosed realism of 1901 about the prospects for democracy in Cuba and the Philippines, this idealistic faith is visible. The two nations were not, at that time, ready for democracy, but Wilson speaks of them as organic beings—as children in the process of growth. They were not then ready for "adult" government, but one day they would be—they would be prepared for that moment, gradually, by history, just as the Americans had been more than a century earlier.

The notion of America as the "adult" in affairs of government is important to understanding Wilson's particular brand of foreign-policy idealism and how it grew out of his long-held historical sense. Democracy was, in the end, the ideal and universal form of government. But some peoples and nations had been prepared for it by history, while others had not yet been prepared. America, then, because it was further down the road of historical progress, served as a leader illuminating the path for other peoples who lagged behind it in historical development. This view helps to explain both Wilson's many interventions in the affairs of other nations during his presidency (which, after all, seem quite at odds with his postwar principle of "self-determination" for all peoples), and also his vision for the League of Nations. Let us turn briefly to these interventions, and then to his vision for the League.

37 After the fashion of G.W.F. Hegel and his disciples who had influenced Wilson, Wilson believed that the key persons and events of history are part of a providential plan for progress. Strong indications of this can be seen in Wilson's treatments of historical figures such as George Washington (Wilson, "A Commemorative Address," April 30, 1889, in *PWW*, 6:178) or Napoleon (Wilson, "The Study of Administration," November 1886, in *PWW*, 5:366). His arguments on behalf of the inevitability of historical progress can be found not only in earlier academic works such as "The Study of Administration" and *The State*, but also in later works like *Constitutional Government in the United States*, where he outlines four historical stages through which all human governments will eventually pass. Wilson, *Constitutional Government in the United States* (New York: Columbia University Press, 1908), 28.

WILSON'S ADVENTUROUSNESS IN FOREIGN POLICY

Wilson demonstrated, from an early point in his presidency, a willingness, even eagerness, to pursue an activist foreign policy. While it is true that Wilson was much more interested in—and prepared for—an aggressive agenda in domestic politics, this did not deter him from throwing American weight around internationally. One of Wilson's principal biographers, Arthur S. Link, maintained that Wilson, along with his Secretary of State William Jennings Bryan, could not resist the temptations to "interference in the internal affairs of other nations on such a scale as the United States had not heretofore attempted." Such action, Link argues, stemmed from a moralist's determination to do good rather than from practical "expedient" considerations,[38] and this seems born out by the facts.

His limited knowledge of foreign affairs, both in theory and practice, notwithstanding, Wilson's activist foreign policy was on display early in his administration. In Asia, he effectively withdrew U.S. backing for the so-called Six-Power Consortium that had been established in 1911 to build a series of railroads in China. Former Secretary of State Philander C. Knox had maintained that U.S. participation in the consortium would, among other benefits, help to maintain the Open Door in China. However, Wilson justified his decision as one made in the interest of recognizing and assisting Chinese autonomy in its own administration and seeking to prevent foreign meddling in Chinese affairs. He went even further, unilaterally recognizing the republican government of China established in 1912. Those actions certainly comported with Wilson's commitment to anti-colonialism and the extension of the blessings of republican government abroad, despite the fact that China's flirtation with republicanism proved to be short-lived.

In Japan, as in China, Wilson hoped to demonstrate American beneficence, though that proved far more difficult. The immigration policies of California progressives and Democrats were the major stumbling block to improved relations. Since fears of the "yellow peril" had led to Theodore Roosevelt's 1907 "Gentlemen's Agreement" with the Japanese, whereby the San Francisco school board rescinded its 1906 decision to segregate

38 Arthur S. Link, *Woodrow Wilson and the Progressive Era: 1910–1917* (New York: Harper & Row, 1954), 81.

Asian students in separate schools, tensions between the two nations had abated somewhat, as evidenced by the warm reception the Great White Fleet was given in Tokyo Bay. Barely healed wounds were reopened, however, when, in early 1913, California legislators undertook to exclude Japanese from owning land in California. Rather than rejecting their plan outright, Wilson pleaded with the statute's supporters to find a means to mitigate its offensive aspects, even suggesting how that might be done.

With public anti-American demonstrations and a strongly worded note of protest from the Japanese government, Wilson was advised by the Joint Board of the Army and Navy to consider the strong possibility of war with Japan, which senior military planners feared would begin with a Japanese assault against the American Protectorate in the Philippines. Wilson forcefully rejected their advice that he send U.S. warships from China to the Philippines to prepare for hostilities. Several weeks earlier, he had dispatched Bryan on an ultimately futile mission to convince the California legislature to abandon its present course in favor of a more racially sensitive bill or, failing that, to secure from California Governor Hiram Johnson a veto when such legislation was presented for his signature. The furor eventually subsided due to spent passions and Japanese exasperation rather than anything the Wilson administration did.

In Latin America, Wilson's many interventions demonstrated his vision of America as a teacher of democracy to historically less advanced nations. He rejected the "dollar diplomacy" of William Howard Taft, but he was not reluctant to intervene in those instances where he believed it necessary to ensure "orderly processes of just government based upon law."[39] The most substantial interventions were in Haiti, Santo Domingo, and, above all, Mexico. In the Caribbean, where the island nations were regularly subject to political tumult and outside intervention, Wilson found it necessary on more than one occasion to send in the marines and naval forces to secure order. Haiti, for example, had defaulted on payment of its debts and was plagued by numerous political assassinations and, eventually, revolution in March, 1915. Wilson dispatched the Marines and imposed a temporary military occupation until order was restored—and Haitian leaders agreed to a treaty which essentially established it as a protectorate of the United States. Similarly, in Santo Domingo, where warring factions threatened to tear the country apart, Wilson worked first

39 Wilson quoted in Blum, *Progressive Presidents*, 83.

to secure a provisional government but was then compelled again to send in the Marines and establish temporary control over the government in 1916—beginning a nearly six-year period of military government there. It was in Mexico, however, that Wilson was most active and his hubristic determination to "teach" good government on greatest display.

In February, 1917, the revolutionary government established two years earlier was overthrown by the forces of General Victoriano Huerta. Huerta continued to be opposed, however, by the Constitutionalists under the leadership of the revolutionary Venustiano Carranza. Wilson initially rejected the calls for intervention in order to protect American lives and property. Unlike a number of European nations, including Britain, he refused to recognize Huerta's regime, which he referred to as a "government of assassins," despite the fact that Huerta did restore order and strive to protect foreigners and their property, if only temporarily. Wilson even went so far as to dispatch a circular note to nations with embassies in Mexico in order to pressure Huerta to accept American mediation that would effectively end his government in favor of the Constitutionalists.[40] As Carranza enjoyed greater military success, Wilson saw an opportunity to aid in forcing Huerta from office, and he subsequently lifted the embargo on the export of arms to Mexico so long as they were destined for Carranza and his erstwhile lieutenant, Pancho Villa. And in April, 1914, Wilson landed Marines in the port city of Vera Cruz to keep a German arms shipment from Huerta's forces. Nearly twenty Americans were killed with seventy-one wounded while Mexican losses were 129 dead and 195 wounded.

Though Carranza ultimately prevailed over Huerta, his military chief, Pancho Villa, had become alienated from his former leader. Hoping to provoke a U.S. intervention and destabilize Carranza, Villa twice attacked Americans early in 1916—once in Mexico and again in the United States—murdering a total of thirty-three Americans. Wilson responded by dispatching General John J. Pershing at the head of an American force to capture or kill Villa and his forces, though Villa consistently eluded the Americans in their futile pursuit. Wilson recalled Pershing's force early in 1917 as war in Europe loomed and ultimately recognized the new government in Mexico under its elected leader Carranza. Nonetheless, Wilson's interventionism only confirmed many Mexicans' impression of

40 Link, *Woodrow Wilson and the Progressive Era,* 113.

the "Yankees" as imperialists driven by notions of Anglo-Saxon superiority—a notion that Wilson himself expressed in his private remark that he intended to "teach the South American republics to elect good men."[41]

THE LEAGUE AND AMERICAN FOREIGN-POLICY LEADERSHIP

Wilson's notion of America as the more historically advanced "adult" in affairs of government is also very much evident in his vision for the League of Nations. In the context of subsequent developments with the United Nations and other multilateral arrangements, we often make the mistake of overlooking important differences between these more recent bodies and Wilson's original idea for the League. Wilson did not contemplate a form of world government along the lines of the United Nations, nor was he ready to turn over American foreign policy—or the direction of international affairs generally—to some assemblage of nations that might not be dominated by American or at least Western leadership.

The League did purport to represent a rejection of balance-of-power politics in favor of a unity of nations that would promote peace and international cooperation. And the League's covenant did call for an Assembly in which each nation would have a vote. However, it also provided for an executive council that included four seats for small nations—but those would not consistently enjoy influence within the League as the seats were rotated on a regular basis. Of the remaining seats, all were permanent and four of the five—the United States, Great Britain, France, and Italy—were of Western origin. Only one non-western nation, Japan, would have a permanent place on the executive council. Thus the "Big Four" Western powers that dominated the negotiations at Versailles would wield the greatest influence over the League.

In this vision for peace, we can see that there are important continuities between Wilson's postwar framework for international affairs and his progressive political philosophy. Again, peoples and nations ought to have the kind of government that history demands in their particular cases. There are, in other words, some peoples and nations for whom the time is ripe, and to whom history has designated a role of leadership in

41 Wilson to Sir William Tyrell, November 22, 1913. Quoted in Link, *Woodrow Wilson and the Progressive Era*, 119.

the process of historical development. And just as some nations, such as America, are the adults in this chain of historical progress, so there are other nations that are the children—"they are children and we are men in these deep matters of government" was how Wilson put it with respect to Cuba and the Philippines.[42] The racial connotations of such a view were an inherent part of Wilson's progressive principles, and of the Hegelianism out of which they grew. For Wilson, progress in history is based upon the advance of certain races, which lead all of the others. In his book *The State*, Wilson claimed that certain races had been "progressive,"[43] and in "The Study of Politics" he claimed that certain superior races had had a modern spirit and were thus the leaders in the progression toward modern democracy. Compared to his own race, Wilson contended, "other races have developed so much more slowly, and accomplished so much less."[44]

While Wilson's troubling views on race are certainly acknowledged in the better histories, they are not connected to his progressive political philosophy as much as they deserve to be. This connection is essential to understanding the nature of Wilson's foreign-policy idealism and its relationship to his earlier historical realism. For Wilson, democracy was indeed the universal ideal for which all nations and peoples were destined; his postwar diplomacy surely reflected this belief. But he also believed that America was in a far superior position of historical preparedness for modern democracy, and thus moderated his democratic faith with a special place for leadership by historically advanced elites. In this respect Wilson's internationalism was simply a manifestation of the

42 Wilson, "Ideals of America" in *PWW*, 12:222–23.

43 Wilson, *The State* (Boston: D.C. Heath & Company, 1898), 2–3, 17.

44 Wilson, "The Study of Politics," September 1891, in *PWW*, 7:280–81. Wilson's troubling views on race—which were not unique to him among the original progressives—become more evident the more one learns of his core political principles, especially his dialectical theory of progress. The old, facile way of explaining such views was to point to Wilson's roots in America's South, but the problem with that approach is that Wilson was not anything remotely close to a southern partisan. For a longer treatment of this question, see my *Woodrow Wilson and the Roots of Modern Liberalism*, 43–45. On the general connections of progressivism and racism, see, for example: William L. Anderson and David Kiriazis, "Rents and Race: Legacies of Progressive Policies," *The Independent Review* 18, no. 1 (Summer 2013): 115–133; David W. Southern, *The Progressive Era and Race: Reaction and Reform, 1900–1917* (Wheeling, IL: Harlan Davidson, 2005). On the connection between Wilson's Eurocentric, Anglo-American beliefs and his foreign policy in particular, see Lloyd E. Ambrosius, *Woodrow Wilson and American Internationalism* (New York: Cambridge University Press, 2017).

broader dilemma of progressivism outlined in the book thus far: to what extent does its promotion of government by elites undercut its advocacy of democracy?

We can see how the particulars of Wilson's approach to foreign policy are most useful in bringing into sharper focus the overall principled vision of politics advanced by America's progressives. How that vision helped to shape the future of American government is the subject of the next part of the book.

PART III

★

PROGRESSIVISM AND GOVERNMENT TODAY

CHAPTER SEVEN

★

THE PROGRESSIVE ORIGINS OF THE ADMINISTRATIVE STATE

The principles and policies of America's original progressives have received renewed attention over the last decade, both in academia and in public discourse. Today's progressive politicians and intellectuals have themselves pointed to their roots in the original progressive movement; moreover, the connections between the original progressive calls for reform and the language and shape of our politics today have become increasingly obvious. Some of these connections have been shown in the preceding chapters; in what follows, the relevance of original progressivism to government today will be more fully explored. There is no better place to begin than with our administrative state. This chapter deals with the general principles of the administrative state and its roots in the original progressive movement; Chapter Eight focuses on doctrines in the federal courts which have facilitated the rise of the administrative state and the connection of those doctrines to progressive ideas.

The term "administrative state" has come to have a variety of meanings, but at its core it points to the situation in contemporary American government, created largely although not entirely by Franklin Roosevelt's New Deal, whereby a large, unelected bureaucracy is empowered with significant governing authority. The fundamental question for many of those making reference to an "administrative state" is how it can be squared with government by consent and with the constitutional separation-of-powers system.[1] Nominally, the agencies comprising the bureaucracy reside within the executive branch, but their powers transcend the traditional boundaries of executive power to include both legislative and judicial functions; these powers are often exercised in a manner largely independent of presidential control and of political control altogether. Given the vast array of activities in which the national government has involved itself in the post-New Deal era, the political branches of government have come to rely heavily on the expertise of bureaucratic agencies, often ceding to them significant responsibility to set, execute, and adjudicate national policy. The major policy debates during the current and most recent presidential administrations show that the administrative state is of the utmost relevance: with President Obama's healthcare and environmental initiatives, or with President Trump's immigration initiatives, to name just a few of the most obvious examples, debates have centered around the extent to which agencies have authority to make and carry out policy in the absence of clear legislative warrant. As the constitutional branch tasked with making law—Congress—has increasingly ceded this responsibility,[2] the administrative state has stepped into the gap.

The difficulty with this state of affairs is that the administrative state co-exists uneasily and often incoherently with the principles of constitutional government upon which the nation was founded and under which, at least in form, it continues to operate. This is by no means a novel observation; within the literature on constitutional and administrative law, many on both the Right and the Left have pointed to such a development.[3] This state of affairs is also evident from the

1 See, for example, Joseph Postell, *Bureaucracy in America: The Administrative State's Challenge to Constitutional Government* (Columbia: University of Missouri, 2017).

2 See, for example, Christopher DeMuth, "A Constitutional Congress? How the Legislative Branch Can Resume Its Rightful Role," *Weekly Standard* 20, no. 7 (Oct. 2014): 25–33; David Schoenbrod, *Power Without Responsibility: How Congress Abuses the People Through Delegation* (Yale University Press: 1993); John Marini, *Unmasking the Administrative State: The Crisis of American Politics in the Twenty-First Century* (New York: Encounter Books, 2019).

3 From the point of view of criticizing this development, see Gary Lawson, "The Rise and Rise of the Administrative State," *Harvard Law Review* 107 (1994): 1231–1254; from the point of view of celebrating it, see Cass R. Sunstein, "Constitutionalism after the New Deal," *Harvard Law Review* 101 (1987): 421–510. For another insightful account, see Eric R. Claeys, "The National

tortured logic of federal court opinions, as judges must regularly bow to the reality of the administrative state while doing so within the formal framework of a legal or constitutional order that seems to provide little place for that reality. These facts show us why the administrative state is bound up with the rise of progressivism, since the ideas of the progressives formed a foundation in the American political tradition for moving away from the principles and political science of the founding. This chapter, therefore, aims to examine the political ideas that gave rise to the contemporary situation in administrative law and policymaking, and especially to uncover the foundations of these ideas in the political thought of the Progressive Era. Some introduction, however, to the current situation and its relationship to the principles of original constitutionalism is in order, and will show how the growth of the modern administrative state is tied to the movement in the United States from the old liberalism to the new.

We know by now that the founders' principal aim was to protect individual natural rights in a democratic system of government, and that they did so through the political science of the Constitution. *Federalism* and the *separation of powers* were the two primary organizational features of this political science. Both features were predicated, at least partly, on the notion that dividing power made it more likely that it would be exercised in a rational manner more conducive to the securing of rights. In the case of separation of powers, the legitimate authority of the union would be exercised by three co-equal departments of government, each making sure that the others remained within the confines of their proper constitutional places.[4] The fundamental aim of the separation of powers, which, as the fathers of progressive liberalism correctly understood, came not only from Locke's *Second Treatise* but more directly from Montesquieu's *Spirit of the Laws*,[5] was to safeguard rights against the possibility of arbitrary government. Madison in *Federalist* 47, echoing Thomas Jefferson,

Regulatory State in Progressive Political Theory and Twentieth-Century Constitutional Law," in Ronald J. Pestritto and Thomas G. West, eds., *Modern America and the Legacy of the Founding* (Lanham, MD: Lexington Books, 2006). A considerable intellectual debt is owed to Lawson's work, which has influenced the way in which I have structured the constitutional questions in this chapter and the next.

4 See Publius, *The Federalist*, ed. Jacob E. Cooke (Middletown, CT: Wesleyan University Press, 1961), No. 51:347–49.

5 See Locke, *Second Treatise*, chapter 12 ("Of the Legislative, Executive, and Federative Power of the Commonwealth"); and Montesquieu, *Spirit of the Laws*, Part 2, Book 11, chapter 6 ("On the Constitution of England").

redefined "tyranny" to mean the absence in government of the separation of powers.[6]

It is from this fundamental aim of separation of powers that we can discern three important tenets of American constitutionalism that bear directly on the administrative state, although this is by no means an exhaustive list. The first is the principle of non-delegation. If the separation of powers means anything at all, it means that one branch of government may not permit its powers to be substantially exercised by another branch.[7] The second tenet is a corollary of the first: there may be no combination of functions within a single branch. As Madison, quoting Jefferson in the passage from *Federalist* 47 mentioned above, elaborates: "The accumulation of all powers legislative, executive and judiciary in the same hands . . . may justly be pronounced the very definition of tyranny."[8] Under this second tenet of the separation of powers, those making the law would also have to be subject to its being enforced upon them by an independent authority; those involved in execution could not make up

---

6 *Federalist* 47:324; Thomas Jefferson, *Notes on the State of Virginia*, Query XIII: "The Constitution of the State, and Its Several Charters," in *The Portable Thomas Jefferson*, ed. Merrill D. Peterson (New York: Penguin Books, 1977), paragraph 4.

7 See *Federalist* 48:332. Lawson elaborates on this principle by showing the logic of non-delegation contained in the Constitution's "vesting" clauses, whereby legislative power is granted almost wholly to Congress, the executive power to the president, and the judicial power to the Supreme Courts and lower courts. Lawson, "Rise and Rise," 1237. See also David Schoenbrod, *Power Without Responsibility: How Congress Abuses the People Through Delegation* (New Haven: Yale University Press, 1993), for a comprehensive explanation of the constitutional and political defects of delegation.

8 *Federalist* 47:324. John A. Rohr attempts to use Madison's subsequent statement in this paper—that an injustice occurs only when "the *whole* power of one department is exercised by the same hands which possess the *whole* power of another department" (47:325–26)—to contend that the separation-of-powers principle cannot be used as an effective critique of the combination of functions in the modern administrative state. He even claims that by this statement "Publius has defined any likely violation of separation of powers out of existence for the entire government as well as for any administrative agency that we know today." While it may be the case that Rohr's defense of the administrative state would be made much easier if *The Federalist* were as unconcerned about the separation of powers as he contends, his interpretation nonetheless contradicts the very purpose of *Federalist* 47. Madison's point in the paper is to respond to critics who were claiming that the various checks and balances (presidential veto of legislation, Senate confirmation of executive appointments, etc.), where one branch exercises some small portion of the powers of another branch, violated the separation-of-powers principle. He follows up this point in the subsequent paper, number 48, by explaining how checks and balances keep the separation-of-powers provisions from becoming mere "parchment barriers" (48:333). The whole point here is to explicate checks and balances as a defense mechanism *against* the combination of powers; Rohr would, instead, have us believe that *Federalist* 47 is Publius's way of facilitating such a combination. *To Run a Constitution* (Lawrence, KS: University Press of Kansas, 1986), 18–19.

the law as they went along, but would instead have to enforce laws that had been previously established by a separate authority; and those on whom the law was enforced could have their cases judged by an authority entirely separate from that which had brought prosecution. The third tenet of the separation of powers is the responsibility of administration to the republican executive. The government remains "wholly popular," in the words of *Federalist* 14,[9] because those who carry out the law (administrators, under the traditional meaning of the term) are directly answerable to the president, who is elected. The Constitution grants all of "the executive power" to the president and requires him to "take care that the laws be faithfully executed."[10] Administration—as vigorous as some of the founders surely envisioned it—was thereby placed wholly within a single branch of government, and a clear line of political accountability for administrators was established.[11]

For the American pioneers in progressive liberalism, this older, limited understanding of government stood in the way of the policy aims they believed the state ought to pursue in a world that had undergone significant evolution since the time of the founding. At the most fundamental level, therefore, the separation of powers was a deadly obstacle to the new liberalism, since it was an institutional system intended to keep the national government directed toward the relatively limited ends enumerated in the Constitution and the Declaration of Independence. Beyond this fundamental difference, the three tenets of the separation of powers mentioned above posed a particular problem for the progressives' vision for national administration at the outset of the twentieth century. The range of activities they wanted the government to regulate was far too broad for Congress to handle under the original vision of legislative power. Instead, to varying degrees, the fathers of progressive liberalism envisioned a congressional delegation of regulatory power to an enlarged national administrative apparatus, which would be much more capable of managing the intricacies of a modern, complex economy because of its expertise and its ability to specialize. And because of the complexities involved with regulating a modern economy, it would be much more efficient for a single agency, with its expertise, to be made responsible

9 *Federalist* 14:84.

10 U.S. Constitution, Article II, sections 1, 3.

11 One of the best explications of this principle is found in Justice Antonin Scalia's dissent in *Morrison v. Olson*, 487 U.S. 654 (1988), at 697–734.

within its area of competence for setting specific policies, investigating violations of those policies, and adjudicating disputes. The fulfillment of progressivism's administrative vision, therefore, required the evisceration of the non-delegation doctrine and the adoption of combination of functions as an operating principle for administrative agencies. Furthermore, the progressives believed that administrative agencies would never be up to the mission they had in mind if those agencies remained subservient to national political institutions. Since modern regulation was to be based upon expertise—which was, its founders argued, objective and politically neutral—administrators should be freed from political influence. Thus the constitutional placement of administration within the executive and under the control of the president was a problem, as the progressives looked to insulate administrators not only from the chief executive but from politics altogether.

The achievement of these aims for national administration in the course of the twentieth century, at the expense of separation-of-powers constitutionalism, has been described in the legal literature and elsewhere, especially in Gary Lawson's seminal essay, "The Rise and Rise of the Administrative State." As Lawson explains, the Supreme Court ceased applying the non-delegation principle after 1935, and allowed to stand a whole body of statutes that enact the new vision of administrative power.[12] These statutes, to varying degrees, lay out Congress's broad policy aims in vague and undefined terms, and delegate to administrative agencies the task of coming up with specific rules and regulations giving them real meaning. Lawson cites, for example, securities legislation giving to the Securities and Exchange Commission (SEC) the power to proscribe the use of "any manipulative or deceptive device or contrivance in contravention of such rules and regulations as the Commission may prescribe as necessary or appropriate in the public interest or for the protection of investors." The agency, on the basis of its expertise, and not Congress, on the basis of its electoral connection, is charged with determining the policy that best serves the public interest. In another example, legislation on broadcast licenses directs that the Federal Communications Commission (FCC) shall grant licenses "if public convenience, interest,

12 Lawson, "Rise and Rise," 1240. He cites two cases as the last instances of the Court applying the non-delegation doctrine: *Schechter Poultry v. United States*, 295 U.S. 495 (1935) and *Panama Refining Co. v. Ryan*, 293 U.S. 388 (1935).

or necessity will be served thereby."[13] More recently, the Rehnquist Court made clear that there would be no revisiting the abandonment of non-delegation. In the case of *Mistretta v. United States* (1989), the Court upheld the statute which delegated to the U.S. Sentencing Commission the power to set sentences (or sentencing guidelines) for most federal crimes. If any case were going to constitute grounds for non-delegation review, it would have been this one. Congress created the Sentencing Commission as, essentially, a temporary legislature with no purpose other than to establish criminal penalties and then to go out of existence.[14] But *Mistretta* simply served as confirmation that the federal courts were not going to bring the legitimacy of the administrative state into question by resurrecting the separation of powers.[15]

The second tenet of separation of powers—the prohibition on combining functions—has fared no better in modern constitutional and administrative law. As Lawson explains, "the destruction of this principle of separation of powers is perhaps the crowning jewel of the modern administrative revolution. Administrative agencies routinely combine all three governmental functions in the same body, and even in the same people within that body." His example here is the Federal Trade Commission (FTC):

> The Commission promulgates substantive rules of conduct. The Commission then considers whether to authorize investigations into whether the Commission's rules have been violated. If the Commission authorizes an investigation, the investigation is conducted by the Commission, which reports its findings to the Commission. If the Commission thinks that the Commission's findings warrant an enforcement action, the Commission issues a complaint. The Commission's complaint that a Commission rule has been violated is then prosecuted by the Commission and adjudicated by the Commission. The Commission adjudication can either take place before the full Commission or before a semi-autonomous administrative law judge.

13 Lawson, "Rise and Rise," 1240. He cites here these sections of U.S. code: 15 U.S.C. Sec. 78j(b); 47 U.S.C. Sec. 307(a).

14 *Mistretta v. United States*, 488 U.S. 361 (1989).

15 There is some reasonable speculation that the Court may take a fresh look at delegation in the near future, based on *Gundy v. United States*, decided at the conclusion of the 2018–19 term. The potential significance of *Gundy* is discussed in Chapter Eight.

> If the Commission chooses to adjudicate before an administrative law judge rather than before the Commission and the decision is adverse to the Commission, the Commission can appeal to the Commission.[16]

The FTC is a particularly apt example, since it was the "quasi legislative" and "quasi judicial" character of the FTC that was upheld in 1935, in the landmark Supreme Court case of *Humphrey's Executor v. United States*—the first time that the Court so clearly acknowledged that agencies technically within the executive branch could exercise substantially non-executive functions.[17]

Progressivism has also succeeded, at least partly, in defeating the third tenet of the separation-of-powers framework, by weakening the political accountability of administrators and shielding a large subset of agencies from most political controls. While the independence of so-called "independent regulatory commissions" and other "neutral" agencies is not as clearly established as delegation and combination of functions, the federal courts have certainly recognized the power of Congress to create agencies that are presumably part of the executive (where else, constitutionally, could they be?) but are nonetheless shielded from direct presidential control. Normally, this shielding is accomplished by limiting the president's freedom to remove agency personnel. The *Humphrey's* case, for example, overturned the president's removal of an FTC commissioner by reasoning that the Commission was more legislative and judicial than it was executive.[18] More recently, the Supreme Court upheld the Independent Counsel provisions of the Ethics in Government Act (the provisions were subsequently repealed), concluding that even an office as obviously executive in nature as a prosecutor could be shielded from presidential control.[19] These rulings reflect the acceptance of a key tenet of the modern administrative state: that many areas of administration are based upon expertise and neutral principles, and must therefore be freed from the influence of politics. That such a notion has become ingrained in

16 Lawson, "Rise and Rise," 1248.

17 *Humphrey's Executor v. United States*, 295 U.S. 602 (1935). See also the more recent case of *Withrow v. Larkin*, 421 U.S. 35 (1975), which upholds and confirms the combination of functions in the administrative state.

18 *Humphrey's Executor v. United States*. See also Nolan Clark, "The Headless Fourth Branch," in *The Imperial Congress*, ed. Gordon S. Jones and John A. Marini (New York: Pharos Books, 1988), 268–292.

19 *Morrison v. Olson*, 487 U.S. 654 (1988).

the American political mindset was evidenced by the near universal outrage expressed over the Supreme Court's 2000 decision in *FDA v. Brown and Williamson*. In this surprising exception to its standard deference for agencies, the Court ruled that before the Food and Drug Administration (FDA) could promulgate and enforce regulations on tobacco, Congress first had to pass a law actually giving the agency the authority to do so.[20] The decision was denounced because it would subject tobacco regulation to the control of the people's elected representatives in Congress (where tobacco-state legislators might derail it), instead of giving carte-blanche to the FDA scientists to regulate in accord with their own expertise.

The acquiescence in the realms of law, politics, and culture to the concepts of delegation, combination of functions, and insulating administration from political control is explained by what legal scholars call the victory of "functionalism" over "formalism," or what political theorists might loosely translate as "pragmatism" over "originalism." Simply defined, a functionalist or pragmatic approach begins not with the forms of the Constitution, but with the necessities of the current age, thereby freeing government from the restraints of the Constitution so that the exigencies of today can be met. As Peter L. Strauss argues, "Respect for 'framers' intent' is only workable in the context of the actual present, and may require some selectivity in just what it is we choose to respect."[21] This sentiment elevating expedience and efficiency over the separation of powers was expressed very clearly by Justice Blackmun in his opinion for the Court in *Mistretta*: "Our jurisprudence has been driven by a practical understanding that in our increasingly complex society, replete with ever changing and more technical problems, Congress simply cannot do its job absent an ability to delegate power under broad general directives."[22]

The rise of the administrative state that is such an integral feature of progressive liberalism thus required the defeat of the separation of powers as a governing principle, at least as it was originally understood, and its

20 *FDA v. Brown & Williamson Tobacco Corp.*, 529 U.S. 120 (2000). This is, strictly speaking, a statutory case as opposed to a non-delegation (i.e. constitutional law) case, and the Court does not, in its opinion, indicate any reversal of its long-established delegation jurisprudence. Rather, the significance of the case comes from the Court's refusal, in a high-profile controversy, to read into the law a deference to agency expertise that was not there in the first place.

21 Peter L. Strauss, "Formal and Functional Approaches to Separation-of-Powers Questions: A Foolish Inconsistency?" *Cornell Law Review* 72 (1987): 493. See also Strauss, "The Place of Agencies in Government: Separation of Powers and the Fourth Branch," *Columbia Law Review* 84 (1984): 573–669.

22 *Mistretta v. United States*, 488 U.S. 361, at 372.

replacement by a system that allows delegations of power, combination of functions, and the insulation of administration from the full measure of political control. In actual practice, the biggest steps toward defeating separation-of-powers constitutionalism took place during the New Deal, which was animated by a strong optimism about the capabilities, public spiritedness, and objectivity of administrators. Nowhere was this optimism embodied more fully than in James Landis, the New Deal architect of the administrative state, who is the topic of the chapter's next section. I proceed in reverse chronological order, beginning with Landis, in order first to identify the central premise of the modern administrative state before investigating where this premise might have originated. While Landis himself was not part of the Progressive Era, his optimism reflected the progressive political theory that had come at least a generation earlier; it was a manifestation of the idea of separating politics and administration, originated in America by Woodrow Wilson and Frank Goodnow. And so the final parts of the chapter address the progressive vision of replacing the separation of powers with the separation of politics and administration, and thus look to the role of Wilson and Goodnow as founders of the administrative state today.[23] The further impact of progressive principles on the major doctrines of administrative law will be taken up in Chapter Eight.

---

23 The premise of this chapter runs counter to Rohr's *To Run a Constitution*, a major work on the origins of the administrative state that also delves into the writings of Wilson and Goodnow, among others. While I argue that today's administrative state is illegitimate in the eyes of the founders' constitutionalism, Rohr attempts to demonstrate a continuity between the two. Rohr's work does, however, offer a mixed view on the role of Wilson and Goodnow. At some points, he suggests that Wilson and Goodnow contradicted the Constitution in their vision for administration, but that in doing so they gave administration a bad name. While Wilson and Goodnow's particular form of administration contradicted the constitutional tradition, the modern administrative state does not. See *To Run a Constitution*, esp. 4–5, 111–12; see also Rohr, "The Administrative State and Constitutional Principle," in Ralph Clark Chandler, ed., *A Centennial History of the American Administrative State* (New York: The Free Press, 1987), 116–120, 124. But elsewhere, Rohr argues on behalf of the continuity between Wilson's thinking and that of the founders; see Rohr, "The Constitutional World of Woodrow Wilson," in Jack Rabin and James S. Bowman, eds., *Politics and Administration: Woodrow Wilson and American Public Administration* (New York: Marcel Dekker, 1984), 43–44. While Rohr contends that the modern administrative state does not necessarily adopt the principles of Wilson and Goodnow, I endeavor to show here that the ideas of Wilson and Goodnow are quite influential in the later thinking of Landis and in the principles of the administrative state today. For another account asserting the continuity between the twentieth-century expansion of the administrative state and earlier constitutional practice, see Jerry L. Mashaw, *Creating the Administrative Constitution: The Lost One Hundred Years of American Administrative Law* (New Haven: Yale University Press, 2012).

A note of caution before proceeding: when speaking of Wilson and Goodnow as founders of the administrative state, or of Landis as a New Deal facilitator of the growth of administration, I do not suggest that we see in the modern administrative state the complete fulfillment of the ideas of these men. The primary features of administration today—delegation, combination of functions, limited presidential control—are grounded in the notion of separating administration from politics. But like most political phenomena, this separation does not go quite as far in practice as it did in theory. In spite of the dramatic push toward establishing significant administrative discretion over policymaking, it still matters very much, for example, what happens in Congress and the presidency. The point of this chapter is, however, to explore the *animating ideas* behind the growth of the administrative state in the twentieth century, and to suggest the ways in which such ideas developed out of opposition to the *animating ideas* of the founding. The principles of Wilson and Goodnow, later adopted by Landis, are in this way central to the very premise of the modern administrative state.

LANDIS AND THE OBJECTIVITY OF THE ADMINISTRATIVE CLASS

When Franklin Roosevelt assumed the presidency in 1933, he embarked on a mission to enlarge vastly the scope of national government. This mission was not simply a response to the economic circumstances of the day, but was instead a conscious effort to put into practice the vision of a centralized, regulatory government that had been conceived by the progressives a generation earlier. Such a mission was made clear by Roosevelt in the 1932 presidential campaign, where he identified Wilson as a key source of New Deal principles.[24] Roosevelt advisor Felix Frankfurter looked to assemble a team to assist the new administration in crafting a plan of implementation for the goals on which Roosevelt had campaigned. Among others, Frankfurter called on his junior colleague at Harvard Law School, James Landis. Commissioned to work on securities legislation, Landis believed that the only way for the national

---

24 Franklin D. Roosevelt, "Campaign Address on Progressive Government," September 23, 1932, in Samuel I. Rosenman, ed., *Public Papers and Addresses of Franklin D. Roosevelt*, vol. 1 (New York: Random House, 1938), 742–56, especially 749–51.

government to manage capably the scope of affairs outlined in the New Deal program was to establish and empower a variety of regulatory agencies, whose expert staffs would be given significant discretion to implement Roosevelt's broad goals. It was through his work on securities legislation, and his subsequent service on the FTC and SEC, that Landis became the animating force behind the growth of modern administration as we know it today.[25]

Landis wrote two substantial works of interest on the principles of the administrative state. The first was his seminal work, *The Administrative Process*, which was based upon lectures Landis delivered after leaving the SEC in 1937 to become Dean of Harvard Law School. As Harvard administrative law scholar Louis L. Jaffe has written, "his lectures in 1938 became inevitably a celebration, a defense, and a rationalization of the magnificent accomplishment in which he had played so brilliant a part."[26] Landis left Harvard in 1946 to return to public service as chairman of the Civil Aeronautics Board, but his experience there was disappointing, as President Truman did not reappoint him at the end of his term. Landis ended up working for the Kennedy family and thus was an advisor to John F. Kennedy during his presidential campaign and the early part of his presidency. It was in this capacity that Landis wrote his *Report on Regulatory Agencies to the President-Elect* in 1960, which contains some very useful reflections on the status of the administrative state that he had helped to form.

Against Constitutional Formalism

In both of Landis's major works, the traditional forms of the Constitution are critiqued from an evolutionary point of view. Landis contended that there can be no fixed understanding of the ends and scope of government; rather, the role and even the structure of government must be constantly adjusted so that it can deal with the exigencies of the present. The growth of modern administration, which Landis fully conceded does not fit within the form of American constitutionalism, is a manifestation of this

25 For biographical information on Landis, see Thomas K. McGraw, *Prophets of Regulation* (Cambridge: Belknap Press of Harvard University Press, 1984), 153–209. See also Donald A. Ritchie, *James M. Landis: Dean of the Regulators* (Cambridge: Harvard University Press, 1980).

26 Louis L. Jaffe, "James Landis and the Administrative Process," *Harvard Law Review* 78 (December 1964): 320.

evolutionary critique. "In terms of political theory," Landis explained, "the administrative process springs from the inadequacy of a simple tripartite form of government to deal with modern problems."[27] In an entirely functionalist or pragmatic mode, the ultimate standard for Landis is *efficiency*. Government ought not do what the Constitution prescribes; rather, it ought to do that which enables it to deal most efficiently with the problems of the present. "There is no doubt," Landis reasoned, "but that our age must tolerate much more lightly inefficiencies in the art of government."[28]

Landis was fully aware that with the advent of national administration as he envisioned it, the very understanding of the ends of government in the United States had changed. Under the original view, he knew, government was erected for the sake of securing individual rights. The framers of the Constitution thus acted correctly when they implemented the separation-of-powers framework; this was a framework, Landis agreed, that would keep the national government focused on rights-protection as its fundamental end. But modern government had to move beyond the separation of powers, since the end of government had changed from rights-protection to what Landis called the "promotion of the welfare of the governed," or, more generally, "well being." For Landis, the establishment of the Interstate Commerce Commission (ICC) in 1887 marked the key turning point in America's self-understanding of the ends and scope of government. "What was important" about the ICC, Landis explained, "was the deliberate organization of a governmental unit whose single concern was the well-being, in a broad public sense, of a vital and national industry." As for the understanding of the old government that the end of government was rights protection, Landis simply explained that "concessions to rectify social maladjustments thus had to be made."[29]

One of the major concessions to which Landis referred is that the new vision of national administration does not comport with the separation-of-powers structure of the Constitution. As explained above, the original view of administration placed it wholly within the executive branch of government, subject to the superintendence of an elected president vested

27 James M. Landis, *The Administrative Process* (New Haven: Yale University Press, 1938), 1–2.

28 Landis, *Administrative Process*, 46.

29 Landis, *Administrative Process*, 8–10.

with "the executive power."[30] But for Landis, administration cannot be confined to exercising solely executive powers. In order for an agency to operate with maximum efficiency in its regulation of an industry for the purpose of "well being," rulemaking, investigatory, prosecutorial, and adjudicatory powers need to be combined and placed at its disposal.[31] This kind of combination is precisely what Landis liked about the ICC, where "a government had to be provided to direct and control an industry, and governance as a practical matter implied not merely legislative power or simply executive power, but whatever power might be required to achieve the desired results."[32] "The resort to administrative process," he subsequently explained, "is not, as some suppose, simply an extension of executive power."[33] Thus Landis reasoned that the Constitution cannot be read to require strict adherence to the separation of powers. Instead, the organization of the government's powers must be determined by the facts on the ground, and so he urges that interpreters look to the "constitutional history"—that is, how the Constitution had been interpreted to accommodate historical changes—as opposed to the forms of the Constitution itself.[34] This new reading of the Constitution amounts to an admission that there exist legitimate powers of the national government that are not directly granted by the Constitution. Landis lamented that some critics insisted on finding a place for administration within the existing constitutional structure. This lament is what characterizes his response to the Brownlow Commission, which had been appointed by President Roosevelt in 1936 for the purpose of exerting executive supremacy in national government. Its membership consisted of Luther Gulick, Charles Merriam, and Louis Brownlow, who served as its chairman.[35] The Commission had been critical, to a degree, of administrative discretion. For Landis, the Commission had responded "hysterically" to the administrative process, and he mocks its label of administration as a "fourth branch." Such criticism, he explained comes from too strong

---

30 U.S. Constitution, Article II, Section 1.

31 Landis explains that he would like for administrators to have the power to make modifications to legislation, and also explains that administration cannot work unless agencies have the authority to impose their own sanctions. See Landis, *The Administrative Process*, 52, 89.

32 Landis, *The Administrative Process*, 10.

33 Landis, *Administrative Process*, 15.

34 Landis, *Administrative Process*, 47–48.

35 See "Report of the President's Committee on Administrative Management," 74th Congress, 2nd Session (Washington: Government Printing Office, 1937). See also Donald R. Brand, "Progressivism, the Brownlow Commission, and the Origins of the American Administrative State," in Pestritto and West, *Modern America and the Legacy of the Founding*.

a fixation on the number "three" in thinking about the organization of government.[36]

The Nature and Extent of Administrative Power

The greatest reason that Landis's vision of administration could not be reconciled with original American constitutionalism was that he could not tolerate any notion of limiting the discretionary authority of administrators. Not only would administrators need to have at their disposal the combination of legislative, executive, and judicial powers, but Landis did not like talk of placing general limits on the extent to which administrators could employ these powers. Such talk, Landis reasoned, would violate the functionalist tenet of using necessity to determine the scope of state power. "Generalization as to the allowable limits of administrative discretion is dangerous," he argued. He pointed to the Securities and Exchange Act of 1934, which he helped to draft, as an example of how to create an agency with powers flexible enough to meet unforeseen exigencies. The discretionary language with which the Act empowered the SEC was a vast improvement, Landis contended, over the 1933 Securities Act, which had placed authority for securities regulation in the FTC and limited the ways in which commissioners could operate.[37]

Landis conceded that his vision of administration had to overcome a substantial objection: that it threatened rights by combining prosecutorial and adjudicatory powers in the same set of hands. Recognizing the need to answer this objection, Landis suggested that his lectures on the administrative process would offer a response to it. His response, however, simply falls back on the functionalist tenet of *necessity* or *efficiency*. He defended the combination of functions within agencies by describing the history of how such a combination came about—by explaining that necessity thrust such a change upon government. Furthermore, Landis believed that there are more than sufficient safeguards within agencies to guard against potential abuses; these safeguards, he contended, may not be "traditional," but they are adequate.[38]

Ultimately, the main requirement Landis seems to have had for ensuring competence in administration is the shielding of administrators

36 Landis, *The Administrative Process*, 25, 47.

37 Landis, *Administrative Process*, 52–55.

38 Landis, *Administrative Process*, 91–101.

from political influence. Since administration was politically neutral and based upon the administrator's expertise in a particular area, political control could only corrupt the quality of administrative decisionmaking. Administrators should, therefore, have the discretion to apply their expertise and to make their own determination of how best to serve the public interest in particular cases within their jurisdiction, free from specific guidance of those elected by the people to serve their interests. In what has to be one of the clearest expressions of this sentiment that one is likely to see anywhere, Landis stated:

> One of the ablest administrators that it was my good fortune to know, I believe, never read, at least more than casually, the statutes that he translated into reality. He assumed that they gave him power to deal with the broad problems of an industry and, upon that understanding, he sought his own solutions.[39]

Landis's *Administrative Process* catalogues the virtues that he believed are generated by securing maximum independence for administrators from political influence. In addition to the rule of expertise, Landis also emphasized consistency in administration as a primary virtue.[40] As a rule, administrators should have long tenure, which would both insulate them from political control and ensure consistency even across periods of political change.[41]

This drive to separate administration from politics made Landis a strong admirer of the Supreme Court's *Humphrey's* decision in 1935. As explained above, this decision limited the president's ability to remove commissioners of the FTC, thus creating an important precedent for shielding administrators from political influence. "The real significance of the Humphrey doctrine lies," Landis observed, "in its endorsement of administrative freedom of movement."[42] Landis himself was involved in this case in two ways. First, Landis was serving as a clerk for Justice Louis Brandeis when the Supreme Court, in the 1926 case of *Myers v. United States*,[43] handed down the precedent that *Humphrey's*

39 Landis, *Administrative Process*, 75.
40 Landis, *Administrative Process*, 113.
41 Landis, *Administrative Process*, 23.
42 Landis, *Administrative Process*, 115.
43 *Myers v. United States*, 272 U.S. 52 (1926).

subsequently overturned. Writing for the Court in *Myers*, Chief Justice Taft laid out a broad precedent requiring presidential control over (and thus the ability to remove at will) executive branch officers. Both Landis and Brandeis recognized the threat that this ruling posed to the development of a modern administrative apparatus with significant discretionary powers and independence from the realm of politics, and so Landis worked closely with Brandeis on his *Myers* dissent. Landis and Brandeis were particularly alarmed that Taft had gone out of his way to include independent commissions among the executive entities over which the Constitution required direct presidential control. In the second instance of Landis's involvement, the individual whose estate brought suit for back wages in the *Humphrey's* case was William E. Humphrey, who was a member of the FTC when Landis himself was appointed to the Commission by Franklin Roosevelt. Humphrey was a holdover on the Commission, and thus a continuous thorn in the side of New Dealers like Landis. Ironically, it was Landis himself who convinced the Roosevelt administration that the president had the authority to remove Humphrey at will, since Landis was so familiar with the *Myers* precedent. When Roosevelt eventually lost the case because he had followed Landis's advice, Landis was nonetheless quite pleased: the defeat for the president was meaningless in comparison with the great independence for administrators that the *Humphrey's* decision helped to secure.[44] This incident also helps to show that Landis was much more concerned with the freedom of administrators from politics than was Roosevelt. It was, after all, partly as a result of Roosevelt's belief that administrators should be tied more closely to his political agenda that he appointed the Brownlow Commission, the conclusions of which Landis ridiculed in *The Administrative Process*.[45]

When Landis reflected back on the status of administration in his 1960 work, he continued to urge an even greater independence for administrators from political influence. To the extent that administrative agencies had failed to live up to the vision with which they were created, Landis made clear that the problem was not insufficient political control, but rather an insufficient separation of administration from politics. This is why Landis criticized *ex parte* contacts in administrative

44 For an account of these episodes, see Ritchie, *Dean of the Regulators*, 24–25, 49.

45 Ritchie, *Dean of the Regulators*, 85–86.

decisionmaking[46]—where administrators seek or receive input from other parties in the political institutions—and why he warned that politics was playing too great a role in the appointment of administrators. As he elaborated:

> Advances have been nullified by the appointment of members of these agencies on political grounds, and by not advancing to posts of significance within the agencies men experienced by long service in their business. Largely on political grounds, outsiders lacking necessary qualification for their important tasks have been appointed. There has also been too much of the morale-shattering practice of permitting executive interference in the disposition of causes and controversies delegated to the agencies for decision.[47]

Landis readily acknowledged that keeping administrative decisionmaking free from the influence of politics, and providing administrators with the latitude to exercise legislative, executive, and judicial powers, weakened the protection for individual rights contained within the traditional doctrine of the rule of law. The rule-of-law principle, after all, requires that administrators act only in accord with a pre-established rule. Absent such a principle, individuals and companies have no idea what they have to do in order to avoid the enforcement power of the state, thus putting them at the mercy of administrators who, literally, make up the rules as they go along. Landis complained, however, that the modern need for efficiency and discretion in administration simply made it impossible for administrators to be bound by such an inflexible system.[48]

Furthermore, administrators would be hampered by subjecting their decisions to review by an independent court. This bedrock protection for rights, Landis explained, interfered with the notion that administrators were the most expert at their field and thus were the most qualified to adjudicate disputes where individuals or companies were accused of wrongdoing.[49] He even lamented that the problem with allowing

46 James M. Landis, *Report on Regulatory Agencies to the President-Elect*, Committee on the Judiciary of the U.S. Senate, 86th Congress, 2nd Session, December 1960, section I.D.

47 Landis, *Report on Regulatory Agencies*, section II.

48 Landis, *The Administrative Process*, 49–50. For an excellent illustration of how progressive principles of administration undermine the rule of law, see *SEC v. Chenery*, 332 U.S. 194 (1947) and its related cases.

49 Landis, *The Administrative Process*, 123–124.

individuals or companies to have their cases heard in traditional courts is that such courts must be bound by the "limitations" of the law and judicial procedure put into place to protect rights. They must rely only on evidence presented at trial, for example. When administrators adjudicate, by contrast, they do not have to be bound by the evidence presented, but can instead employ their own expertise and understanding of what is truly in the public interest. "For [the administrative] process to be successful in a particular field," Landis argued, "it is imperative that controversies be decided as 'rightly' as possible, independently of the formal record the parties themselves produce."[50] At the very least, Landis considered it essential that agency fact-finding not be second-guessed by an independent judiciary; otherwise, "the very efficiency of the system becomes threatened."[51] These sentiments make perfect sense when one recalls that, for Landis, the ends of government had evolved. Getting a decision "right" in terms of the "well being" of the general public interest was, to Landis, a far more important purpose of government than following specific rules and procedures designed to ensure the maximum protection for individual rights.

Why Trust Administrators?

It would not be quite correct to say that Landis disregarded the importance of individual rights. It is the case, rather, that Landis so strongly trusted the objectivity and expertness of administrators that he could not conceive it likely that they would reach unjust decisions, if only they were given sufficient freedom to do their jobs. And it is this trust—or what one commentator has called his "exuberant optimism"[52]—that is really at the core of Landis's entire outlook on reforming government. As we will see in subsequent parts of this article, Landis was a true progressive at heart; his trust in the enlightenment and disinterestedness of administrators stands as an instructive contrast to the permanent self-interestedness that

---

50 Landis, *The Administrative Process*, 38–39. For additional examples of Landis's criticism of rule of law, see 30, 35, 133–135.

51 Landis, *The Administrative Process*, 133.

52 Jaffe, *Landis and the Administrative Process*, 319. Jaffe was one of the main critics of Landis's optimism, and he argues in this volume that the special circumstances of the New Deal blinded Landis to administration's general susceptibility to corruption. For a listing of other accounts criticizing Landis's excessive optimism, see Ritchie, *Dean of the Regulators*, 213n6.

the framers of the U.S. Constitution saw in human nature.[53] Just as this sobriety about the potential for tyranny led the framers to circumscribe carefully the authority of the national government, Landis's passionate optimism fueled his call for maximum discretion for administrators. This is not to suggest that the framers denied discretionary power to the national government—no reader of *Federalist* 23, or many other papers of *The Federalist*, for that matter, could draw such a conclusion; rather, they understood that such discretion had to be channeled through the forms of the Constitution in order to be safe for liberty. Thus, as Alexander Hamilton explained in *Federalist* 23 and elsewhere, the vigorous discretion that the national government must have is made safe by the "most vigilant and careful attention of the people."[54] For the people to exercise this kind of vigilance, the officers who exercise discretion must do so in a system of clear, electoral accountability. It is precisely this kind of accountability to the realm of politics from which Landis, by contrast, wanted to free administrators.

For Landis, there is something special about civil servants which somehow raises them above the ordinary self-interestedness of human nature. As we will see, for Landis's forebears in the Progressive Era, such confidence came from a faith that the progressive power of history had elevated public servants to a level of objectivity. They would, accordingly, be able to disregard their own private or particular inclinations in order to dedicate themselves to the objective good. Landis himself spoke glowingly of the selflessness of administrators, describing them as "men whose sole urge for public service is the opportunity that it affords for the satisfaction of achievement."[55] Because of this disinterestedness, restraints on their discretion were unnecessary. And Landis took this notion even further, suggesting that the selflessness and objectivity of administrators created a kind of moral imperative that the country allow them to rule:

> Government today no longer dares to rely for its administration upon the casual office-seeker. Into its service it now seeks to bring men of professional attainment in various fields and to make that service

53 See, for example, *Federalist* 6, where Publius addresses the Anti-Federalist and Enlightenment notion that human nature had improved and become less dangerous. He characterizes those holding such notions as "far gone in utopian speculations." *Federalist* 6:28.

54 *Federalist* 23:150.

55 Landis, *The Administrative Process*, 28.

> such that they will envisage governance as a career. *The desires of these men to share in the mediation of human claims cannot be denied; their contributions dare not casually be tossed aside.* The grandeur that is law loses nothing from such a prospect. Instead, under its banner as a commanding discipline are enlisted armies of men dedicated to the idea of justice.[56]

For Landis, this dedication and the expertise of administrators cure any potential problem that might come from removing the traditional separation-of-powers protections for individual rights. In the case of granting adjudicatory power to administrators, for example, Landis explained that this is a good thing both for individuals and the common good, because the expertise of administrators makes them more competent than traditional courts and thus more likely to reach a just result. Therefore, he argued, "it is only delay that results from the insistence upon independent judicial examination of the administrative's [*sic*] conclusion."[57]

Reconsiderations?

Landis's faith in the competence and objectivity of administrators had not receded when he wrote his 1960 evaluation of the system he helped to create. It is true that Landis was disappointed with the record of what agencies had done with their discretion, and he had also had his own unsatisfactory experience with national administration. He even made what must have been a painful concession, admitting that "a deterioration in the quality of our administrative personnel has taken place, both at the top level and throughout the staff."[58] But Landis did not draw from his disappointment over the actual experience of administration the conclusion that agencies might not have been so deserving of the trust he had placed in them or of the latitude they were given as a consequence of the New Deal. "Their continued existence is obviously essential for effective government," Landis wrote. "The complexities of our modern society are

56 Landis, *The Administrative Process*, 154. Emphasis added.

57 Landis, *The Administrative Process*, 142–43. See also 125. In *Withrow v. Larkin*, where the Supreme Court upheld combining prosecutorial and adjudicative functions in the same set of agency hands, Justice White employed a Landis-like trust of administrators, writing of a "presumption of honesty and integrity in those serving as adjudicators." *Withrow v. Larkin*, 421 U.S. 35, at 47.

58 Landis, *Report on Regulatory Agencies*, I.C.

increasing rather than decreasing.... [They] all call for greater surveillance by government."[59] Landis's 1960 evaluation is thus animated by a call for agencies to do even more, and for them to exercise even greater discretion in making national policy. If anything, agencies had not abused their discretion but had, instead, been too deliberative and cautious.[60]

The question for Landis in 1960, therefore, was how administration could be helped along to fulfill the great role that he still envisioned for it. First, Landis urged more money and more manpower. It was a frequent observation of Landis's report that agency inaction seemed to come, at least partly, from too great a workload. With greater budgets and staff, agencies would be able to regulate even more zealously.[61] Second, Landis saw a need to attract higher quality personnel into administrative positions. The problem was not that administrators had abused their trust, but rather that they had not been trusted enough. The way to attract better administrators, Landis argued, was to put even more power in administrative positions, thus demonstrating to the most talented individuals that national administration was a place where they could make a real difference. So Landis advocated further insulating administration from politics, and contended that political interference had harmed the morale of agencies and had even kept good men away from administration entirely. The other way to attract higher quality administrators was to offer higher compensation and longer tenure. Longer tenure would, especially, give administrators "freedom from worry" about political influence.[62] Landis also worried about excessive procedural impediments to agency action. Perhaps more than anything else, regulatory activity had been slowed because agencies were being overly cautious in their procedures. Again, the problem was not too much discretion for agencies, but too little. As Landis observed, "The tendency here is again further to judicialize [*sic*] the administrative process and, in the opinion of many observers, to over-judicialize it to a point where stagnation is likely to set in."[63]

If Landis's faith in the competence and objectivity of administrators was at odds with the founders' sobriety over the self-interestedness of human nature, experience with the poor quality of administration did not

59 Landis, *Report on Regulatory Agencies*, Introduction.
60 Landis, *Report on Regulatory Agencies*, I.A, I.C, Summary.
61 Landis, *Report on Regulatory Agencies*, I.F, II.A.9.
62 Landis, *Report on Regulatory Agencies*, II.B.
63 Landis, *Report on Regulatory Agencies*, I. See also I.A.

lead him to change his mind. When Landis fretted in 1960 that administrators were making decisions out of concern for advancing their careers, or that administrators might be attracted by more money or increased job security, he did not draw the conclusion that these observations might just be evidence that the founders were correct about the self-interestedness of human nature. He wanted, instead, to see administrators take on an even greater role in national governance.

At first glance Landis's faith in the objectivity of administrators, expressed in 1938 and affirmed in 1960, may seem at odds with a subsequent development in 1970s administrative law often referred to as "capture theory." This development refers to a growing sentiment, especially among environmental interest groups, that administrators too frequently became "captured" by the industries and businesses they were supposed to regulate. These interest groups began to turn, in the 1970s, to increasingly receptive federal courts, seeking intervention either against agency inaction or against agency action deemed to be insufficiently vigorous.[64] In one sense, such action by interest groups and courts suggests a lack of confidence in the ability of administrators to do their jobs—not a sentiment one would easily associate with Landis. But it is also the case that Landis's views in 1960 prefigured the sentiments of activists in the 1970s. That is, Landis wanted agencies to do more—to be more active and zealous in regulating. And Landis, too, worried about the "capture" of regulators:

> Industry orientation of agency members is a common criticism, frequently expressed in terms that the regulatees have become the regulators.... The real problem relates to those who are originally oriented towards the public interest but who gradually and honestly begin to view that interest more in terms of the private interest.[65]

Landis and the 1970s activists thus shared a vision about the proper role of administration; both believed that administrators needed to be out front

64 Gary Lawson has an excellent account of this phenomenon, to which my understanding of it is indebted. See Gary Lawson, *Federal Administrative Law*, 2nd edition (St. Paul, MN: West Group, 2001), 245–255. For examples of the kinds of cases which reflect court action in response to "capture theory," see especially: *Citizens to Preserve Overton Park v. Volpe*, 401 U.S. 402 (1971); *Motor Vehicles Manufacturers Association of the U.S. v. State Farm Mutual Automobile Ins.*, 463 U.S. 29 (1983).

65 Landis, *Report on Regulatory Agencies*, II.C.

in acting on behalf of the public good. Both shared, in other words, in the original, New Deal vision for the role of agencies in national governance. Landis did not call, of course, for increasing judicial intervention in order to make administrators fulfill his vision for them; he thought more money, power, and freedom of action would solve the problem. But the basic understanding of the broad role and mission of administration remained relatively consistent throughout the post-New Deal period—no one, in other words, sought to revive the non-delegation doctrine as a means of correcting any problems that were perceived with agencies or those who staffed them.

WOODROW WILSON AND THE ORIGINS OF THE POLITICS-ADMINISTRATION DICHOTOMY

The key principle at work in the development of the administrative state described so far—especially in James Landis's vision for it—is the destruction of separation-of-powers constitutionalism and its replacement by the separation of politics and administration. And while Landis and the New Dealers were responsible for taking this principle and transforming it into reality, it did not originate with them. The idea of separating politics and administration—of grounding a significant portion of government not on the basis of popular consent but on expertise—was introduced into the United States by progressive reformers who had, themselves, learned the principle from German historicism and state theory. In this regard, no one was more important to the origins of the administrative state in America than Woodrow Wilson and Frank Goodnow.

The idea of shielding administration, at least to some degree, from political influence had been around in the United States for some time—at least since the reaction against the nineteenth-century spoils system, in which many jobs in the federal bureaucracy were doled out on the basis of one's affiliation with the party currently in power, as opposed to one's actual merit or skill. While the establishment of the Civil Service Commission, through the Pendleton Act of 1883, marked a significant victory for opponents of the spoils system, it took the progressives, starting with Wilson and Goodnow, to take this rather narrow inclination against the influence of politics in administration and make it part of a thoughtful, comprehensive critique of American constitutionalism and part of a broader argument for political reform. And while the opponents of the spoils system certainly wanted to shield administration from political cronyism, they did not offer a vision of a vastly expanded role for administration; the progressives, by contrast, made such an expansive role a vital cog in their reform argument. As indicated in Chapter One, Wilson introduced the concept of separating politics and administration—of treating administrative governance as an object of study entirely separate from politics—in a series of essays in the latter part of the 1880s. Goodnow expanded upon this Wilsonian concept in the 1890s, and eventually published a book in 1900 titled *Politics and Administration*. Goodnow is often given more credit today for his role in the origins of administrative law, both because his seminal writings on the topic were more voluminous than Wilson's and because administrative law was the field in which Goodnow worked and published for decades. Wilson's administrative writings, by contrast, were but one element of his academic work, and his presidency naturally occupies most of the attention he receives from scholars. But there is very little in Goodnow's understanding of politics and administration, and in his critique of separation-of-powers constitutionalism, that does not build on the principles of Wilson's work from the 1880s, when Wilson was in the early stages of a prolific academic career that would see him in posts at Bryn Mawr College, Wesleyan University, and Princeton (of which he became president) prior to his entry into political life in 1910.

As Landis's writing makes clear, the fundamental assumption behind the vast discretion that new liberals wanted to give to administration was a trust in or optimism about the selflessness, competence, and objectivity of administrators—an outlook that comports comfortably with the progressive view of human nature laid out in the book thus far. If the framers had instituted the separation-of-powers checks on government out of fear of majority faction—fear that the permanent self-interestedness of human nature could make government empowered by democratic majorities a threat to the natural rights of citizens—then the advocates of administrative discretion concluded that such fears, even if well founded in the early days of the republic, no longer applied in the modern era. Thus administration could be freed from the shackles placed upon it by the separation of powers, in order to take on the new tasks that progressives had in mind for the national state. This key assumption behind the separation of politics and administration is exemplified in Wilson's political thought.[66]

We know from Chapter One that Wilson blamed separation-of-powers theory, in particular, for what he believed to be the inflexibility of national government and its inability to handle the tasks required of it by the modern time. He saw the separation of powers as a hindrance because, as Landis would later explain, the modern era values efficiency over anything else. As Wilson claimed in 1885, efficiency had become the preeminent principle in government because history had brought us to an age where the administrative functions of government were most important: "The period of constitution-making is passed now. We have reached a new territory in which we need new guides, the vast territory of *administration*."[67]

Wilson's work on empowering administration with significant discretion to regulate national progress seems to have taken off immediately following his graduate education at Johns Hopkins University. It was at Hopkins that Wilson imbibed deeply in the administrative writings of German authors who belonged to the Hegelian tradition, especially Bluntschli, and where he learned from teachers like Ely, who had studied under Bluntschli at Heidelberg. Wilson's first sustained work on administration came right at this time, in an unpublished essay written in November, 1885, titled "The Art of Governing." This work led to the writing, the following year, of Wilson's seminal essay, "The Study of Administration," where the case for separating politics and administration is made explicitly for the first time in the United States.[68] Wilson

66 For a different point of view—one that suggests important continuities between Wilson's administrative vision and that of the American founders—see Herbert J. Storing, "American Statesmanship: Old and New," in *Toward a More Perfect Union: Writings of Herbert J. Storing*, ed. Joseph M. Bessette (Washington, DC: AEI Press, 1995), 412–14; Paul P. Van Riper, "The American Administrative State: Wilson and the Founders—An Unorthodox View," *Public Administration Review* 43 (November/December 1983): 479–80; and Rohr, "Constitutional World," 43–44. For a more detailed response to these arguments, particularly as they relate to Wilson, see my *Woodrow Wilson and the Roots of Modern Liberalism*, 237–238.

67 Wilson, "The Art of Governing," November 15, 1885, in *PWW*, 5:52. Emphasis original.

68 Some scholars suggest that Wilson did not really urge a strict separation between politics and administration. See Kent A. Kirwan, "The Crisis of Identity in the Study of Public Administration: Woodrow Wilson," *Polity* 9 (Spring 1977): 332; Larry Walker, "Woodrow Wilson, Progressive Reform, and Public Administration," *Political Science Quarterly* 104:3 (1989): 511; John M. Mulder, *Woodrow Wilson: The Years of Preparation* (Princeton: Princeton University Press, 1978), 118; Phillip J. Cooper, "The Wilsonian Dichotomy in Administrative Law," in Rabin and Bowman, eds., *Politics and Administration*, 79-94; Kendrick A. Clements, "Woodrow Wilson and Administrative Reform," *Presidential Studies Quarterly* 28:2 (Spring 1998): 320–336. Cle-

subsequently elaborated on this case in notes he prepared for an annual lectureship at Johns Hopkins from 1888 to 1897. But even prior to entering graduate school, Wilson's views on administration had been taking shape, as evidenced by his 1882 essay "Government By Debate." It was in this essay that Wilson first suggested freeing administration from political influence because large parts of national administration were, he contended, apolitical and based on expertise. Administrative departments, Wilson wrote then, "should be organized in strict accordance with recognized business principles. The greater part of their affairs is altogether outside of politics."[69]

Wilson's thesis in his works on administration was that it was far better and more efficient for a professional class of experts, instead of a multiplicity of politicians with narrow, competing interests, to handle the complex business of the modern state. To the objection that entrusting administrators with such discretion might not comport with the Constitution's distribution of power, Wilson responded that administrative principles and constitutional principles were distinct, and thus constitutional limitations could not easily be applied to the exercise of administrative authority. The constitutional principle of checks and balances, for example, interfered with efficiency and should not be applied to the exercise of administrative power. "Give us administrative elasticity and discretion," he urged: "free us from the idea that checks and balances are to be carried down through all stages of organization."[70] Relying heavily on European models of administrative power, Wilson laid out a vision for administrative discretion that could easily be used as an encapsulation for what Landis would later write in *The Administrative Process*. Wilson wrote, in 1891:

---

ments even suggests that Wilson's previous assertion of a strict separation between politics and administration "was not really what he meant to say" (322).

69 Wilson, "Government By Debate," December 1882, in *PWW*, 2:224. Wilson's precise role as a founder of the modern discipline of "public administration" has been the topic of some debate. For examples of those who see Wilson as the founder of public administration, see Arthur S. Link, "Woodrow Wilson and the Study of Administration," chap. in *The Higher Realism of Woodrow Wilson and Other Essays* (Nashville: Vanderbilt University Press, 1971), 44; Leonard D. White, *Introduction to the Study of Administration* (New York: MacMillan, 1929), 5–9. For examples of those who contest Wilson's status as the founder of public administration, see Lynton K. Caldwell, "Public Administration and the Universities: A Half-Century of Development," *Public Administration Review* 25:1 (1965): 53–58; Daniel W. Martin, "The Fading Legacy of Woodrow Wilson," *Public Administration Review* 48 (March/April 1988): 632–35; Van Riper, "An Unorthodox View," 479.

70 Wilson, "Notes for Lectures at the Johns Hopkins," January 26, 1891, in *PWW*, 7:122.

> The functions of government are in a very real sense independent of legislation, and even constitutions, because [they are] as old as government and inherent in its very nature. The bulk and complex minuteness of our positive law, which covers almost every case that can arise in Administration, obscures for us the fact that *Administration cannot wait upon legislation, but must be given leave, or take it, to proceed without specific warrant in giving effect to the characteristic life of the State.*[71]

Wilson well understood that this wide latitude for administrative action undermined the separation of powers, which he attacked and contrasted with what he called the "actual division of powers," where there are many "legislative and judicial acts of the administration."[72]

As would later be the case with Landis, Wilson's argument for freeing administrators from close political control was grounded in a confidence in the expertness and objectivity of the administrative class. For years Wilson had been urging special education for future administrators at elite universities. He argued that "an intelligent nation cannot be led or ruled save by thoroughly trained and completely-educated men. Only comprehensive information and entire mastery of principles and details can qualify for command." Wilson had faith in the power of expertise, of "special knowledge, and its importance to those who would lead."[73] He later referred to "the patriotism" and "the disinterested ambition" of the new administrative class.[74] Wilson is thus a critical figure for the progressive vision of administration, because he is largely responsible for applying Hegelian optimism about the objectivity of administrators to the American system. Wilson assumed, just as Hegel had in the *Philosophy of Right*, that a secure position in the bureaucracy, with tenure and good pay, would relieve the civil servant of his natural self-interestedness, thereby freeing him of his particularity and allowing him to focus solely on the objective good of society.[75] This is exactly the assumption relied upon by

71 Wilson, "Notes for Lectures at the Johns Hopkins," 7:121. Emphasis added.

72 Wilson, "Notes for Lectures at the Johns Hopkins," 7:134–138.

73 Wilson, "What Can Be Done for Constitutional Liberty," March 21, 1881, in *PWW*, 2:34–36.

74 Wilson, "Notes for Lectures at the Johns Hopkins," in *PWW*, 7:122.

75 See G.W.F. Hegel, *Philosophy of Right*, trans. T.M. Knox (Oxford: Oxford University Press, 1967), 191–92. For criticisms of this assumption of administrators' disinterestedness, see Herbert J. Storing, "Political Parties and the Bureaucracy," in *Toward a More Perfect Union,* 312; Robert D. Miewald, "The Origins of Wilson's Thought: The German Tradition and the Organic State," in Rabin and Bowman, eds., *Politics and Administration*, 18–19, 27.

Landis, both in 1938 and later in 1960, when Landis called explicitly for improving the pay and tenure of bureaucrats in order to improve their public spiritedness.

Wilson's model for this conception of administrators, he freely acknowledged, was almost entirely foreign to American constitutionalism. Yet it was his own notion of the distinction between politics and administration, Wilson argued, that cleared the way for importing what was essentially a Prussian model of administration into the United States. Precisely because administration was to be insulated from politics, an administrative system that had come from a monarchy could be brought to America without harming America's republican political institutions. Chapter One's brief summary of Wilson's memorable argument from the "Study of Administration" is worth elaborating at greater length here:

> It is the distinction, already drawn, between administration and politics which makes the comparative method so safe in the field of administration. When we study the administrative systems of France and Germany, knowing that we are not in search of *political* principles, we need not care a peppercorn for the constitutional or political reasons which Frenchmen or Germans give for their practices when explaining them to us. If I see a murderous fellow sharpening a knife cleverly, I can borrow his way of sharpening the knife without borrowing his probable intention to commit murder with it; and so, if I see a monarchist dyed in the wool managing a public bureau well, I can learn his business methods without changing one of my republican spots.[76]

Or, as Wilson asked elsewhere in the "Study," "Why should we not use such parts of foreign contrivances as we want, if they be in any way serviceable? We are in no danger of using them in a foreign way. We borrowed rice, but we do not eat it with chopsticks."[77] And so Wilson knew that his vision for administration was a novelty in America. In fact, when he later taught administration in the 1890s, he said that there was only one author other than himself who understood administration as a separate discipline: Frank Goodnow.[78]

76 Wilson, "The Study of Administration," November, 1886, in *PWW*, 5:378.
77 Wilson, "Study of Administration," 5:378.
78 Wilson, "Notes for Lectures," in *PWW*, 7:118–120. Wilson's mention of Goodnow came in an 1894 revision he made to these notes.

GOODNOW AND THE DEVELOPMENT OF THE POLITICS–ADMINISTRATION DICHOTOMY

When Wilson identified Goodnow as the only other American of whom he was aware to treat administration as an object of study separate from politics, he was referring to Goodnow's *Comparative Administrative Law*, published in 1893. That book certainly put Goodnow on the map, although his real contributions to the modern understanding of administration's place in the political order came primarily with the publication of *Politics and Administration* in 1900. Two other works—*Social Reform and the Constitution* (1911) and *The American Conception of Liberty and Government* (1916)—later helped to clarify Goodnow's progressive agenda, especially for the courts, and to fill out his views on the fundamental purposes of civil government. Goodnow produced almost all of this work while a professor at Columbia University, where he had been brought by his mentor, John Burgess, to teach political science and law, and where he became the first to teach administrative law in the United States. Prior to teaching at Columbia, Goodnow had spent a year studying in France and Germany; he would go on to finish his career at Johns Hopkins, where he served as president until his retirement in 1929.[79] Although a student of Burgess, Goodnow did not adopt Burgess's political conservatism. Instead, Goodnow looked for ways that American national government could be modified to accommodate progressive policy aims; this goal could best be accomplished, Goodnow believed, by freeing up administration to manage the broad scope of affairs that progressives believed needed government intervention.

The Evolving Ends and Scope of Government

Like Wilson, Goodnow argued that government needed to adjust its very purpose and organization to accommodate modern necessities;[80] and, like Wilson, he believed that history had made obsolete the founders' dedication to protecting individual rights and their consequent

79 Samuel C. Patterson, "Remembering Frank J. Goodnow," *PS* 34:4 (December 2001): 875–81; Charles G. Haines and Marshall E. Dimock, "Introduction" to *Essays on the Law and Practice of Governmental Administration: A Volume in Honor of Frank Johnson Goodnow*, ed. Haines and Dimock (Baltimore: Johns Hopkins Press, 1935), vii–viii.

80 Frank J. Goodnow, *Social Reform and the Constitution* (New York: Macmillan, 1911), 1.

design of a carefully limited form of national government. In *Social Reform and the Constitution*, Goodnow complained about the "reverence" for the Constitution, which he regarded as "superstitious" and an obstacle to genuine political and administrative reform.[81] In *Politics and Administration*, Goodnow made clear that his push for administrative reform was not simply or even primarily aimed at correcting the corruption of the spoils system. Rather, administrative reform was, for Goodnow, instrumental to the end of achieving progressive, big-government liberalism. Progressives had in mind a wide array of new activities in which they wanted national-government involvement; such involvement could not be achieved with the old system of placing administration under political direction:

> Before we can hope that administrative officers can occupy a position reasonably permanent in character and reasonably free from political influence, we must recognize the existence of an administrative function whose discharge must be uninfluenced by political considerations. This England and Germany, and France though to a much less degree, have done. To this fact in large part is due the excellence of their administrative systems. Under such conditions the government may safely be intrusted with much work which, until the people of the United States attain to the same conception, cannot be intrusted to their governmental organs.[82]

Understanding administrative reform this way—as a means to securing the broader aims of progressive liberalism—is what makes the work of Goodnow, and Wilson too, so much more significant to the development of modern American thought and politics than had been the case with the civil-service reformers.

Goodnow and his fellow progressives envisioned an almost entirely new purpose for the national government. Government itself, therefore, had to be viewed through an historical lens. The principles of the original Constitution, Goodnow reasoned, may have been appropriate for the founding era, but now, "under present conditions[,] they are

81 Goodnow, *Social Reform and the Constitution*, 9–10.

82 Goodnow, *Politics and Administration* (New Brunswick, NJ: Transaction, 2003 [orig. pub. 1900]), 86–87.

working harm rather than good."[83] As previously explained, the error of the founders was in failing to see the historical contingency of their principles.[84] The modern situation, Goodnow argued, called for less focus on constitutional principle and form, and much greater focus on empowering and perfecting administration. He even repeated, using almost the same words, Wilson's proclamation from 1885 that the nation had to move from constitutional to administrative questions. Wrote Goodnow: "The great problems of modern public law are almost exclusively administrative in character. While the age that has passed was one of constitutional, the present age is one of administrative reform."[85] In order to address the administrative questions that history was pressing upon the nation, Goodnow urged a focus not on the "formal" governing system (i.e. the rules and procedures of the Constitution) but on the "real" governing system, which becomes whatever is demanded by the necessities of the time.[86]

The focus of original liberalism on government's permanent duty to protect individual rights was an impediment to the marked expansion of governmental power that progressives desired; thus the ideas that animated the original conception of government had to be discredited. As shown in Chapter One, Goodnow understood the political theory of the founding quite well. He knew that the notion that government's primary duty was to protect rights came from the theory of social compact—a theory which progressives took as an obstacle to their aims for the expansion of national government since it led, in their view, to outmoded mechanisms like the separation of powers. The founding-era concern for individual liberty was to blame: "It was the fear of political tyranny through which liberty might be lost which led to the adoption of the theories of checks and balances and of the separation of powers."[87]

Goodnow's critique of the founders' political theory came from the perspective of historical contingency. Their understanding of rights and the role of government, he argued, was based upon pure "speculation,"

83 Goodnow, *Social Reform and the Constitution*, 2.

84 Goodnow, *The American Conception of Liberty and Government* (Providence: Brown University Colver Lectures, 1916), 20.

85 Goodnow, *Comparative Administrative Law*, student edition (New York: Putnam, 1893), iv. See Wilson's similar statement in "The Art of Governing," in *PWW*, 5:52, quoted above.

86 Goodnow, *Politics and Administration*, xxxi, 1–3.

87 Goodnow, *The American Conception of Liberty and Government*, 11.

and "had no historical justification."[88] Here Goodnow employed the same critique as his fellow Hegelian Wilson, who had written in 1889 that the idea of social compact had "no historical foundation."[89] Instead of an understanding of rights grounded in nature, where the individual possesses them prior to the formation of government, Goodnow urged an understanding of rights that are granted by government itself. Recall the remarks quoted in Chapter One, where he reflected favorably upon European trends in understanding rights as contingent upon government: "The rights which [an individual] possesses are, it is believed, conferred upon him, not by his Creator, but rather by the society to which he belongs. What they are is to be determined by the legislative authority in view of the needs of that society. Social expediency, rather than natural right, is thus to determine the sphere of individual freedom of action."[90]

Goodnow found it necessary to critique the theory of natural rights because, he knew, it was the foundation for the requirement of government based upon consent.[91] The principle of government by the consent of the governed was a problem for Goodnow and those with his vision of administrative power. Goodnow's vision required significant deference to expertise. The empowering of administrators, as he saw it, was justified not because the administrators had the consent of the people, but because they were experts in their fields. This is why Goodnow wanted to improve administration not by making it more accountable to politics and to the consent of the governed, but less. He observed and conceded that the doctrines of "sovereignty of the people and of popular participation in the operations of government" were an integral part of American political culture. And he therefore acknowledged that this aspect of the culture would be a difficult hurdle for his vision of administration to overcome. "Our governmental organization developed," he explained, "at a time when expert service could not be obtained, when the expert as we now understand him did not exist."[92]

88 Goodnow, *The American Conception of Liberty and Government*, 9.

89 Wilson, *The State*, 13.

90 Goodnow, *The American Conception of Liberty and Government*, 11.

91 For a good explanation of the foundation of consent in the Declaration of Independence, see Thomas G. West, *The Political Theory of the American Founding: Natural Rights, Public Policy, and the Moral Conditions of Freedom* (Cambridge University Press: 2017), 116–127.

92 Goodnow, *The American Conception of Liberty and Government*, 45. See also 36.

Discretion for Administrators and the Separation of Politics and Administration

Since administrative experts were now available, Goodnow urged that they be employed and empowered with significant discretion to manage the new tasks that progressives had in mind for the national government. In *Politics and Administration*, Goodnow featured chapters on the "Function of Politics" and the "Function of Administration." Both chapters have exactly the same aim: to show that politics ought to be kept out of administration's way. Put differently, the function of politics is to refrain from influencing administration, and the function of administration is to exercise discretion by avoiding the influence of politics. Goodnow's distinction between the roles of politics and administration came from what he believed had been the corrupting influence of politics on national administration. While Goodnow, for example, championed the potential of the party system (as a means of circumventing the separation of powers), he did so only under the condition that party politics be kept entirely out of administration.[93] Administrative decisionmaking, Goodnow argued, was politically neutral and required expertise. Where administration had been "subjected too much to the control of politics in the United States," he claimed, the effect had been the "decreasing of administrative efficiency."[94] Thus the political institutions, Goodnow concluded, ought to concern themselves only with ensuring that administrators remained neutral, and were to be kept out of influencing the *substance* of administrative decisions. He explained: "All that the legislature, or any political body, can do is to see to it, through the exercise of its control, that persons discharging these administrative functions are efficient and impartial. Their general conduct, but not their concrete actions, should be subject to control."[95]

Goodnow was well aware that insulating administration from political control in this way ran up against the traditional, constitutional role for administration, where administrators are subservient to the chief executive. He explained that his conception of administration was novel, considering as it did the sphere of administration to lie outside the

93 Goodnow, *Politics and Administration*, 37.
94 Goodnow, *Politics and Administration*, 43.
95 Goodnow, *Politics and Administration*, 81.

sphere of constitutional law; indeed, this new conception is exactly what Wilson had given Goodnow credit for in 1894. Emphasizing the distinction between the constitutional and administrative spheres, Goodnow remarked that the student of government "is too apt to confine himself to constitutional questions, perhaps not considering at all the administrative system."[96] It is for this reason of considering administration as an object of study outside of the Constitution that Goodnow's landmark book on administrative law—*Comparative Administrative Law*—relies almost entirely upon an account of foreign administrative systems.[97] He knew, as Wilson did, that such a concept was a novelty in the American political tradition. Modern administrative law, therefore, would take it for granted that the political branches of government had to cede significant discretion to administrative agencies; the new body of law would be dedicated to establishing a framework for governing the *extent* and *organization* of this discretion.[98] Chapter Eight will detail the important doctrines that grew out of this new body of law.

Careful readers of Goodnow's work will note that, in making his case for freeing administration from political influence, he did not speak of a strict or rigid separation between politics and administration; indeed, Goodnow noted that the boundary between the two is difficult to define and that there would inevitably be overlap.[99] But this overlap seems to be in one direction only, in a manner that enlarges the orbit of administration; that is, Goodnow seemed to contemplate instances where administrative organs will exercise political functions, but apparently did not contemplate instances of political organs engaging in administrative activity. He characterized the function of politics as "expressing" the will of the state, while the function of administration is to "execute" the will of the state. But he made clear that the overlap between politics and administration would come in the form of administrative agencies taking a share in "expressing" as well as "executing" state will:

> No political organization, based on the general theory of a differentiation of governmental functions, has ever been established which assigns

96 Goodnow, *Politics and Administration*, 5–6.

97 Goodnow, *Comparative Administrative Law*, v.

98 Goodnow, *Comparative Administrative Law*, 1:10–11.

99 See, for example, Goodnow, *Politics and Administration*, 16. For an account of this point, see Patterson, "Remembering Goodnow," 878.

> the functions of expressing the will of the state exclusively to any one of the organs for which it makes provision. Thus, the organ of government whose main function is the execution of the will of the state is often, and indeed usually, intrusted with the expression of that will in its details. These details, however, when expressed, must conform with the general principles laid down by the organ whose main duty is that of expression. That is, the authority called executive has, in almost all cases, considerable ordinance or legislative power.[100]

The notion that Goodnow might see administration as subordinate to politics—as confined only to executing previously expressed will[101]—is hereby called into question. And Goodnow's statement essentially laid the foundation for the abandonment of the non-delegation doctrine. He elaborated: "As a result, either of the provisions of the constitution or of the delegation of the power by the legislature, the chief executive or subordinate executive authorities may, through the issue of ordinances, express the will of the state as to details where it is inconvenient for the legislature to act."[102]

Goodnow shed further light on the role administration might play in "expressing" the will of the state when he categorized the kinds of decisions in which administrative agencies are legitimately involved. When administrators, he explained, make "executive" decisions, they are subordinate to previously expressed will. But in reasoning that would later be adopted by the Supreme Court in the *Humphrey's* case, Goodnow contended that administrators engage not only in "executive" decisions but also those that are quasi-legislative and quasi-judicial. In doing so, administrators not only execute the will of the state, but also play a role in its expression. When merely executing state will, Goodnow explained that it is appropriate for administrators to be subject to the supervision of politics. But when expressing state will in its quasi-legislative or quasi-judicial role, administration requires freedom from political influence. As Goodnow wrote: The "executive function must therefore of necessity be subordinated to the function of politics. No such close connection, however, exists between the function of politics and the other branches of

---

100 Goodnow, *Politics and Administration*, 15.

101 For an example of Goodnow's making such a claim, see *Politics and Administration*, 24.

102 Goodnow, *Politics and Administration*, 17.

the administration of government. No control of a political character can bring it about that administrative officers will discharge better their *quasi-*judicial duties, for example...."[103] In other words, when administrators are merely functioning as executives by following previously expressed will, political accountability can be brought to bear; but it is at the point when they exercise even more power, acting as legislators or judges by aiding the expression of state will, that they must be the most free from political accountability.

Why Trust Administrators?

The key to trusting administrators with the kind of discretion that Goodnow envisioned was his profound faith in the expertness and objectivity of the administrative class—just as it had been for Wilson and would be for Landis. Administrators could be freed from political control because they were "neutral"—their salary and tenure would take care of any self-interested inclinations that might corrupt their decisionmaking, liberating them to focus solely on truth and the good of the public as a whole. As Goodnow explained, "such a force should be free from the influence of politics because of the fact that their mission is the exercise of foresight and discretion, the pursuit of truth, the gathering of information, the maintenance of a strictly impartial attitude toward the individuals with whom they have dealings, and the provision of the most efficient possible administrative organization."[104] A natural objection here would be that freeing administrators from political control is a recipe for corruption—that it is precisely through the electoral connection of public officials that we "make their interest coincide with their duty," as Hamilton puts it in *The Federalist*.[105] But for Goodnow, it is just this connection to electoral politics that would make administrators corrupt, while the absence of accountability to the electorate somehow makes them pure. Politics, Goodnow explained, is "polluted" and full of "bias," whereas administration is all about the "truth."[106]

Goodnow's confidence in the objectivity of administrators, like Wilson's, is a sign of his Hegelianism, and it shows that he accepted

103 Goodnow, *Politics and Administration*, 79.

104 Goodnow, *Politics and Administration*, 85.

105 *Federalist* 72:488.

106 Goodnow, *Politics and Administration*, 82.

Hegel's premise that bureaucrats could be freed of their particularity and will only the objective good of the state. In his introduction to the recent edition of *Politics and Administration*, bureaucracy scholar John A. Rohr even concludes that Goodnow's "Hegelian starting point" doomed his attempt at crafting a realistic administrative reform.[107] Goodnow himself worried, in 1900, that the emphasis in American political culture on popular sovereignty and individual rights would pose a formidable obstacle to the enactment of his vision for administration. The people, given their historical background, might resist deferring to a permanent, administrative class:

> When we take into account on the one hand the environment in which men lived in this country prior to the middle of the nineteenth century, and on the other hand the prevailing political philosophy with its emphasis on individual liberty, and popular sovereignty, and its abhorrence of a permanent governing class, we can well understand the development of the idea which was so commonly held that rotation in office was a cardinal doctrine in American government.[108]

Goodnow also worried that this public hostility to "experts" would make it hard to attract talented individuals into the bureaucracy, although he subsequently consoled himself with the possibility that change was on the horizon. In 1916, Goodnow hoped he was seeing a change in attitude, where the people were becoming less attached to their sovereignty so that experts could be allowed to rule:

> Generally speaking, however, the power of the people to elect directly public officers is diminishing. The change is not, however, as has been pointed out, due to any decrease in the belief in the general theory of popular sovereignty. The people through the referendum and initiative are exercising greater power than ever over the determination of questions of policy. They have, however, in the interest of efficient government, been willing to surrender powers of choosing public officers which they at one time regarded with great jealousy.[109]

---

107 John A. Rohr, "Introduction" to Goodnow, *Politics and Administration*, xxviii–xxix.

108 Goodnow, *Politics and Administration*, 46.

109 Goodnow, *The American Conception of Liberty and Government*, 62.

Goodnow's New Categories of State Power

Goodnow's vision for administrative governance is grounded in a set of categories he employs to describe the different types of state power. Contrary to the American separation-of-powers framework, which divides power into three categories, Goodnow's framework contains only two. When the state exercises power, Goodnow argued in *Politics and Administration*, it does it either by "expressing" will or by "executing" will that has previously been expressed.[110] This is an elaboration of an expression that Goodnow had employed in his first book, *Comparative Administrative Law*, where he referred to the "expression of the will of the state."[111] The distinction between "expressing" and "executing" translates directly into Goodnow's distinction between "politics" and "administration"—the very distinction at the heart of the administrative state today. As he explained, "There are, then, in all governmental systems two primary or ultimate functions of government, viz. the expression of the will of the state and the execution of that will. There are also in all states separate organs, each of which is mainly busied with the discharge of one of these functions. These functions are, respectively, Politics and Administration."[112] As had been the case with Wilson's "Study of Administration," Goodnow emphasized the separation between politics and administration in order to pave the way for importing a foreign administrative science into the American system of government. Since administration, under this scheme, is not involved in politics—since it is only involved in "executing" previously expressed will—Goodnow saw no danger in adopting a monarchic system of bureaucracy in a democratic regime. As previously discussed, however, Goodnow did not always talk so strictly or rigidly about the separation between politics and administration, and acknowledged that there are many instances where administration will have a role in "expressing" as well as "executing" state will.

110 Goodnow, *Politics and Administration*, 9. Goodnow thus relies on a division of power which, at least at the surface, comports more with Locke's division (between legislative and executive) than with Montesquieu's (between legislative, executive, and judicial). Rohr cites this connection to Locke for the purpose of arguing that Goodnow is not completely "out of touch with American political thought" (Rohr, *To Run a Constitution*, 88). But this is only a superficial connection to Locke, as the purpose of Locke's separation is to protect individual rights from the arbitrary exercise of state power, whereas the purpose of Goodnow's is to provide the most efficient mechanism for the delivery of state power.

111 Goodnow, *Comparative Administrative Law*, 2:106.

112 Goodnow, *Politics and Administration*, 22.

Within that part of the state responsible for "executing" will, Goodnow made a further division into three parts. It is this division of the executive that is central to his argument for the independence of administration and that represents the most unique part of his overall argument for reform. The three elements of the executive are: 1) the judiciary; 2) the administrative agencies; 3) what would traditionally be called the constitutional executive—the president, state governors, etc.[113] What most immediately stands out here, of course, is the inclusion of the judiciary within the executive. Goodnow explained that the founders had erred in following Montesquieu's placing of the judiciary as its own independent branch of government. Judges, Goodnow reasoned, were essentially involved in the *execution* of previously expressed will or law, just like the other elements of the executive.[114] In addition to the inclusion of the judiciary within the executive, it is also worth noting the distinction that Goodnow made between the president and the administrative agencies; whereas the Constitution would have to consider agencies simply as an extension of the presidency (the president being vested with all of "the executive power"), Goodnow clearly separated agencies from the political office of president.

Goodnow's conception of the executive is also unique in that it considers both courts and agencies to be part of administration. The executive, he explained, involves both the "administration of justice" (by the courts) and "administration of government" (by agencies). And within the "administration of government," agencies can perform different functions; some of these are purely executive, but others take on more of a judicial or even legislative character.[115] What matters most is that neither kind of administration—that done by the courts nor that done by agencies—is confined to the mere execution of previously expressed will. These traditionally administrative elements commonly cross over into the realm of politics, helping to express as well as execute the will of the state. This is true of courts in particular, since they interpret both the law and the Constitution itself.[116]

Goodnow emphasized the independence from political influence that American courts had traditionally enjoyed. But whereas the original

113 Goodnow, *Politics and Administration*, 17.

114 Goodnow, *Politics and Administration*, 11–13.

115 Goodnow, *Politics and Administration*, 72–73.

116 Goodnow, *Politics and Administration*, 36.

idea behind this independence had been the securing of individual rights,[117] for Goodnow it serves as a vehicle for granting vast discretion to administration. The key is Goodnow's placing of the courts and agencies alongside one another in the realm of administration. Since the courts had traditionally enjoyed independence from politics, and since agencies are partners with the courts in the realm of administration, then agencies (like courts) ought to enjoy independence from political control. Administration—whether it be "administration of justice" in the courts, or "administration of government" in the bureaucracy—is politically neutral and ought not be influenced by the vicissitudes of elections, even though, as Goodnow himself made clear, administration must necessarily involve itself in not only executing but in giving expression to the will of the state.[118] As Rohr puts it, "by assimilating administrators to judges whom he includes within the concept of executive and excluding constitutional executives from administration, Goodnow neatly carves a niche for the administrator to exercise legitimately a certain degree of independence."[119] Put another way, Goodnow tapped into a traditional feature of American constitutionalism—the relative independence of the judiciary—to argue for something quite untraditional—the independence of administration from political control.

Goodnow's employment of independent courts to secure a similar independence for administrative agencies is useful in placing in its proper perspective the "capture" phenomenon of the modern administrative state. As previously explained, much of modern administrative law consists of fights between agencies and judges, who are spurred on by interest groups to intervene in agency decisionmaking out of a belief that agencies are too lenient on regulated entities. From one point of view, such a phenomenon demonstrates that agencies no longer have the discretion that they once enjoyed. But understood from Goodnow's perspective, such wrangling between courts and agencies would be largely inconsequential, or merely at the level of an intra-family squabble, since both courts and agencies are considered by Goodnow to be part of administration. What mattered for Goodnow is not whether courts or agencies have the upper hand, but rather that both of them, as part of administration, are

117 See *Federalist* 78:522–24, where Hamilton explains that the federal courts required independence from politics because of the necessity to safeguard individual liberty.

118 Goodnow, *Politics and Administration*, 39–42, 45–46, 78.

119 Rohr, "Introduction," xxvii.

independent of politics. And this is the important point for those of us who are interested in the fate of traditional constitutionalism in today's administrative state: it ought to matter less exactly which unelected entity is most influential in policymaking (agencies or courts), and ought to matter more that such power has been delegated in the first place by the elected branches of government.

CONCLUSION

Today's administrative state is built on the death of the non-delegation doctrine. It is on the basis of abandoning non-delegation that administration can be separated from politics—that administrators can act, in other words, with discretion as they employ their expertise free from political influence. Constitutional and administrative law today really do not concern themselves with whether or not administrative agencies can have such discretion delegated to them, or whether or not they may exercise legislative and judicial powers in addition to their executive powers. Instead, the law assumes these things to be entirely legitimate, and concerns itself with the questions of how, and to what extent, such discretion can be exercised. Thus the entire enterprise of the modern administrative state owes its existence to the abandonment of separation of powers as an operative constitutional principle, and its replacement by a system separating politics and administration. While such a separation was relied upon by the likes of Landis to build up the administrative state, it originated in the Progressive Era, in the work of Wilson and Goodnow.

Goodnow seems to have built on Wilson's basic principles, and made a very significant contribution by his unique argument on the role of the courts. In particular, Goodnow's use of judicial independence to make the case for administrative independence was unprecedented in progressive thought. And it is why we have in Goodnow's thought the two pillars of today's liberal state: unelected judges who make law through constitutional interpretation, and unelected bureaucrats to whom significant policymaking power is delegated on the basis of their expertise.

Modern administrative law largely focuses on sorting out power between judges and agency administrators. Understanding how that plays out goes a long way towards grasping how policy is really made today in American government. And it rests on a set of critical legal doctrines that have been established in the judiciary since the New Deal. Those doctrines are tied to progressive principles in important ways, as the next chapter will show.

CHAPTER EIGHT

★

PROGRESSIVISM AND THE LAW IN TODAY'S ADMINISTRATIVE STATE

The preceding chapter traced the origins of today's administrative state to the progressive thought of Woodrow Wilson, Frank Goodnow, and James Landis, emphasizing the principle of separating administration from politics as the administrative state took shape over the course of the twentieth century. Here we examine how the progressive principles of the administrative state continue their influence on American government today, particularly in its legal doctrines. A brief consideration of politics and the policymaking process in America today will show that the administrative state is more impactful than ever, and that it may well be the most significant legacy of the progressive movement.

Begin with the fact that Congress—the institution assigned by the Constitution with the task of making policy—has become increasingly paralyzed due to the ideological polarization in the country. In its place, the agencies of the administrative state have increasingly been relied upon to step into the void. This state of affairs is evident in most of the major policy debates of the day, where the disputes often center around decisions made by the executive, usually through an administrative agency. On the environment, for example, while Congress has not enacted any significant legislation since the amendments to the Clean Air Act in

1990, the Environmental Protection Agency (EPA) has been aggressive in its regulatory activity on greenhouse gas emissions. Major legislation was defeated in Congress in 2009, but the EPA has been busy since that point with a series of major rulemakings pertaining to greenhouse gases. Policy on immigration and citizenship has been made in like manner: while Congress has been largely inactive, the executive—through the Department of Justice (DOJ)—has been the originator of several major immigration policy initiatives. In the Obama administration, the DOJ granted legal status to immigrants under policy initiatives like "DACA," whereby the children of those who immigrated illegally into the United States were extended status and benefits in the absence of any overt legislative warrant. And the Trump administration has been equally active, though in the other direction, as its DOJ has launched major initiatives restricting travel from foreign nationals as well as asylum applications. In the arena of healthcare, while Congress itself enacted the Affordable Care Act in 2010, most of the actual policymaking has come from the administrative agencies tasked with the law's implementation, since the law itself is extremely vague. It was the Department of Health and Human Services (HHS), for example, that made the policy requiring insurance plans to cover contraceptives, which has become one of the most controversial issues in healthcare policy today. And, as a final example, consider recent attempts to extend federal regulation over the internet: "net-neutrality" legislation was considered by Congress for years without coming close to enactment, until the Federal Communications Commission (FCC) under President Obama took matters into its own hands and enacted the policy through the regulatory process—a policy that was later rescinded by the FCC under the Trump administration.

In addition to the lead role taken by administrative agencies in the promulgation of all of these policies, they have something else in common: all of them have gone on to be the subject of extensive litigation in the federal courts, which is where the fate of such policies is often settled. The favored strategy of opponents has been to litigate as opposed to legislate. This choice was particularly evident during the Obama administration, where the opposition party controlled at least one house of Congress for the majority of the president's tenure. But instead of taking the more straightforward approach of opposing the administration's policymaking ventures through its own legislative activity—especially by using the power of the purse—Congress frequently took the president to court. Opponents of President Trump's policies have done likewise. And as the major policy disputes in the country have thus played out in its courtrooms, increasing attention has naturally been paid to the legal issues pertinent to administrative policymaking, and especially to the constitutional questions that go to the heart of the administrative state. Opponents of administrative action have raised important constitutional objections that had been thought, for a long time, to be settled law. And in addition to constitutional law, administrative law is now drawing increased public attention. As courts are more frequently asked to consider the statutory and constitutional limits on administrative policymaking, more scrutiny is being paid to the major doctrines that courts have developed to govern these questions since the origins of the administrative state in the 1930s. Obscure questions previously of concern only to a narrow band of legal scholars—"*Chevron* deference" or the meaning of the Administrative Procedure Act (APA), for example—have now become part of the public discourse. Scholarship on administrative law—both skeptical[1] and supportive[2]—has correspondingly been on the rise.

LEGAL ACCOMMODATION FOR ADMINISTRATIVE DISCRETION

As we learned in Chapter Seven, administrative agencies came to occupy a position of significant policymaking authority due to the embrace of progressive principles by the New Deal architects of the administrative state, and due to the accommodation of the administrative state's novel legal structure by federal courts. This legal accommodation proceeded in two arenas: *constitutional law*, where formalism gave way to functionalism, and *administrative law*, which originated in the twentieth century to govern what judicial supervision remained of administrative agencies. With respect to the constitutional accommodation, which was detailed in Chapter Seven, we will only recall here that the administrative state was

1 Philip Hamburger, *Is Administrative Law Unlawful?* (University of Chicago Press, 2014); Joseph Postell, *Bureaucracy in America: The Administrative State's Challenge to Constitutional Government* (University of Missouri Press, 2017).

2 Gillian Metzger, "1930s Redux: The Administrative State Under Siege," in *Harvard Law Review* 131 (2017): 1–95; Jerry Mashaw, *Creating the Administrative Constitution: The Lost One Hundred Years of American Administrative Law* (Harvard University Press, 2012).

built on three main pillars, each of which clashes with core constitutional principles.

The first pillar was the congressional delegation of discretionary and regulatory power to the executive—especially to an enlarged national administrative apparatus which, it was contended, would operate under the advantages inherent in expertise and specialization. The second pillar was the combination of powers—legislative, executive, and judicial—into single entities within the administrative apparatus, thus benefitting from the efficiency of centralizing all core agency functions in the same set of hands. The third pillar was the insulation of administrators from political control. For the progressive fathers of the administrative state, its legitimacy stemmed not from consent but from science. This is why the Constitution's unitary executive, where the president exercises all of the executive power because he is the lone executive officer accountable to voters, needed to be transformed by the independence of administrative agencies.

By the late 1930s, federal courts had given way on all three of these pillars. The Supreme Court ceased applying the non-delegation principle after 1936,[3] and allowed to stand a whole body of statutes whereby Congress delegates significant discretionary power to executive agencies. Single federal agencies are also now regularly permitted to exercise all three powers of government—legislative, executive, and judicial. And the courts have permitted the weakening of the political accountability of administrators and the shielding of a large subset of agencies from most political controls. The most common way this shielding is accomplished is by statutes that limit the president's freedom to remove agency personnel.

Having recalled how the *constitutional* restraints on the national administrative state were eroded, we turn our attention here to the manner in which federal courts came to rely on a growing body of *administrative* law to govern the scope of national administrative power. This body of law is grounded in the APA of 1946 and the precedents that have been established as courts have applied that law (along with the specific, "organic" statutes that give life to individual agencies) during the growth of the administrative state over the last seventy-five years. Initially intended to rein in national administrative power after the

3 *Carter v. Carter Coal Co.*, 298 U.S. 238 (1936).

courts had loosened the constitutional restraints on it in the 1930s, the manner in which the APA has been interpreted has led, for the most part, to even greater discretion for national bureaucracies in both procedure and substance.

On *procedural* questions, the APA was thought to be a check on the discretion of agencies by means of the many trial-like steps it lays out for formal agency rulemaking and adjudication. Affected parties are given, in these steps, significant rights to participate in the decision-making process and to present their own evidence and cross-examine witnesses, among other things. However, in several landmark cases from the 1970s, the Supreme Court greatly narrowed the category of administrative actions to which these formal procedures apply. In the case of *United States v. Florida East Coast Railway* from 1973, the Court construed the triggering language for formal procedures so narrowly as to virtually eliminate formal rulemaking as a viable category of administrative law.[4] And in 1978, the Court strictly limited the procedural restraints that could be imposed on agencies engaged in informal rulemaking in the case of *Vermont Yankee v. Natural Resources Defense Council*, thereby reducing the ability of affected parties to challenge agency decision-making in independent, Article III federal courts.[5]

As these precedents have developed on the *procedural* side, judicial deference to national administrative power on *substantive* questions has come to be even greater, though this is a somewhat more recent development. In one respect, such deference seems perfectly consistent with the basic tenets of the administrative state: national bureaucracies were created because the national government was taking on many of the police powers that had previously been handled at the state and local level, and it needed the expertise of administrative agencies to accomplish the task. The federal courts concluded, not unreasonably, that the administrators in the bureaucracy were the experts on the substance of the policies that they had been created to implement, and that judges should not substitute their own, amateur understanding of policy for substantive decisions made by national administrators.

4 *United States v. Florida East Coast Railway Co.*, 410 U.S. 224 (1973).

5 *Vermont Yankee Nuclear Power Corp. v. Natural Resources Defense Council*, 435 U.S. 519 (1978). This isn't to suggest that the rulemaking process is now straightforward—far from it. But agencies—as well as those affected parties with deep resources—have figured out how to manage the process, and the overall historical trend has been to loosen restrictions on agency action.

Courts thus adopted a sharply deferential posture to the substance of agency decision-making.

The difficulty with this principle, however, comes in the fact that much of the substance of what agencies do involves interpreting the laws they are charged with implementing; and interpretation of law is supposed to be the province of the independent judiciary. The Clean Air Act, for example, places certain requirements for expensive pollution-control equipment on "stationary sources" of pollution; but the Act does not define "stationary source." Does a single factory—which may contain a number of different emitting devices—constitute a single "stationary source," or is each discrete emitting device within a single factory its own "stationary source," thus requiring the factory to make a potentially crippling investment in a multitude of diverse control devices? This seems like an obscure question (as administrative cases often are), but it had major economic consequences, affecting the profitability of an entire industry and the jobs of many workers. And since Congress did not clearly address this question in the legislation, did it intend for agency to step in and, effectively, make the law on the question? How much latitude do agencies get to fill in the gaps left by legislation, much of which, in our time, has become broad and vague?

In the question posed by the example, which was at issue in the 1984 case of *Chevron v. Natural Resources Defense Council*, the Supreme Court concluded that gaps in the law are to be filled in by the agency charged with its implementation—that when Congress does not directly address a question in the statute, that lack of clarity is *in itself* a kind of express intent that the agency should have the power to do so, and that courts reviewing agency action are to grant significant deference to the agency's interpretation of the law.[6] That conclusion established what is known as the "*Chevron* Doctrine," which has become the most important principle in American administrative law. With it, we have gone from the old, constitutional understanding—that for executive agencies to implement policy the legislature must first enact law giving them warrant to do so—to the understanding of national administration today—that when Congress *fails* to enact a policy, that failure or void can itself be understood as a warrant for national administrators to make policy on the basis of their own expertise. Much of contemporary administrative

6 *Chevron U.S.A., Inc. v. Natural Resources Defense Council, Inc.*, 467 U.S. 837 (1984).

law—and, thus, much of our understanding of the power of the administrative state today—comes from court decisions applying the Chevron Doctrine to a wide variety of administrative action. It is unsurprising that critics of discretionary policymaking by agencies point to *Chevron* as a principal target for reform, along with its companion doctrine from *Auer v. Robbins* establishing judicial deference when agencies interpret their own regulations.[7]

RECONSIDERING PROGRESSIVE ACHIEVEMENTS?

The legal accommodation to the rise of the administrative state was a principal feature in the story of the American judiciary for the bulk of the twentieth century. Yet there is at least a question today of whether or not these progressive gains may be undergoing some reconsideration. The best evidence for this lies in the increasingly fierce battles over nominations to federal courts, and to the Supreme Court in particular. As constitutional originalists have gradually taken positions on the federal courts since the 1980s, today's progressives have intensified their efforts to preserve the legal achievements of the last eighty years. In part the aim is to preserve the major precedents on social issues, where courts have handed progressives major victories on questions that always seem to lie at the heart of confirmation battles, such as abortion and homosexual marriage. But in addition to closing ranks on these social issues, progressives have become increasingly alarmed at what originalist jurists might do to their gains in establishing and growing the administrative state. As detailed at the outset of this chapter, the administrative state has become the principal vehicle for making progressive policy today. The fight-to-the-death character of recent confirmation battles seems to be due, in part, to some evidence that the Supreme Court, in particular, may be taking a second look at its functionalist accommodation of the administrative state. In small ways, this reconsideration began in the 1970s, but has lately become more serious. We will first consider the major constitutional challenges that have arisen to the administrative state—those pertaining to appointment and removal of agency personnel, as well as the potential revisiting of the non-delegation doctrine—followed by challenges in the arena of administrative law.

7 *Auer v. Robbins*, 519 U.S. 452 (1997).

Appointment and Removal

Presidential control over personnel in the executive branch was considered by the Constitution's framers to be a critical means of ensuring that national administration remained consistent with the regime's republican character. Since the president is the only elected official in the executive branch, a "unitary executive" was essential to holding administrators accountable to the people, even if indirectly.[8] Unitary control over administration comes in the president's ability to appoint and remove the most important agency personnel. First consider the appointment power—a critical question for the viability of the administrative state today—where the Constitution specifies that employees who are "officers of the United States" must be appointed under the methods of the Constitution's appointments clause. Defenders of the administrative state have sought to remove as many administrators as possible from the umbrella of the appointments clause, as the need to undergo the constitutional process of appointment creates a burden in staffing and empowering administrative agencies. So the question is, who exactly, among agency personnel, are "officers" requiring the constitutional method of appointment?

An early, but slight, blow was struck against the administrative state on this question with the Supreme Court's 1976 decision in *Buckley v. Valeo*.[9] In its attempt to shield an agency—in this case, the Federal Elections Commission (FEC)—from the influence of the president, Congress had devised a rather odd method of appointing commissioners,[10] which led to the Court's striking down part of the statute on separation-of-powers

---

8 See the defense of a unitary executive in Publius, *The Federalist*, ed. George W. Carey and James McClellan (Indianapolis: Liberty Fund, 2001), No. 70: 363-69. The extent of the president's removal power was not fully settled at the constitutional convention, and the Constitution itself is explicit about appointment but not about removal. There was a major debate about the issue in the First Congress, where the principle of the unitary executive was relied upon by James Madison and others in adopting the option of sole presidential removal in the legislation creating the first executive departments. For the best account of this debate, see Charles C. Thach, Jr., *The Creation of the Presidency, 1775–1789* (Johns Hopkins Press, 1969), 140–65. Moreover, respecting the characterization of the president as the only elected executive officer, it is noted that the Vice President is also an elected officer, but his election is tied to the president's, and the only constitutional powers exercised by the Vice President are actually legislative, in his capacity as President of the Senate.

9 *Buckley v. Valeo*, 424 U.S. 1 (1976).

10 The 1974 amendments to the Federal Election Campaign Act of 1971 directed that the six voting members of the Commission be appointed in the following manner: two appointments each by the President, the Speaker of the House of Representatives, and the President Pro Tempore of the Senate.

grounds—the first time it had done so since the 1930s. *Buckley* held that FEC commissioners were indeed "officers," and that they therefore needed to be appointed in accord with the forms of the Constitution.[11] The statute in this case failed to do that. Yet *Buckley* was very much an outlier, as courts in subsequent cases typically took great pains to find that agency personnel did not rise to the level of exercising "significant authority," which was the bar set by *Buckley* to trigger the Constitution's appointment process for "officers."

In its 2018 term, however, in the case of *Lucia v. SEC*, the Supreme Court seriously undercut this functionalist reading of *Buckley* and the appointments clause, finding that Administrative Law Judges (ALJs) are indeed "officers," and thus require the constitutional mode of appointment.[12] ALJs are a staple of the administrative state, exercising considerable power in many agencies, even though—prior to the *Lucia* decision—their appointment was deemed to be outside the bounds of the Constitution's prescribed methods for "officers." The *Lucia* case is especially significant in that it arose from a controversy under the Dodd-Frank financial-regulation law, which is the model law for advocates of an independent administrative state.

The removal power over agency personnel raises similar issues, as the aim for advocates of the administrative state is to shield agency personnel, as much as possible, from presidential control. The landmark case on this question is *Humphrey's Executor v. United States*, from 1935—a case, as detailed in Chapter Seven, greatly responsible for enabling the administrative state by allowing Congress to create agencies in the executive branch but to insulate them from presidential control.[13] The Supreme Court later expanded on this precedent in the *Morrison v. Olson* case from 1988, where it permitted even a federal prosecutor—as pure an executive official as one can find—to be shielded from presidential control.[14]

But the Court has since started retreating from its constitutional revisionism in removal-power cases. The first significant step in this direction came in 2010, when it ruled against a new agency created by the Sarbanes-Oxley law: the Public Company Accounting Oversight Board (PCAOB). The Board answers to the Securities and Exchange Commission (SEC),

11 *Buckley v. Valeo*, 424 U.S. 1 (1976), at 109–43.

12 *Lucia v. SEC*, No. 17-130, slip op. at 12 (U.S. June 21, 2018).

13 *Humphrey's Executor v. United States*, 295 U.S. 602 (1935).

14 *Morrison v. Olson*, 487 U.S. 654 (1988).

and is appointed by the SEC, but its members may not be removed at will. This arrangement effectively sets up a double-layer of insulation from presidential control: the SEC cannot remove Board members at will, and the President cannot remove SEC commissioners at will. This is too little control for the president, the Supreme Court concluded in the case of *Free Enterprise Fund v. PCAOB*, decided in 2010.[15]

In this case, and also in the *Lucia* case, the Court claimed it was doing nothing radical, and that it was keeping within its post-1930s functionalist precedents. That is technically true, but the momentum had clearly shifted—a shift that did not go unnoticed by defenders of the administrative state like Justice Stephen Breyer. In his dissent in the *PCAOB* case, Breyer pointed out that if the Court now objects to shielding agencies from presidential control, the implications for the administrative state could be profound.[16] And the Court does indeed seem to be attempting to walk the tightrope of returning toward constitutional formalism while also pretending to be faithful to precedent like *Humphrey's* or *Morrison*. The most obvious indication of this phenomenon came in the Court's blow, at the end of the 2020 term, against the Consumer Financial Protection Bureau (CFPB).

The CFPB is the crown jewel of the Dodd-Frank law, with a constitutionally questionable structure, even as administrative agencies go: a single administrator, not removable by the president, whose funds are not subject to annual congressional appropriations. In *Seila Law v. CFPB*, the Supreme Court struck down a major piece of the agency's structure on removal-power grounds, holding that the insulation of the agency administrator from presidential control violated the Constitution's separation-of-powers doctrine.[17] The Court's controlling opinion in the case employed reasoning similar to a panel of the United States Court of Appeals for the DC Circuit in *PHH v. CFPB*, in an opinion authored by then-judge Brett Kavanaugh in 2017.[18] While that panel's judgment was subsequently reversed in 2018 by the full circuit sitting *en banc*,[19] it did not take long after Kavanaugh's ascension to the Supreme Court for his originalist reasoning on the CFPB to become the law of the land.

---

15 *Free Enterprise Fund v. Public Company Accounting Oversight Board*, 561 U.S. 477 (2010).

16 *Free Enterprise Fund v. PCAOB*, 561 U.S. 477 (2010) (Breyer, J., dissenting), at 514.

17 *Seila Law v. Consumer Financial Protection Bureau*, No. 19-7, slip op. (U.S. June 29, 2020).

18 *PHH Corporation v. Consumer Financial Protection Bureau*, No. 15-1177 (D.C. Cir. Feb. 16, 2017).

19 *PHH Corp. v. CFPB*, No. 15-1177 (D.C. Cir. Jan. 31, 2018).

And while the Court employed its severability doctrine in declining to invalidate the entire agency,[20] its insistence that the agency's administrator be subject to ordinary presidential control was a clear rejection of the progressive vision for separating administration from politics.

Delegation

While courts have entertained constitutional challenges to the administrative state on appointment and removal-power grounds, until very recently there has been no indication that any reconsideration of the administrative state's structure might be underway with respect to its first main pillar: delegation. Without the ability of Congress to enact broad directives and to delegate to administrative agencies the power to legislate specific rules under these directives, the administrative state as we know it could not exist. As mentioned above, courts made this accommodation in the 1930s, and have swatted back subsequent attempts to revive the doctrine of non-delegation. A major example of this unwillingness to revisit the delegation question came in 1989 with the Supreme Court's decision in *Mistretta v. United States*.[21] As explained in Chapter Seven, this case featured a constitutional challenge to the U.S. Sentencing Commission on non-delegation grounds, where challengers pointed out that Congress had, in the Sentencing Commission, effectively created a second legislature to exercise purely Article I powers; its only duties were legislative in nature—to come up with criminal penalties for a variety of federal crimes as part of the federal government's move from indeterminate to determinate sentencing. The Court's accommodation of the administrative state and abandonment of non-delegation was confirmed in direct language: "Our jurisprudence has been driven by a practical understanding that in our increasingly complex society, replete with ever changing and more technical problems, Congress simply cannot do its job absent an ability to delegate power."[22]

If the U.S. Sentencing Commission was able to survive a non-delegation challenge, it was difficult to imagine what administrative entity could not. But the 1989 Supreme Court was populated by, at most, one or two originalists. The present makeup of the Court is decidedly

---

20 *Seila Law v. CFPB*, No. 19-7, slip op. at 35-42 (U.S. June 29, 2020).

21 *Mistretta v. United States*, 488 U.S. 361 (1989).

22 *Mistretta v. United States*, 488 U.S. 361 (1989), at 372.

different, of which there could be no clearer indication than the bomb that was figuratively dropped in the *Gundy v. United States* case from the term ending in 2019. On the surface the case is unremarkable, since it continued the practice of upholding congressional delegations of legislative authority to administrative entities. Specifically, in the 2006 Sex Offender Registration and Notification Act (SORNA), Congress had delegated to the Attorney General the authority to make rules concerning the applicability of registration requirements to pre-Act offenders, and the Court upheld the constitutionality of the delegation. But the opinion of the Court was only signed by a plurality of four justices, who were the only four to affirm the Court's decades-long accommodation of delegation to administrative agencies.[23] In dissent, three justices took direct aim at the constitutionality of delegation, contending that the principles of the Constitution require the Court to revisit its long-ago abandonment of the non-delegation principle. Writing for the dissenters, Justice Gorsuch calls the SORNA delegation an "extraconstitutional arrangement" where Congress was attempting to "endow the nation's chief prosecutor with the power to write his own criminal code."[24] And he extends the logic of his criticism to the manner in which Congress undertakes much of its legislative work today: "The Framers understood... that it would frustrate 'the system of government ordained by the Constitution' if Congress could merely announce vague aspirations and then assign others the responsibility of adopting legislation to realize its goals."[25] This is exactly how Congress prefers to operate today—as Justice Kagan herself recognizes in her opinion for the Court: "if SORNA's delegation is unconstitutional, then most of Government is unconstitutional."[26] While it would be more accurate to say that if SORNA's delegation is unconstitutional, then much of the *administrative state's rulemaking power* is unconstitutional, Justice Kagan's comment nonetheless captures the threat to the administrative state posed by the reasoning of the dissenters. Their reasoning is relevant in this case because a fourth justice with originalist leanings—Justice Alito—concurred in the Court's judgment but indicated sympathy with the dissent's desire to revive the non-delegation principle. The case was

23 *Gundy v. United States*, No. 17-6086, slip op. (U.S. June 20, 2019).

24 *Gundy v. United States*, No. 17-6086, slip op. at 1 (U.S. June 20, 2019) (Gorsuch, J., dissenting).

25 *Gundy v. United States*, No. 17-6086, slip op. at 5 (U.S. June 20, 2019) (Gorsuch, J., dissenting).

26 *Gundy v. United States*, No. 17-6086, slip op. at 17 (U.S. June 20, 2019).

heard by only eight of the justices, and Justice Alito noted that there were not, among the eight, enough votes to revisit the Court's delegation jurisprudence—even if, presumably, he were one of those in favor of revisiting it. His separate opinion concurring only in the Court's judgment leaves little room for doubt where he might come down should a fifth vote materialize in favor of reviving non-delegation: "If a majority of this Court were willing to reconsider the approach we have taken for the past 84 years, I would support that effort."[27] The significance of Justice Kavanaugh's ascension to the Court, just a few months after *Gundy* was handed down, was lost on no one, as his originalism in separation-of-powers cases had been well established during his tenure on the Court of Appeals. And Justice Kavanaugh himself underscored the point by going out of his way to make an unusual separate statement on an otherwise unsigned order in the case of *Paul v. United States* during his first term. This statement praised the Gorsuch dissent in *Gundy* and noted that it "may warrant further consideration in future cases."[28]

Deference

As the main *constitutional* pillars of the administrative state—delegation and freedom from presidential removal—have lately drawn scrutiny, there have also been important developments with the major deference doctrines of *administrative law*. These are doctrines, as explained above, that limit a court's freedom to undertake *de novo* review of agency interpretations of statutes and of their own regulations. Without such deference—especially *Chevron* deference to agency statutory interpretation—the discretionary rulemaking power of the administrative state would be substantially curtailed. *Chevron* has been controversial since it was first decided in 1984, underscored by the fact that even the Supreme Court at the time could not quite agree on what it had done.[29] And since

27 *Gundy v. United States*, No. 17-6086, slip op. at 1 (U.S. June 20, 2019) (Alito, J., concurring).

28 *Paul v. United States*, No. 17-8830, slip op. at 1 (U.S. November 25, 2019) (Statement of Kavanaugh, J., respecting the denial of certiorari). The vacancy on the Court created by the death of Justice Ginsburg as this book was coming to press serves to underscore the point, as it seems likely that the vacancy will have been filled with a jurist of more originalist leanings by the time the book is released.

29 *Immigration and Naturalization Service v. Cardoza-Fonseca*, 480 U.S. 421 (1987), at 423; Stevens's view of the meaning of the *Chevron* doctrine would seem to be particularly relevant, since he was the author of the Court's opinion in *Chevron*.

then its applicability has been limited in a variety of ways; in more recent cases, those limitations have become more evident and more robust. A brief review of the basics of the so-called "*Chevron* Test" will allow us to see how this is the case.

The basic holding of *Chevron* is that when the meaning of a statute is unclear, courts are to defer to any reasonable interpretation made by the agency, and are not to engage in their own *de novo* interpretation of the statute. This formulation gives rise to a two-step test, where courts reviewing agency interpretations first determine if a statute is clear, or if Congress has left a gap for the agency to fill. If the statute is clear, the analysis stops, and the reviewing court goes with the clear meaning of the statute, giving no deference to the agency. If the statute is unclear, the next step is for the court to defer to the agency's interpretation of it, as long as it is not unreasonable. Considered straightforwardly, this approach grants very considerable power to agencies, since it is not unusual for statutes to be vague. But limits to *Chevron* are increasing, as are direct assaults on its fundamental reasoning.

First, courts have limited the kinds of agency action to which the *Chevron* methodology applies. Within a couple of decades after *Chevron*, the Supreme Court had made clear that its deference doctrine was only to be applied in instances of major agency action where Congress intended such action to have the "force of law," thus excluding from deference common kinds of agency actions like "policy statements, agency manuals, and enforcement guidelines. . . ."[30] The scope of *Chevron* was further limited in *United States v. Mead*, where the Court said that *Chevron* should not be applied as a hard and fast rule, but was instead subject to a case-by-case analysis of congressional intent in writing the relevant statute.[31] These limitations on *Chevron* were substantial enough to draw vigorous objections from advocates of judicial deference.[32]

An even more serious limitation on *Chevron* has come in what is being called the "major questions" doctrine—more serious because it has been invoked precisely when the Court is considering agency action on the most prominent public policy issues. Raised initially in

30 *Christensen v. Harris County*, 529 U.S. 576 (2000), at 577.

31 *United States v. Mead Corp.*, 533 U.S. 218 (2001), at 218–19.

32 *Christensen v. Harris County*, 529 U.S. 576 (2000) (Scalia, J., concurring), at 589; *United States v. Mead Corp.*, 533 U.S. 218 (2001) (Scalia, J., dissenting), at 239.

litigation over the Food and Drug Administration's (FDA) attempt to regulate tobacco in the 1990s, this exception to *Chevron* was employed even more recently when the Court considered agency action under the controversial Affordable Care Act (ACA or "Obamacare"). In these cases where, under the Court's precedents, *Chevron* would otherwise seem to apply, the Court has said that major or contentious issues of public policy merit an exception to the assumption in *Chevron* that ambiguities in the law are indicative of Congressional intent for the agency to make policy. The Court finds it implausible that Congress would intend to make major policy determinations by means of saying nothing about such determinations in a statute. As the Court reasoned about tobacco regulation in 2000, "we must be guided to a degree by common sense as to the manner in which Congress is likely to delegate a policy decision of such economic and political magnitude to an administrative agency."[33] And, as it reasoned in 2015 about a major unresolved question in the Obamacare legislation, "had Congress wished to assign that question to an agency, it surely would have done so expressly."[34]

All of this narrowing of the range of agency actions to which *Chevron* deference applies has come to be called "Step Zero" of the *Chevron* test—an initial analysis that must be undertaken that may short-circuit the deference process before it even begins. And once it begins, courts have, since the early days of *Chevron*, often been willing to leave no stone unturned during Step One, using extensive statutory construction to avoid finding that a law is ambiguous and thus merits *Chevron* deference to the agency's interpretation.[35] There are now, in other words, an increasing number of options available to judges who wish to find reasons to avoid triggering *Chevron*, though lower courts may be more constrained in straying from the *Chevron* formula than the Supreme Court.

An even more recent phenomenon in the scaling back of *Chevron* is developing in Step Two cases—cases where *Chevron* has been triggered and courts are bound to defer to any agency interpretation that is

33 *FDA v. Brown & Williamson Tobacco Corp.*, 529 U.S. 120 (2000), at 133.

34 *King v. Burwell*, No. 14-114, slip op. at 8 (U.S. June 25, 2015).

35 See, for example, *Dole v. United Steelworkers*, 494 U.S. 26 (1990), at 28–40; *FDA v. Brown & Williamson Tobacco Corp.*, 529 U.S. 120 (2000), at 133-59; *King v. Burwell*, No. 14-114, slip op. at 15–20 (U.S. June 25, 2015).

not unreasonable. Ordinarily, once the analysis reaches this stage, these have been easy wins for the agency. Courts may not substitute their own reading of the law for the agency's at Step Two; they must simply verify that what the agency has done could be plausible to a reasonable person. There are some very recent examples at the Supreme Court level, however, of the Court's increasing unwillingness to find automatically for the agency at Step Two. Twice in highly significant litigation over Obama-administration environmental policies, the Court refused to defer to the agency even though it reached the highly deferential second step of the *Chevron* process. In *Utility Air Regulatory Group v. EPA* (2014) and again in *Michigan v. EPA* (2015), the Court paid lip service to the *Chevron* process, but used Step Two to invalidate the EPA's interpretations of the Clean Air Act.[36] Admittedly, this more robust use of Step Two is still in its infancy and thus it would be premature to make too much of it at this point. But there is no question that, when combined with the other ways in which the Court has limited the applicability of *Chevron* described above, the momentum is going in the direction of a curtailment of judicial deference to agency statutory interpretations—and these interpretations are often the principal foundation for agencies' discretionary policymaking power. It does not seem out of bounds to ask if *Chevron* is not, at this point, mere window-dressing, at least at the Supreme Court level: the Court of late has mouthed fidelity to the structure of *Chevron*, but in practice has discovered for itself ample means of avoiding *Chevron*'s actual consequences.

What lies behind this momentum? It is difficult to miss that underneath all of this tinkering with the scope and mechanics of the *Chevron* process lies an increasing skepticism of the fundamental reasoning for judicial deference itself. While the most direct attacks on the principle of deference remain—for now—confined to Supreme Court concurrences and dissents, these concurrences and dissents have been joined by a growing number of justices. Moreover, in those recent cases where the Court has upheld the deference regime, it has saved it by allowing its scope to be considerably narrowed. (In this respect, the phenomenon is not unlike what we have seen with limits to the president's removal power over agency personnel: those limits have been upheld, as described above,

36 *Utility Air Regulatory Group v. Environmental Protection Agency*, No. 12-1146, slip op. at 16–17 (U.S. June 23, 2014); *Michigan v. EPA*, No. 14-46, slip op. at 6–11 (U.S. June 29, 2015).

but only by means of narrowing their scope; the momentum there seems clear enough.)

Examples of direct assaults on the principle of deference itself have become increasingly common. In *Michigan v. EPA*, Justice Thomas wrote a separate concurrence to contend that the entire regime of judicial deference to agencies is unconstitutional. Among other points, he argues that agency "interpretations" are, for all practical purposes, policymaking actions, and thus violate the separation of powers by doing in the administrative state what the Constitution reserves for the legislature alone.[37] A broader group of justices raised deep concerns with *Chevron* in 2013 due to its potential to leave agencies as the final authority on the extent of their own powers under the law. If the power of an administrative agency is defined in and limited by the statute that creates it, and if, under *Chevron*, courts are to give deference to agencies when they interpret such statutes, then this means that courts must defer to agencies even when agencies interpret statutes to determine the extent of their own powers. This scenario led Chief Justice Roberts to conclude, in a three-justice dissent, that "the Framers could hardly have imagined . . . the authority that administrative agencies now hold over our economic, social, and political activities," and to warn that "the danger posed by the growing power of the administrative state cannot be dismissed."[38] And even Justice Scalia, who had been the strongest cheerleader for *Chevron* deference during most of his tenure on the Court, had pretty clearly come to be a skeptic in his final years.[39]

More recently Justice Gorsuch contended that judicial deference "sits uneasily" with the Constitution's vesting of the judicial power exclusively in the Article III courts. Citing both older and more recent precedents, Gorsuch argued that a core component of that judicial power is "the duty of interpreting [the laws] and applying them in cases properly brought before the courts." As Chief Justice Marshall put it, "[i]t is emphatically the province and duty of the judicial department to say what the law is." And never, this Court has warned, should the "judicial power . . . be shared with [the] Executive Branch."[40]

37 *Michigan v. EPA*, No. 14-46, slip op. at 3 (U.S. June 29, 2015) (Thomas, J., concurring).

38 *City of Arlington v. Federal Communication Commission*, 569 U.S. 290 (2013) (Roberts, C.J., dissenting), at 313–315.

39 *Perez v. Mortgage Bankers Association*, 135 S.Ct. 1199 (2015) (Scalia, J., concurring), at 1210.

40 *Kisor v. Wilke*, No. 18-15, slip op. at 22 (U.S. June 26, 2019) (Gorsuch, J., concurring).

Gorsuch's reasoning was applied in this case to the question of judicial deference to agency interpretations of their own regulations ("*Auer* deference"), but there is nothing in it that would not apply equally to *Chevron*-style deference on interpretations of statutes. Moreover, this constitutional reasoning was endorsed by three other justices (Thomas, Alito, and Kavanaugh), and a fifth—Chief Justice Roberts—wrote separately to indicate that, while he was not joining Gorsuch's reasoning with respect to *Auer*, he considered *Chevron* an entirely different matter that might warrant reconsideration in a future case.[41]

These most recent arguments were from the Supreme Court's *Kisor v. Wilke* decision handed down in 2019—a decision, many will be quick to point out, that upheld the *Auer* doctrine of deference to agency interpretations of their own prior, vague regulations. But the opinion upholding the *Auer* regime represented a mere plurality of four justices, and even these justices were only able to save *Auer* by substantially limiting its applicability. It is not clear how much of *Auer* deference has actually survived from the limitations placed on it by Justice Kagan in her opinion for the Court, where she emphasizes that it is "just a 'general rule'" that "does not apply in all cases." She attempts to save *Auer* by explaining that it is "not the answer to every question of interpreting an agency's rules," and by going on to enumerate an extensive set of circumstances under which deference would not apply.[42] Combined with statements, above, from a majority of the Court that this tepid upholding of *Auer* does not apply to future consideration of *Chevron*, it seems reasonable to surmise that judicial deference is due for a major reconsideration.

The specifics of individual cases make it difficult to predict what the vehicle for such a reconsideration might be, though the Justice Department's recent ban on "bump-stock" mechanisms for firearms raises the appropriate issues and is currently the subject of a Petition for Writ of Certiorari to the Supreme Court. The agency's ban on bump-stocks came in a rule that was based on its interpretation of the term "machine gun" used first in the National Firearms Act of 1934, then in the Gun Control Act of 1968 and subsequent federal statutes.[43] Lower courts, in upholding the rule, employed the *Chevron* analysis, finding the term "machine

41 *Kisor v. Wilke*, No. 18-15, slip op. at 2 (U.S. June 26, 2019) (Roberts, C.J., concurring).

42 *Kisor v. Wilke*, No. 18-15, slip op. at 11-12 (U.S. June 26, 2019).

43 Final Rule, Bump-Stock-Type Devices, 83 Fed. Reg. 66, 514, Dec. 26, 2018.

gun" to be ambiguous and deferring to the agency's interpretation of the term to include bump-stocks.[44] In their appeal to the Supreme Court, the petitioners call for *Chevron* to be overruled, and make their case on the basis of several constitutional and statutory objections that have been raised in this chapter and voiced by several of the justices in recent cases.[45] Whether the Court, for legal or political reasons, chooses not to take up *Chevron* in this particular vehicle, a reconsideration of *Chevron* deference seems likely in the not-too-distant future.

Restraints on Agencies Through "Arbitrary and Capricious" Review

The narrative thus far with respect to constitutional and legal restraints on the administrative state has pointed to the long period of permissiveness since the 1930s, followed by a relatively recent trend toward reconsideration of agency discretion. Yet there is one area of law where no reconsideration seems in the offing, because courts have been able to check agency discretion for a long time: by employing Section 706 of the APA, which allows reviewing courts to invalidate agency action deemed "arbitrary and capricious."[46] This provision of the APA applies to agency policymaking, as opposed to the agency legal interpretations that are the objects of *Chevron* and *Auer* deference. Read plainly, the meaning of the APA is straightforward: when the law directs agencies to make policy, they must show that they have reasons for it—that the policy is the result of some discernible reasoning process. While reviewing courts do not get to substitute their own reasoning for that of the agency, they do get to ensure that the agency does more in justifying its actions than what a parent might say to an inquisitive child: "because I said so." Courts have come to call this area of the law "hard look review,"[47] indicating that they must see in the reasons presented by agencies evidence that the agency took a "hard look" at the policy question.

This area of review is worth mentioning in the context of this chapter

44 *Guedes v. Bureau of Alcohol, Tobacco, Firearms, and Explosives et al.*, No. 19-5042, slip op. at 45–54 (D.C. Cir. April 1, 2019).

45 *Petition for Writ of Certiorari to the Supreme Court of the United States in Guedes v. BATFE* (Aug 29, 2019).

46 5 U.S. Code § 706 (2016).

47 *Industrial Union Department, Afl-Cio v. Hodgson*, 499 F.2d 467 (D.C. Cir. 1974), at 471–72; *Motor Vehicle Mfrs. Association v. State Farm Ins.*, 463 U.S. 29 (1983), at 40–43.

because it has become, of late, a principal vehicle for courts to stymie the policies of executive agencies. By one recent count, federal courts had invalidated actions of the Trump administration at least sixty-three times over the president's first two years in office.[48] A substantial portion of these rulings invoked arbitrary and capricious or "hard look" review in concluding that the administration had not provided sufficient reasoning to justify its actions, and applied the standards to major policy areas such as the environment, immigration, and the census. As presidents have come to rely on executive action to make or change policy—a trend as evident in the Obama Administration as in the Trump Administration—litigating on "hard look" grounds has become a favored method of the administration's opponents.

On one hand, "hard look" review is sometimes embraced by those who are wary of the administrative state's power, as it can be a check on administrative discretion in cases where fundamental rights are affected. On the other hand, there is reason to question the desirability of this trend from the perspective of republican principles. Presidents making regulatory policy changes often do so because they have campaigned on the policies and feel as if they have an endorsement from voters to move administrative agencies in a particular direction.[49] Such was certainly the case with Trump Administration action on the environment and immigration, as it was with Obama-era policies on the environment. Yet the courts have maintained that such democratic reasons will not, as a rule, be acceptable in the hard-look review process. The major controlling case here is *Motor Vehicle Manufacturer's Association v. State Farm* (1983), in which the Supreme Court disallowed Reagan administration changes in regulations on automobile passive restraint systems. Reagan had campaigned in 1980 on the issue of reducing the regulatory burden on domestic automobile manufacturers, contributing to his election victory in states like Michigan. When he came into office his administration justified rescinding certain automobile regulations by arguing that the regulatory changes came out of a change in political leadership in a democratic country—that the voters had the prerogative, through their election of the chief executive, to affect regulatory policy. But the Court

48 Fred Babash and Deanna Paul, "The Real Reason the Trump Administration is Constantly Losing in Court," *Washington Post*, March 19, 2019.

49 *Motor Vehicle Mfrs. Association v. State Farm Ins.*, 463 U.S. 29 (1983) (Rehnquist, J., concurring in part/dissenting in part), at 59.

was explicit in rejecting that reasoning as insufficient.[50] Instead, the Court insisted on seeing technical reasons for the policy change, which is a point worth emphasizing: the aim of the Court was not to stand up for individual rights in an instance of democratic excess. The guiding principle was neither republicanism nor liberalism but the supremacy of agency *expertise*, and that has become the standard in these kinds of cases.

PROGRESSIVISM OR REPUBLICANISM?

Courts' continued reliance on arbitrary and capricious review, combined with recent trends portending a reconsideration of the constitutional and administrative-law pillars of the administrative state, suggest that agencies may be entering an era where they will have less discretion to make policy. But considered more fundamentally, this development does not in itself suggest a turn away from progressive ideas or a return to more republican principles. This is because neither of the two options that have been on the table since the emergence of the administrative state necessarily bode well for republicanism. On one side we have deference for unelected administrative agencies—by way of delegation and the deference doctrines such as *Chevron* and *Auer* that have come out of administrative law. On the other side, more recently, we have what seems to be an increased willingness of courts to supervise agency policymaking—thereby shifting some power away from unelected agency administrators and toward unelected federal judges. Recall from Chapter Seven that Frank Goodnow's vision for the progressive administrative state conceived of agencies and courts as partners in modern administration, the principal reason for which was the independence of both from electoral politics. Recent trends shifting supervision of policymaking into federal courts do not greatly challenge this vision. Such a challenge would require a reassertion by Congress of its constitutional duty to make law; with the growing divide and intransigence in Congress, however, the involvement of agencies and courts in making policy seems unlikely to diminish.

50 *Motor Vehicle Mfrs. Association v. State Farm Ins.*, 463 U.S. 29 (1983), at 46–59.

CHAPTER NINE

★

PROGRESSIVISM IN STATE AND LOCAL GOVERNMENT

For all of its impact on national government, progressivism had much more immediate and radical effects on state and local government.[1] Indeed, while progressive Presidents, especially Woodrow Wilson, oversaw significant policy achievements—the national income tax, the Federal Reserve Act, and the Federal Trade Commission Act to name just a few—the progressives were unable to achieve much formal structural change in American government itself beyond the direct election of Senators in the Seventeenth Amendment, as significant as that was. The full institutional effects of progressivism at the national level—in the growth of the administrative state, for instance—had to wait for subsequent waves of modern liberalism to show their strength.

In many states and localities, however, progressives were more immediately able to push through sweeping structural changes. Many of these changes pertain to the common ways in which most Americans interact with government and have become such a familiar part of Americans' political participation that their departure from our constitutional

1 An earlier version of this chapter was co-authored with Taylor Kempema, and published by the Heritage Foundation. See Ronald J. Pestritto and Taylor Kempema, "The Birth of Direct Democracy: What Progressivism Did to the States," The Heritage Foundation, February 25, 2014, accessed March 20, 2020, http://report.heritage.org/fp49.

principles is hardly noticed. This chapter will address itself to these changes by examining what progressivism did to state and local government: what happened in those states and municipalities where progressivism effected the most profound changes in government and what the consequences of these developments have been for republican liberty.

PROGRESSIVE DIRECT DEMOCRACY

It has been established that progressives disagreed fundamentally with James Madison and most of the other American founders on the basic facts about human nature and its impact on democratic government. In particular, they did not share the founders' view that the greatest threat to republicanism was majority faction. The founders' fear of tyranny of the majority was outdated, progressives contended; the real problem of their day was tyranny of the minority. The people, argued Theodore Roosevelt, were calling for their government to take action—to regulate corporations and propertied interests, for example—yet the institutional structure handed down from the founding placed too much distance between the people's will and those in government who actually make policy.[2]

This is why one category of progressive efforts at the state and local levels was aimed principally at getting around the institutions that stood between popular opinion and governing. If, for instance, a state legislature refused to heed a popular call for regulation of railroad rates (because, as progressives contended, it was under the control of railroad special interests), then the people should be able to go around the legislature and enact such regulation directly through a popular ballot initiative. Related reforms included the popular referendum, by which a measure approved by the legislature could nonetheless be rejected by the voters, and the recall, by which officeholders could be ousted before the constitutionally prescribed conclusion of their terms. Theodore Roosevelt was the best known of those calling for adoption by states of the initiative, the popular referendum, and the recall of elected officials in order to circumvent recalcitrant institutions of government. Roosevelt also called for the direct primary in order to circumvent unaccountable party leaders.[3]

2 Theodore Roosevelt, "The Right of the People to Rule," in Ronald J. Pestritto and William J. Atto, eds., *American Progressivism: A Reader* (Lanham, MD: Lexington Books, 2008), 251–252.

3 Roosevelt, "Right of the People to Rule," 253–254.

Roosevelt went beyond some other progressives in calling for popular referenda on key state judicial decisions. He was incensed that some state courts had been striking down progressive legislation on constitutional grounds (including legislation enacted in New York under his governorship). And he demanded that the people in individual states be given the opportunity—by direct ballot initiative—to retain laws that had been overturned by state courts.[4] The institutions of government were not carrying out the will of the people as he saw it, and that meant that these institutions had to give way.

Progressive writer Herbert Croly—founding editor of *The New Republic*, whose *Promise of American Life* had, upon its publication in 1909, profoundly influenced Roosevelt and helped push him back into national politics—shared Roosevelt's belief that genuine democracy had to be achieved not by going through but by going around political institutions. Late nineteenth-century politics was dominated by corrupt bosses and political machines to which the people had been forced to resort when the regular political institutions had proved incapable of meeting their needs. If the legal and constitutional restraints on government could be cleared out of the way, Croly reasoned, government might be able to meet these needs. Direct democracy was the vehicle through which this goal could be accomplished.[5]

Even Woodrow Wilson, who as a rule had more regard for institutions than either Roosevelt or Croly (he did not, for instance, share Roosevelt's antipathy for the judiciary), joined the progressive cry for direct democracy. Not only did he advocate the direct primary and direct election of Senators,[6] which was ubiquitous among progressives of all stripes, but he also joined in the calls for the initiative, the referendum, and the recall.[7]

---

4 Roosevelt, "Right of the People to Rule," 254. In making this case, Roosevelt relied specifically on the sentiments of Justice Oliver Wendell Holmes, whom he had appointed to the U.S. Supreme Court and who dissented from cases like *Lochner v. New York*, 198 U.S. 45 (1905), in which the Supreme Court had struck down as unconstitutional state legislation regulating work hours. He also made reference to the New York case of *Ives v. South Buffalo Railroad*, 201 N.Y. 271 (1911), in which the top state appellate court had overturned a worker's compensation law enacted under Roosevelt's governorship.

5 Herbert Croly, *Progressive Democracy* (New York: The Macmillan Company, 1914), 254–256.

6 Woodrow Wilson, *The New Freedom* (New York: Doubleday, Page and Company, 1913), 229–232.

7 Wilson, *New Freedom*, 236–238. This did not include, he clarified, the recall of judges. See 239–242.

Wilson believed that the people were out ahead of their government and that a self-interested minority was pushing an excessively strict interpretation of the Constitution to prevent change that was long overdue. He relied upon the remark of an Englishman—presumably the nineteenth-century liberal realist Walter Bagehot—that "to show that the American Constitution had worked well was no proof that it is an excellent constitution, because Americans could run any constitution."[8] Not only had legislatures become corrupt (something Wilson himself had witnessed in his battles with the Democratic Party bosses during his governorship of New Jersey), but the very idea of fixed terms allowed corrupt legislators and administrators temporary immunity from having fallen out of favor with public opinion.

Like other progressives, Wilson saw state direct democracy measures as means of tying institutions more directly and immediately to the public will. He spoke of "the growing consciousness that something intervenes between the people and the government" and argued that "there must be some arm direct enough and strong enough to thrust aside the something that comes in the way."[9] Wilson, like all progressives, sought to use the mechanisms of direct democracy to tie policymaking more tightly to immediate public opinion. Yet, while no progressive sought to circumvent institutions entirely, there were differences among them on the necessary degree and duration of such mechanisms. Some saw them as important temporary measures, to be used occasionally when the ordinary institutions of government had become corrupt and needed correction. Others had a more ambitious vision for direct democracy, seeing it as a permanent and regular complement to traditional institutions.

PROGRESSIVE CHANGES IN STATE GOVERNMENT

Many states heeded progressive calls to make state government more directly democratic, and where changes did occur, they did so to varying degrees. The most popular measures by far were the ballot initiative, the referendum, and the direct primary. Yet this was not the only assault on the institutions of state government. In addition to circumventing state legislatures through direct democracy measures, progressives also

8 Wilson, *New Freedom*, 234.
9 Wilson, *New Freedom*, 236.

sought to delegate power away from the political institutions in other ways, most notably by delegating some legislative power to commissions and other "experts." Both kinds of moves—direct democracy and delegation of power to "experts"—came from the progressive belief that politics itself had become corrupt and beholden to special interests, and thus that power had to be diverted away from traditional political institutions.

These moves pull in opposite directions: On the one side, direct democracy measures seek to empower popular majorities and give them greater voice in state government, while on the other, delegation of power away from politicians (for whom the people vote, after all) to unelected administrators certainly reduces the accountability of policymakers to the electorate. The major progressive movements to change state governments contained both of these seemingly contradictory elements.

The Initiative, Referendum, and Recall

While several progressive measures—most notably the direct primary—were designed to "purify" political institutions, this was insufficient for many progressives who sought to bypass political institutions altogether. The ballot initiative and referendum were their principal mechanisms of choice. Both the ballot initiative and the referendum were devices that placed legislation or constitutional amendments directly before the voters. Initiatives did so by circumventing the legislature, relying instead on a petition process to force a vote on a particular issue either in the legislature or by the general public. Referenda were put on the ballot as a consequence of action in the legislature, giving voters the opportunity to approve or reject what the legislature had done.

These devices were used most widely in the West, where South Dakota first adopted them in 1898 and was joined soon thereafter by Utah, Oregon, Nevada, Montana, and Oklahoma. From 1908 to 1915, fifteen other states adopted some variant of these devices, including several states in the East and South. The momentum slowed around 1915, and the devices did not spread thereafter to many other states. The use of the recall followed a similar pattern of rise and decline and, depending upon the state, could be used for all elected offices or be restricted to specific ones. In the case of the recall, conservatives were successful in fighting it where they focused attention on efforts to implement the recall of judges. Even many progressives who were sympathetic to the recall recognized the threat to individual liberty should voters win the power to remove judges who made unpopular decisions.

The origin of direct democracy in Oregon is a good illustration of the kinds of concerns that led to direct democracy in many states. As historian Steven L. Piott has observed, agitators for direct democracy in Oregon cited the influence of corrupt political machines on the electoral process. The process yielded the election of those who were described as "business failures" and "farmless farmers," and corporations were often thought to manipulate the selection of state legislators. In 1892, writer J. W. Sullivan's group Direct Legislation won a sympathetic ear at a meeting of the state Farmers' Alliance, which is credited with providing a spark for the direct democracy measures that were passed later in the decade.

At roughly the same time, direct democracy gained steam in California, where many resented what was believed to be the control of state politics by the Southern Pacific Railroad. Sullivan, who had published his book *Direct Legislation* in 1895, gave speeches in California, and ultimately, the Direct Legislation League of California was formed and became a national movement. As would be the case with many states, the first concrete moves toward direct democracy were made at the municipal level: San Francisco and Los Angeles, in particular, were able to draft their own city charters due to the home rule provisions of California's 1879 constitution.

In Washington, the influence of railroad interests was also a source of complaint on which progressives seized; particularly galling to both shippers and farmers was the common practice of government officials receiving free railroad passes. In Michigan, the issues were similar, and they framed the debate between a progressive governor—Hazen Pingree—and a conservative legislature that resisted his attempts to enact railroad-rate regulation and other progressive policies. Egged on once again by Sullivan, local direct-legislation groups sprouted up and led ultimately to the calling of a constitutional convention in 1906.[10]

10 Steven A. Piott, *Giving Voters a Voice: The Origins of the Initiative and Referendum in America* (Columbia: University of Missouri Press, 2003), 32, 148–151, 186, 199–200.

In other states where direct legislation was adopted, the causes appear to have been similar—the influence of corrupt political machines and resentment over the dominance of particular interests in the political process—in addition to having gained momentum from the states that pioneered the effort.

The initiative and referendum finally became part of the Oregon constitution in 1902 after a process that required passage of the devices in two legislative sessions and approval by voters. Legislative approval came in 1899 and again in 1901, and voters approved the devices by a margin of more than 10 to 1 in 1902. The measures altered Oregon's constitution, requiring a petition of 8 percent of qualified voters to place an initiative on the ballot and 5 percent of qualified voters to force a referendum on a legislative measure.

In California, sweeping direct democracy measures were adopted in 1911. Like Oregon, California adopted a measure requiring an 8 percent threshold for initiatives and 5 percent for referenda, but unlike Oregon, it also adopted a recall mechanism for all statewide officeholders, allowing recall elections where petitioners had secured the signatures of 20 percent of the number of people who had voted in the previous election. While the initiative and referendum had no trouble being adopted, the recall provisions met with stiff resistance—even some progressives hesitated to include state judges. In the end, however, in spite of arguments marshaled by opponents about abandoning representative government and falling victim to the tyranny of the majority, both the legislature and state voters overwhelmingly approved all of the direct democracy devices.

The state of Washington also adopted the initiative and the referendum at roughly the same time, with legislative approval in 1911 and voter approval in 1912. There was more resistance to the measures there, where the state Senate made supporters increase petition requirements (to 10 percent for initiatives and 6 percent for referenda) and allowed the legislature to amend laws passed by initiative two years after their enactment.

In Michigan, the constitutional convention held in 1906 yielded only watered-down direct democracy measures, but by 1912, voters had become much more intense about the issue even though the legislature had enacted several laws favored by progressives in the session following the 1910 election, including railroad regulation, revision of the state tax structure, a state primary law, and a workers' compensation law. In 1912, led by progressive Democratic governor Woodbridge N. Ferris, the legislature enacted the initiative and referendum, which were subsequently approved by voters in 1913.[11]

Policies Enacted via Direct Legislation

The so-called Oregon System of direct democracy not only was one of the earliest enacted, but also led to the most far-reaching policy changes. The system was used extensively and very quickly after it was made available to voters. While South Dakota had actually been the first to adopt direct democracy mechanisms, Oregon did much more with them. Between 1902 and 1913, 108 ballot initiatives were brought before the voters, and 44 percent of them were approved. Major policies were enacted by initiative in 1908, when voters adopted the recall, enacted corrupt practices legislation, expressed non-binding endorsement of the direct election of U.S. Senators, and took the first steps toward a proportional representation system for the state legislature. Even after progressives took control of the governorship and state legislature in 1911 and were thus able to enact progressive legislation without having to resort to the ballot initiative, the thirst for direct democracy did not wane. The election of 1912 included thirty-seven initiatives and referenda, many of them proposing quite radical changes in the structure of state government, though most of them were not adopted.

In Washington and other states, the new direct democracy devices were not used nearly as frequently as they were in Oregon. In Washington, as in Michigan, the legislature was not so progressive, and the ballot initiative and referendum were used there primarily to thwart legislative attacks on direct democracy. State legislators enacted several restrictions on the initiative and referendum process—requiring, among other things, that all petition signing be done in the offices of voter registration officials and only on certain days of the week—but these legislative enactments were overwhelmingly disapproved by voters in the referendum election of 1916. In Michigan, very little use was made of the initiative process once it was adopted.[12]

11 Piott, 40, 164, 167, 192–194, 204.

12 Piott, 44–50, 197, 204–205.

The Direct Primary

While most of the new devices of direct democracy had a mixed record of use in the decades following their adoption, there was one fairly common use. In many states, the initiative process was employed to establish a critical change in state government that was often resisted by legislators: the direct primary. Progressives took aim at the role of parties in the nominating process, contending that the process was undemocratic because it placed control of ballot access in the hands of unaccountable party bosses. Officeholders thus became beholden to those who held the key to the ballot—the party bosses—instead of to the rank-and-file voters who ought to be their true constituency.

For many progressives, the direct primary was an important step toward their ultimate goal of eliminating the role of parties altogether. For Croly, reducing or eliminating the role of parties came from the same principle as circumventing the legislature with direct democracy mechanisms: The point was to undo the representative democracy that the Framers of the Constitution had thought essential. "The two-party system," wrote Croly, "like other forms of representative democracy, proposes to accomplish for the people a fundamental political task which they ought to accomplish for themselves. It seeks to interpose two authoritative partisan organizations between the people and their government."[13] The other major aim of the movement for direct primaries and, ultimately, the elimination of parties altogether was to foster a stronger connection between citizens and the national government itself. As Croly reasoned, the traditional party system "demands and obtains for a party an amount of loyal service and personal sacrifice which a public-spirited democrat should lavish only on the state."[14]

In 1902, Mississippi became the first state to institute a compulsory, statewide primary law. Wisconsin followed suit in 1903, during the governorship of the progressive Robert La Follette. In Oregon, the very first use of the ballot initiative—which had been put into the state constitution in 1902—was to adopt the direct primary statewide. The Oregon legislature had been resisting expansion of the direct primary law, enacted in 1901, to include localities outside of Portland. Under the coordination of

13 Croly, *Progressive Democracy*, 341.
14 Croly, *Progressive Democracy*, 341.

the Direct Primary Nomination League, a new, statewide direct primary initiative was put on the ballot in 1904 and was approved by voters by an almost 4-to-1 margin.[15] In Oregon, as was common in other states, the direct primary measure also included language that attempted to bind state legislative candidates to vote for U.S. Senate candidates who had been endorsed by a majority of primary voters, though such efforts were eventually obviated in 1913 by the Seventeenth Amendment to the U.S. Constitution, which guaranteed the popular election of Senators. By 1916, the only states in the Union that had not yet adopted a primary system of some kind were Connecticut, New Mexico, and Rhode Island.

Commissions and Railroad Regulation

The great paradox of progressivism, as explained above, is that while it sought to circumvent traditional political institutions by pursuing direct democracy mechanisms, it also sought to take power from political institutions in ways that were not so democratic. Where state legislatures were seen as beholden to special interests, progressives often sought the establishment of so-called expert commissions and delegated to them the regulatory power they believed the legislature was incapable of exercising. Ironically, the delegation of power to unaccountable, allegedly nonpartisan administrators was seen as a way of achieving the public good—by removing authority from those whom the people themselves had elected to office. The most common and important instances of such moves involved the regulation of railroads.

Beginning with the establishment of railroad commissions by several states in the 1870s and punctuated by Wisconsin's adoption of La Follette's railroad commission plan in 1905, the delegation of regulatory power to expert commissions became pervasive during the Progressive Era. By 1914, the effects of this regulation were clear: Railroad managers were going to Congress to beg for protection from state railroad commissions. A closer look at activity in five states—Illinois, Iowa, Minnesota, Wisconsin, and California—illustrates the empowerment of commissions and the expansion of state regulation of business.

Railroad regulation began to gain steam in Illinois in 1871, when legislation was introduced to restrict rates and to set up a commission

15 Piott, *Giving Voters a Voice*, 41–42.

to supervise railroads. The momentum was carried forward by farming interests who needed to ship their commodities and wanted to keep rates low. They organized under the "Granger" movement, which successfully agitated for passage of the 1873 Railroad Act in Illinois, aided by the Illinois State Farmers' Association, which wanted regulation of all corporations. The act deemed it "extortion" for any railroad to charge anything other than a "fair rate." And what was a fair rate? This was to be determined by the state's Railroad and Warehouse Commission, which was also established by the act.[16] Commissioners here and elsewhere were typically not elected, but appointed by the governor for fixed terms.

Iowa initially experimented with regulation of railroad rates by the legislature itself, which set a detailed schedule of maximum rates based on the rate published by the Illinois Railroad and Warehouse Commission for 1874. This law was repealed in 1878 and replaced by one that established the state's own supervisory commission. Minnesota followed the same course, initially fixing rates through legislative action in 1871 and then installing a three-member commission in 1874 with a law that mirrored the Illinois Railroad Act. Wisconsin, well before it adopted La Follette's more sweeping plan in 1905, also followed this path in 1874 and also followed the Illinois model. In Wisconsin, the legislature itself set maximum rates, but the commission was empowered to lower rates even further.[17]

California may be the most familiar case of the progressives' assault on railroad interests, but serious regulation did not come there until after the direct democracy provisions were put into the state constitution in 1911. The Southern Pacific Railroad had dominated the state's politics and economy for decades, and the desire to rein in the railroad's influence over state government was the driving force behind the progressive measures that were eventually adopted under the leadership of Governor Hiram Johnson. With the political institutions having ceded authority for railroad-rate regulation to a state commission, there was less inducement for railroad influence in state politics.

The moves in Illinois and elsewhere also illustrate another important feature of progressive calls for delegation of legislative authority to expert

16 George H. Miller, *Railroads and the Granger Laws* (Madison: University of Wisconsin Press, 1971), 84, 90–93.

17 Miller, 114–115, 137–138, 157.

commissions: belief that legislatures were simply not expert enough and lacked sufficient resources to regulate businesses in all of the new ways that progressives had in mind. Such a belief stemmed not so much from the notion that politicians were too beholden to special interests (though progressives certainly believed that too) as they did from the recognition by progressives that they had far more regulation in mind than any traditional legislative body—corrupt or pure—was competent to administer. Historian George H. Miller expresses a sentiment that was typical of this thinking: "Even the purest and most carefully limited assembly was not capable, by itself, of supervising and controlling the railroads of a single state; a permanent, expert body was essential."[18]

Consequences of Commission Government

While the Progressive Era featured the expansive use of commissions in state government, the period immediately following was characterized by attempts to manage the consequences of this movement. In many instances, progressives became victims of their own enthusiasm for delegating regulatory power to commissions, as commissions multiplied and often brought about the very kind of overly complex and inefficient government that progressives themselves had decried. Democracy was commonly thwarted in states due their mazes of commissions with overlapping jurisdiction and lack of political accountability. While many progressives remained devoted to the commission model, many states nonetheless undertook the streamlining and reorganizing of their executive branches as part of an effort to return some power to politically accountable officials.

A common characteristic of states' attempts to reorganize their executive branches was the consolidation of administrative authority into a smaller number of executive departments whose heads would be appointed by the governor in order to provide some measure of political accountability. New Jersey and Minnesota were among the leaders in these efforts. Somewhat comically, both states launched their efforts to rein in commissions by forming special commissions to study the problem and advise on a remedy. New Jersey's efficiency commission focused on the problem of overlapping jurisdictions, noting in just one example

18 Miller, 94.

that the state had five separate commissions or bureaus charged, among other things, with the "preservation and improvement of the oyster industry"—all without doing any evident good for the value of oyster production. Minnesota's "Efficiency and Economy Commission" also attacked the incoherent nature of the state's commission structure and focused on restoring political accountability by recommending the condensing of more than fifty state commissions into six executive departments headed by gubernatorial appointees.[19]

Illinois was also a leader in executive-branch reorganization—in this case by means of a special legislative committee that was formed to investigate the mess resulting from the thirty-four new agencies, boards, and commissions that had been established in the state between 1909 and 1913. This effort led the Illinois legislature to enact in 1917 the Civil Administration Code, which consolidated nearly 130 boards, commissions, and bureaus into nine departments headed by a gubernatorial appointee. Several states followed suit, including Nebraska and Idaho in 1919. By the end of the 1920s, seventeen states had adopted some kind of reorganization legislation aimed at curbing the proliferation of commissions that had been so popular just a decade or two earlier.[20] Reducing the number and inefficiency of commissions, of course, did little to change the fundamental nature of commission government, which remained unaccountable rule by experts.

Legislative Reference Services

Delegation of regulatory power to administrative bodies had been one way, and certainly the most lasting and influential way, to bring expertise to the progressive push for sharply increased state regulation of business. In addition to problems of efficiency, it had also raised serious questions of consent—how can rules be made legitimately without the consent of the people's elected representatives?—and separation of powers—how can executive bodies be granted legislative authority? The reliance by some state legislatures on expert reference services to aid legislators in writing statutes was another way of bringing expertise into regulation without

19 Jon C. Teaford, *The Rise of the States: Evolution of American State Government* (Baltimore: Johns Hopkins University Press, 2002), 72.

20 Teaford, 72–74.

also raising questions of consent and separation of powers in the way that delegation to expert commissions had done.

In the case of legislative reference services, there was no delegation of legislative power to other entities; instead, lawmakers received the guidance of these services during the drafting process, much as today's Congressional Research Service operates at the federal level, with the final laws passed by legislators themselves. The advent of the legislative reference service also reflected the growing abandonment of the idea of the citizen-legislator. Progressives wanted regulation of business at a much greater level than could be accomplished by part-time legislators. With the progressive policy agenda, government needed to be bigger and thus needed to be more than a part-time concern. Legislative reference services were one way of moving things in the direction of professionalization.

The use of legislative reference services became popular between 1900 and 1920. Arguably the most influential advocate for their use was Charles McCarthy of Wisconsin. McCarthy had been appointed the document cataloguer of a special reference collection established for Wisconsin legislators and from that position pushed his arguments for greater reliance on expert research and guidance by legislators in Wisconsin and other states. McCarthy contended that without the guidance of expert advice, lawmaking was amateurish and sloppy, leaving legislators at the mercy of lobbyists.[21]

The movement for legislative reference services picked up in other states. State libraries in California (1904) and Indiana (1906) established special legislative reference sections. As the movement picked up steam, reference services in Nebraska, Indiana, and Illinois actually began to prepare draft legislation between sessions of the legislature so that it would be ready for legislators to review and debate when they reconvened. The degree of involvement in actual legislation by the reference bureaus varied greatly from state to state, but in some states, their influence was significant. In Wisconsin, all bills taken up during the 1929 legislative session had been drafted under the supervision of the special reference service, and 90 percent or more of those considered in Pennsylvania, Illinois, and Indiana had been produced by their respective bureaus.[22]

21 Teaford, 77.

22 Teaford, 79–80.

PROGRESSIVE CHANGES IN MUNICIPAL GOVERNMENT

As wide-ranging as the progressive changes were in state government, most state-level movements grew out of experiments at the municipal level. As with state government, the changes ushered in by progressives in local government have had a lasting effect. Those undertaken by Governor Hiram Johnson in California receive significant attention from scholars—and for good reason, as those changes still greatly affect the politics of our most populous state today. But California's state reforms were modeled after what had gone on in its biggest cities in the 1890s, especially in Los Angeles and San Francisco. Because of the home-rule provisions of California's 1879 constitution, these cities could draft their own charters—the municipal equivalent of constitutions.

In Los Angeles, groups like the Municipal Reform Association and the League for Better City Government sought to limit the power of political machines. Again, much of this was railroad politics, as the Los Angeles machine was controlled by the Southern Pacific Railroad's political bureau in San Francisco. In 1889, Los Angeles added the initiative, referendum, and recall to the city charter and adopted a civil service system. These changes all received overwhelming support from voters (as high as 6-to-1 approval for the initiative and referendum) and were approved by the state legislature in 1903. Other major cities in California followed suit in adopting mechanisms for direct legislation: Sacramento in 1903 and San Bernardino, San Diego, Pasadena, and Eureka in 1905. San Francisco adopted the recall in 1907.[23] And these movements in California's municipalities spread to other states, where local governments likewise led the way for changes that were later to be taken up at the state level.[24]

As a general matter, these kinds of changes in city government stemmed from the public attention that came to focus on corruption in cities in the latter part of the nineteenth century. Muckraking journalists had exposed some of the more scandalous instances of corrupt city government and brought to light the reality of machine control of municipalities. In fact, most major American cities were greatly influenced by political machines: hierarchical organizations that controlled political

23 Piott, *Giving Voters a Voice*, 151.

24 See, for example, the case of Seattle or the cases of cities in Ohio like Cleveland, Columbus, and Cincinnati. Piott, 174–177, 189.

offices and those who voted for public officials. Machine leaders could deliver blocs of votes to candidates, in return for which they would be able to dole out services and favors on behalf of public officials to those constituencies that had voted for them. Machine leaders maintained their power by appealing most often to the downtrodden. By providing social services that were otherwise unavailable, often by means of public officials who were under their control, political machines received the loyalty of their clients and could deliver their votes as they wished. Progressives took aim at these machines both by advocating structural reforms that would reduce the power of traditional political institutions and by seeking to attach machine clients directly to the government itself.

In the 1890s, there were some isolated victories for progressives at the municipal level, though more sweeping changes in city government had to wait until the first decade of the twentieth century. New York's Tammany Hall was temporarily overthrown in 1894, and the Municipal Voters' League was able to wrest control of Chicago's Board of Aldermen from 1895 to 1897, but the more successful and sustained movements that came later ordinarily were led by charismatic leaders who took the mantle of nonpartisanship. Such was the case in Cleveland, where Tom L. Johnson was elected mayor in 1901 and went after the railroads and utilities. Progressives came to realize, through the example of Johnson and others, that major victories over the city machines could be achieved only by weakening the two-party system. They sought consequently to dilute the influence of party bosses by pursuing the direct primary for municipal candidates and by introducing mechanisms of direct legislation. They also fought to maintain home rule—that is, they fought against the management of municipal affairs by state legislatures. The involvement of state legislatures was a problem for progressive reformers in cities because local machines were usually part of larger, state machines. Often, if progressives won a victory at the city level, the local machine bosses would appeal to the state organization, which would then work to influence the state legislature to preempt any municipal reform efforts.

In addition to primaries and mechanisms of direct legislation, progressives at the local level also advocated new means of organizing city government itself through both commission government and city managers.

Commission Government in Municipalities

At the municipal level, as at the state level, progressive attempts to thwart the alleged corruption of political institutions pulled in two opposite directions. While municipalities sought to empower voters by pursuing the direct primary and direct legislation, they also sought to move power away from elected officials and into the hands of nonpartisan experts. These moves made city government simultaneously more democratic (in the case of the primary and direct legislation) and less democratic (in the case of delegating power to unelected experts). The move in cities toward commission government exemplified the latter.

The movement for commission government in cities came about principally by means of an accident. In 1900, Galveston, Texas, was devastated by a hurricane. The city council proved incapable of restoring order, so the city appealed to the state legislature, which appointed a commission of administrators to rebuild the city, essentially granting it legislative as well as executive powers. It seemed to work well in this instance and was also popular; the commissioners continued in office and did so via election after 1903. The commission form of government was then exported to Houston, Dallas, Fort Worth, Austin, and El Paso.

Under the form implemented in Texas, a city commission consisted of five administrators, each of whom had responsibility for a single department of city government. The commission form quickly spread beyond Texas and was implemented in the most widespread fashion in the cities of Iowa. The state legislature there allowed cities over a certain population threshold to adopt the commission form, with commissioners selected in nonpartisan elections, and also to incorporate the mechanisms of direct legislation. It is for this reason that the full-blown commission form of government—paired with mechanisms such as the initiative, referendum, and recall—became known as the "Des Moines Idea."[25]

Even with the popularity of the commission form, the debates over it in the Texas and Iowa state legislatures raised several critical objections from defenders of the republican principles of consent and constitutionalism. Legislators in Texas pointed to the fact that this "reform" actually

25 For details on the development of commission government in the cities of Texas and Iowa, see Bradley Robert Rice, *Progressive Cities: The Commission Government Movement in America, 1901–1920* (Austin: University of Texas Press, 1977), 3–17, 34–46.

gave the people themselves less power by reducing the number of elective offices and delegating legislative authority away from their elected representatives on the city council and into the hands of nonpartisan administrators, elected or otherwise. Historian Bradley Robert Rice notes that, while much opposition surely came from those whose interests would be affected by the change, "some legislators were more detached and sincere in their refusal to countenance the disenfranchisement of the city's voters." Rice's summary of the opposition is worth quoting at length, as it gets to the heart of the opposition between progressive reforms and republican government:

> One [legislator] flatly stated, "I care nothing for the Mayor of Galveston, whether he wants this bill or not, it is not a question of whether the laboring men or the rich men want it; it is a question of the sacred rights of government." Two house members had their impassioned statement of opposition entered in the journal: "We cannot chloroform our consciences by voting for the commission feature of this bill, which disenfranchises free citizens of Texas, destroys the right of local self-government, violates the Constitution of the State, holds in derision the Declaration of Independence, tramples underfoot the fundamental principles of a free republic, and repudiates the teachings, traditions and sentiments of the democratic [*sic*] party."[26]

In Iowa, the objections raised were based not only upon consent, but also on the need to protect liberty through separation of powers. Drake University professor F. I. Herriott was among the most vocal making this argument, observing that the commission form vests commissioners with both legislative and executive powers.[27]

While it is beyond dispute that the commission form of government weakens the power of voters (though not as fully as the city-manager system, discussed below), the irony is that in many cases, these voters essentially disenfranchised themselves by adopting it. One of the principal modes by which commission government was spread was the mechanism of direct democracy. In cities where reformers were making a case to the public for support of commission government, they very often

26 Rice, 13.
27 Rice, 42.

sweetened the pot by including in the proposals various provisions for the direct primary, initiative, referendum, and recall. These direct democracy measures made commission government easier to swallow, and advocates of the commission form figured this out and took advantage of it. The actual use of direct mechanisms, however, was not very common in cities with the commission form.[28]

The City Manager

The rise of the commission form reflected the desire to professionalize city government, which was to take place by moving power away from popularly elected city councils and into the hands of expert administrators. The same principle was at work in a closely related change in city government: the advent of the city manager. Just as progressives believed that city councils had become corrupt and thus ought to give way to administrative commissions, they also believed that powerful mayors were obstacles to progress. They called for replacing strong mayors with nonpartisan, unelected city managers.

In many instances, the city-manager model developed out of the earlier forms of commission government. It became apparent that administrators elected to city commissions were not necessarily experts. For the progressives, the real problem was elections: Those who had to stand for election to their office, even if they were to be "nonpartisan" administrators, necessarily looked more to their own electoral self-interest as opposed to the objective good toward which their expertise was supposed to direct them. The city manager would not stand for election. Instead, a council or commission would be elected on a nonpartisan basis and would then appoint a qualified city manager. In this way, the executive arm of government would be insulated from direct popular control.

This council–manager model, which remains a popular form of city government today, developed in the 1910s and 1920s, as the examples of Dayton and Berkeley illustrate. Dayton's turn to the city-manager model was one of the earliest and, as in the case of Galveston and commission government, came in response to a natural disaster. The city government responded poorly to a major flood in 1913, and subsequent scrutiny of the government uncovered evidence of widespread financial

---

28 Rice, 72–76.

mismanagement. Under the home-rule provisions of the Ohio constitution, the city soon adopted one of the first city-manager systems in the country, with an elected five-member council that would appoint a city manager who would be the head of city government. Berkeley's turn to the city-manager model came after a calamity of a different sort—a deep economic depression in 1921 and 1922. The city adopted the city-manager model the following year, establishing an elected city council for legislative powers and an appointed city manager for executive and administrative powers. Berkeley's city manager was a strong, unitary executive: The council was allowed to deal with city administration only through the city manager and was prohibited from giving orders to any part of the city's administrative apparatus. The city manager could be removed only by a two-thirds vote of the council.[29] This example was followed in countless other cities in the 1920s and 1930s as the city-manager model spread quickly.

The city-manager model also gave rise to the "professionalization" of city government. Progressives sought to undo the kind of local government praised by Alexis de Tocqueville when he visited America in the early part of the nineteenth century. Tocqueville observed that the people became suited for self-government by means of practicing it at the local level: Power in localities was spread widely among a number of citizens who were elected to serve part-time.[30] For the progressives, cities had become too complex for the "amateur," and they turned instead to professional city administrators—not only for the city manager, but for all elements of city administration. Serving as a city administrator was now to be a full-time occupation, taken up by those who had been specially educated and trained for the task. City government was to run less like a manifestation of citizen self-government and more like a business. The influence of elections—which, progressives argued, necessarily created inducements to corruption—would be minimized for the sake of making city government more "professional" and "efficient."

This push for government-as-a-business is why the city-manager model was often accompanied by the "short ballot"—that is, a sharp reduction in the number of elective offices that went hand-in-hand with

29 Frederick C. Mosher et al., *City Manager Government in Seven Cities* (Chicago: Public Administration Service, 1940), 115–129, 265–272.

30 Alexis de Tocqueville, *Democracy in America*, ed. and trans. Harvey C. Mansfield and Delba Winthrop (Chicago: University of Chicago Press, 2002), 56–61.

the concentration of power in the office of the city manager and with the push to remove "amateur" or ordinary citizens from positions of authority. From a Tocquevillean perspective, the trend toward professionalization would necessarily reduce opportunities for ordinary citizens to participate in self-government and would thus run the danger of interfering with citizens' acquiring the habits requisite for maintaining a free society.

THE LEGACY FOR GOVERNMENT TODAY

This book as a whole has explained how the progressive vision of government was aimed at overcoming the republican principles of the American founding. This chapter, in turning to specific reforms at the state and local level, makes the connection between those reforms and the broader progressive vision of government. Progressive changes in state and local government cut against the founders' republican principles in two fundamental ways.

First, the founders wanted to secure both democratic rule and protection for individual natural rights and thus established popular self-government through institutions that would "refine and enlarge the public views."[31] Majority rule through the institutions of government would yield the "cool and deliberate sense of the community"[32] and filter out the factious or tyrannical tendencies of passionate, immediate majority opinion. For the progressives, such thinking exalted the position of the minority at the expense of vigorous government action in pursuit of social justice. The progressives were simply not concerned about potential tyranny by the government in the way that Madison and America's other founders had been. Progressive direct-democracy measures, at both the state and local levels, thus sought to circumvent the refining and enlarging process of America's political institutions.

Second, while the founders certainly believed in vigorous national administration (the lack of it had been a principal objection to the Articles of Confederation), administration for them had to be closely tied to electoral accountability in order to maintain the very idea of self-government. For the progressives, this connection of administration to

31 *Federalist* No. 10, in Carey and McClellan, eds., *The Federalist*, 46.
32 *Federalist* No. 63, in Carey and McClellan, eds., *The Federalist*, 327.

public opinion made government "unprofessional" and impeded the kind of expertise necessary to manage the vast agenda they had in mind for government. Administration would be good, from the progressive viewpoint, only to the extent that it was liberated from electoral accountability, because that accountability is what leads to the opportunity for corruption. If officials did not have to worry about their electoral self-interest, then (progressives reasoned) they would be freer to do the objectively right thing. Progressive efforts to move governing authority—especially in cities—away from elected officials and into the hands of "nonpartisan" commissions and managers reflect this view.

In addition to these deeper effects of the progressive agenda at the state and local levels, there is a very interesting debate on both sides of the political spectrum today as to the *practical* advantages or disadvantages of these progressive reforms for each side's current political aims. Some conservatives will contend that, in recent decades, the mechanisms of direct democracy have made possible many conservative victories at the state level that otherwise would have been unattainable. As much as California has drifted leftward in recent years, conservatives there have used direct democracy to enact policies limiting property taxes (Proposition 13 in 1978), prohibiting the state from using affirmative action (Proposition 209 in 1996), and defining marriage as the union of a man and a woman (Proposition 8 in 2008),[33] to name just a few. In light of these realities, some conservatives would contend that the obvious principled problems of direct democracy need to be weighed against the extent to which it might be used prudentially as a means of restoring limited, republican government. Yet the progressive mechanisms of direct democracy do not predictably lean themselves to any one side of the political spectrum, and the Left has certainly achieved its share of victories with direct democracy. While California voters passed Proposition 13, they also enacted, just a decade later, Proposition 98, an amendment to the state constitution that guarantees that 40 percent of state revenues must go to education and is thus a huge boon to the public employees' unions that anchor the Democratic Party.

There is also the practical question of whether or not direct legislation has even achieved the ends for which it was originally promoted

33 Subsequently rendered inoperative by the courts; see *Hollingsworth v. Perry*, 133 S. Ct. 2652 (2013); *Obergefell v. Hodges*, 135 S. Ct. 2584 (2015).

by America's progressives: the reduction of special-interest influence and the influence of establishment insiders. A comprehensive study by Daniel A. Smith and Caroline J. Tolbert has demonstrated that, nationwide, the initiative process has empowered special-interest groups rather than weakened them. In fact, the initiative process has often been the principal means by which interest groups have altered the balance of power within states. As Smith and Tolbert conclude, "Although Progressive Era advocates of direct democracy had hoped to use the initiative to eliminate interest groups' clout, we find that many political organizations have adapted to the presence of the initiative, educating themselves to use the process to advance their agendas."[34] If it had been a progressive goal to reduce the influence of money in politics, that certainly has not happened through the initiative process, as the sums spent on initiatives in recent decades have come to dwarf spending on races for state political office.[35]

Nor has direct democracy done much to curtail the influence of establishment insiders and party organizations. Parties have become deeply involved in initiative campaigns; not only do they seek particular policy outcomes favorable to their constituencies, but they also see in the initiative process itself many ways to strengthen their own organizations. As Smith and Tolbert conclude from research on the California and Colorado initiative processes:

> [P]arty organizations engage in citizen lawmaking for its procedural effects. Parties have learned that ballot measures have a real educative value because they can spur citizens to vote, divide the opposing party's core constituents, and generate contributions to the party.... Citizen lawmaking clearly has proven to be an ineffective instrument for reining in parties. Indeed, direct democracy may strengthen and energize state and local parties.[36]

These facts about the involvement of parties and money in the initiative process also point to another practical consideration for political

34 Daniel A. Smith and Caroline J. Tolbert, *Educated by Initiative: The Effects of Direct Democracy on Citizens and Political Organizations in the American States* (Ann Arbor: University of Michigan Press, 2004), 88–89.

35 Smith and Tolbert, 90–92.

36 Smith and Tolbert, 140.

strategists on both sides: does reliance on direct democracy divert attention from the thing that partisans need to do in order to achieve their aims: win elections?

Postscript

Chapter Nine concludes with a practical point about winning elections. That is a topic that also makes for a suitable close to the book, as the fate both of progressivism and the natural rights republicanism it sought to replace are clearly before the voters in the election cycles of our day. More than one hundred years after the advent of progressivism, Americans seem to be revisiting the fundamental questions about the nature of our republic. It is common to hear that the country is as divided today as it has been since the 1850s, and that connection seems apt because, like the 1850s, today's debates are not only about policy but about the regime's first principles. In sparring over the extension of slavery into the territories, Abraham Lincoln and Stephen Douglas understood that an even more fundamental question was at stake: was American republicanism all about the ultimate authority of a democratic majority, or was it about the equal protection of natural rights for the majority and minority alike? Some southerners were even willing to concede that the latter *had been* the driving philosophy of the founding, but argued that history had passed by those original principles and that the Confederacy represented the new, more advanced, scientific principles of government. Lincoln's insight at this time was to see that this sharp divide—not over policies but over the question of how the regime should conceive of its core principles—could not continue indefinitely.

In like manner, it is difficult to see in our time how we can continue to govern ourselves through institutions that have been transformed by progressive political philosophy, while simultaneously maintaining the pretense of an attachment to constitutional government. The original progressives understood this divide; they knew that their philosophy of historical contingency, their dedication to the authority of science, and their consequent aim to rule through enlightened administration required an overt rejection of the regime's original principles of constitutional government and natural rights. As the book has shown, they were explicit about this need to abandon founding principles—this is not a revisionist spin but is instead how they understood themselves. For a long time since the original Progressive Era these two distinct regime ideas have coexisted uneasily, but the divides of our own time indicate that we are reaching a point of decision, where we will not be able to continue for much longer with citizens of two different regimes occupying the same country. The progressives understood that in order to consummate the transformation they envisioned, the new regime would ultimately have to replace the original. And so, as Lincoln observed in 1854 with respect to the crisis of his own day, "we have been giving up the old for the new faith," and the question remains whether the victory of the new progressive faith will now be completed.

Index